Partners in Play

Assessing Infants and Toddlers in Natural Contexts

Gail L. Ensher

Tasia P. Bobish

Eric F. Gardner

Carol L. Reinson

Deborah A. Bryden

Daniel J. Foertsch

THOMSON

DELMAR LEARNING

Australia   Canada   Mexico   Singapore   Spain   United Kingdom   United States

THOMSON

DELMAR LEARNING

Partners in Play
Assessing Infants and Toddlers in Natural Contexts
Gail L. Ensher, Tasia P. Bobish, Eric F. Gardner, Carol L. Reinson, Deborah A. Bryden, and Daniel J. Foertsch

Vice President, Career Education SBU:
Dawn Gerrain

Director of Learning Solutions:
Sherry Dickinson

Managing Editor:
Robert Serenka, Jr.

Senior Acquisitions Editor:
Erin O'Connor

Product Manager:
Philip Mandl

Editorial Assistant:
Stephanie Kelly

Director of Production:
Wendy A. Troeger

Production Manager:
J.P. Henkel

Content Project Manager:
Joy Kocsis

Production Assistant:
Angela Iula

Director of Marketing:
Wendy E. Mapstone

Channel Manager:
Kristin McNary

Marketing Coordinator:
Scott A. Chrysler

Cover Design:
Joseph Villanova

Composition:
Pre-Press Company, Inc.

Library of Congress Cataloging-in-Publication Data
Partners in play : assessing infants and toddlers in natural contexts / Gail L. Ensher ... [et al.].
    p. cm.
  Includes bibliographical references and index.
  ISBN 1-4180-3076-7
  1. Child development--Testing. 2. Infants--Development--Testing. 3. Toddlers--Development--Testing. 4. Behavioral assessment of infants. 5. Behavioral assessment of children.
  I. Ensher, Gail L.
  RJ51.D48P37 2007
  618.92'0075--dc22
                            2006007449

NOTICE TO THE READER

Table of Contents

Foreword

Parents and professionals who are veterans of the early intervention service system often have "war stories" to tell about their struggles to obtain services. Many of the tales told involve having children assessed, either for "eligibility" or program planning and monitoring. Indeed, getting *sensible assessment* seems to be one of the greatest obstacles confronted by both parents and professionals. Allow me to tell a story, just one, to set the stage for a few main points relevant to *Partners in Play*. About 25 years ago, I was faced with the job of conducting a community-wide screening effort in order to find 20 children who might be further assessed and made eligible for a newly funded early intervention program. We did what we needed in order to "round-up" children who might be eligible. The results were excellent. We screened about 200 children and identified 30 who then were referred to a local center where psychological services were available. Indeed, "assessment for eligibility and program planning" was touted to be a main service of the center. The school psychologists did what they had been trained to do in their graduate programs, and used the professional tools they were supposed to use. After four weeks, I received a stack of reports from the center. Twenty-four of the 30 reports were stamped "UNTESTABLE"! Bewildered and concerned, I rushed to speak with the people at the center: "What do you mean, 'untestable'? Do you mean that *you* cannot do the assessment, or that you don't have the right training or materials?" Of course, it was not the fault of these well-intentioned professionals; they simply had not been prepared to work with infants, toddlers, or preschoolers, nor did they have assessment materials that permitted the flexible procedures and multi-sources of information so crucial to what is now recognized as developmentally appropriate assessment. (We finally did manage to have 20 of the children declared eligible for our program, but only after a laborious process of collecting observational data, parent reports, and using compelling logic to obtain re-appraisals.) Let me say, here, that it was also at about this time when Gail Ensher and her colleagues began to focus efforts to develop a set of materials to meet the needs of early intervention/early childhood specialists who were continually frustrated, as I was, with conventional assessment. Even though 20 years have passed, early intervention assessment, it seems, has been "developmentally delayed" and has remained centered on procedures that are extrapolations of school-age practices.

Unfortunately, professionals are still often required to use these assessment materials that have been standardized *only* on children with typical development, and to administer these materials to children with developmental differences in the same way they would to children of typical development. Force-fitting children to standard items, objects, and procedures results in labeling children "untestable" or "oppositional/defiant". I am reminded of the Greek legend of Procrustes, who welcomed weary travelers to stay in his house and to sleep in his "special" guest bed. Procrustes claimed that any and all guests would perfectly fit the bed; those taller or shorter than standard would still fit perfectly into the bed. However, the *bed* was not designed to accommodate guests who differed from the standard; rather, Procrustes adjusted the guests to fit the bed; he stretched guests who were too short and chopped off the feet or heads of guests who were too tall! Too often, we have been force-fitting children to methods and materials in a Procrustean approach to assessment.

Today, professionals are permitted to rely on *informed clinical opinion* when the usual required psychometric, standardized materials are not useful. *Partners in Play* offers professionals a way to conduct developmentally appropriate assessment and *to document clinical opinion. Partners in Play* provides flexibility in procedures, uses formal and informal settings, involves significant and genuine parent participation, and is sensitive to differences in culture, sensory/motor abilities, and child disposition. In brief, *Partners in Play* can be the basis for *informed* clinical opinion. I know of no other single source for guiding developmentally appropriate assessment of very young children and for providing documentation for clinical opinion, and all in a playful approach that accommodates and honors differences. It has taken a long time and much hard work, but *Partners in Play* is a success story and a win for all of us who work to promote the welfare of young children.

John T. Neisworth, Ph.D.
Professor Emeritus
Special Education
Penn State University

Preface

Partners in Play (PIP) is a criterion-referenced instrument that was developed for the identification and follow-up of infants and toddlers, birth through three years of age, who might be eligible for early intervention services. As an integrated, "core" assessment, *PIP* generates qualitative and quantitative information central to the development of an Individual Family Service Plan (IFSP), as mandated by the Education of the Handicapped Act Amendments of 1986 (PL 99-457), Individuals with Disabilities Education Act Amendments of 1991 (PL 102-119), and Part C, Individuals with Disabilities Education Act Amendments of 1997 (PL 105-17). The assessment is appropriate for evaluating infants and toddlers with a wide range of actual or suspected delays and abilities such as those placed at risk as a result of environmental factors, children born prematurely, children with Pervasive Developmental Disorders (PDD), and youngsters with other neurological and/or developmental problems. In keeping with best practices in early intervention, parents or primary caregivers are key participants in the assessment process.

PIP has evolved over many years of clinical research and development to fulfill a need for a tool for assessing young children in natural contexts at community-based, home, school, and other clinical settings. In its initial stages, *PIP* was an outgrowth of work on a companion curriculum-based, criterion-referenced instrument, *The Syracuse Dynamic Assessment (SDA)* (Applied Symbolix, 1998). The senior author and a multidisciplinary author team began development of the *SDA* at Syracuse University in 1979, in order to provide a tool to assess the learning and behavior of children from birth to 12 months, who were at risk or developmentally delayed. Over the next several years, additional authors joined the team and contributed their expertise. Collectively, this author group represented the disciplines of communication sciences and disorders, developmental psychology, early childhood special education, occupational therapy, physical therapy, and psychological measurement. Subsequently in 1992, the authors expanded the age range of the assessment from 1–12 months to 1–36 months. They also redefined and reorganized the developmental domains, modifying item formats, and refining other evaluation materials for the suggested toys and materials for administration.

Activities and items of *Partners in Play* have been selected and developed on the basis of extensive field and clinical testing, and in this regard content validity for individual items and clusters of items has been established. In addition, *PIP* recently was used as the primary data collection instrument for a comprehensive doctoral study by a member of the author team (Reinson, 2002). During the latter research, 31 full-term and preterm newborns were followed developmentally for the first 12 months of life, and then re-evaluated periodically throughout their second year of life until they reached 36 months. Further, this assessment has been used extensively in both home and clinical settings over the past 15 years to evaluate infants and toddlers referred to the State Health Department in Onondaga County, New York, to determine their eligibility for early education, center-based, or itinerant home-based services. This experience of administering the assessment has reflected the fact that multiple observers have high rates of agreement in recording information reported by parents or caregivers and in rating children's behavior in both the unstructured and structured components of *PIP*. Accordingly, these evaluations have offered a solid basis for revisions ultimately incorporated into development of the current edition of the assessment.

PIP is designed to encourage and support transdisciplinary team assessment, a model commonly used in early intervention. One professional is selected to interact with the child and caregivers, while other team members observe and record relevant developmental information. This approach underscores the importance of evaluating young children in relatively natural, integrated contexts that are conducive to a meaningful sampling of performance and behavior. In addition, *PIP* has other noteworthy features that are especially appealing for professionals in assessing young children. For example, a substantial portion of the instrument is based on parent or caregiver report and natural observations of the child at play. These features foster an interactive and inviting environment designed to encourage the best possible performance from children across diverse backgrounds. Furthermore, specific information obtained by the caregiver report is confirmed during unstructured or structured play sessions, allowing the team to cross-reference what the parent is reporting as representative of the child's everyday behavior.

PIP differs from most other available instruments in that certain items are administered by the caregiver report, others by observation during guided play scenarios, and still others in play-based activities guided by the examiner or play facilitator. In all three contexts, the child is the center of focus, but the relationship between the child and the adult changes. Administration usually involves two or three sessions for completion of all the components of the assessment, depending on how quickly the child fatigues. Initially, parent or caregiver interviews are carried out to obtain a family-social history and picture of the child's present developmental status. The child thus has time to adjust to the presence of an unfamiliar evaluation team. A period of unstructured caregiver-child play follows, allowing the team to observe the parents or caregivers and the child, approximating typical patterns of interaction. The examiner/facilitator then engages the child in a period of unstructured play, revealing how the child interacts with an unfamiliar adult. In the final component of the assessment, the same examiner/facilitator presents directed, more structured activities (e.g., engaging the child in vocal play with a puppet) and offers prompts and assistance to encourage the child to respond. This strategy of using multiple sources of information acknowledges the interrelatedness of developmental behaviors in the young child and helps the entire team gather information about the child's progress and needs.

In closing, though this tool is used primarily by professionals in assessing young children, *PIP* has served an important role in training students in teacher preparation programs at the college and university level throughout its many years of development. In the latter capacity, the assessment today can be used by faculty in undergraduate programs who teach observation courses dealing with the typical development of infants and young children, courses focused on youngsters with special needs, as well as faculty teaching graduate students who are preparing for work in the fields of teaching in early childhood and early childhood special education, speech therapy, physical and occupational therapy, and psychology. Finally, as we have referenced in the discussion, *PIP* is an assessment that can be used in a variety of community settings including homes, day-care centers, center-based early intervention programs, and other clinical programs that follow the development of infants and young children.

Gail L. Ensher

Acknowledgments

Partners in Play (PIP) would not have been developed without the help of many people. Our greatest appreciation goes to our own families, who taught us the real meaning of parenting, child development, patience, love, and understanding, and to our own parents, who gave so unstintingly of themselves in support of our endeavors over the years.

Several colleagues have had a significant influence in our professional lives, including Burton Blatt, David A. Clark, Larry Consenstein, Eric F. Gardner, Thomas Hutchinson, Albert T. Murphy, John Neisworth, Nancy Songer, and James Pergolizzi. All have been mentors, friends, and examples of the very best in our respective fields.

A number of people have participated in the creation and development of *Partners in Play* over the past 30 years. We owe a sincere debt to those families who opened their homes and allowed us to visit week after week to follow the development of their infants and toddlers. Our colleagues and students also offered substantial feedback throughout the development process. In particular, we are grateful to Amy Good, Carroll Grant, and Sue Ann Kayne.

Finally, we would like to thank all of the graduate students and families who listened to our thoughts and ideas along the way. These individuals truly were responsible for the conception of *Partners in Play* and motivated us to persevere through many years of hard work and refinement.

Special thanks are also due the reviewers of the manuscript:

Irene Cook

    Lecturer, Child, Adolescent, and Family Studies Program
    California State University, Bakersfield

Robin Hasslen, Ph.D.

    Department of Education, Bethel University, St. Paul, MN

Linda Carmichael Gamble

    Adjunct Faculty: Elementary and Early Childhood Education
    College of Education, Health and Rehabilitation, University of Maine at Farmington

Julie Bakerlis

ECE Faculty, Quinsigamond Community College, Worcester, MA

Kay Crowder, M.Ed.

Asst. Professor, Early Childhood Education
Community College of Indiana-Ivy Tech State College, Grabill, IN

Billie L. Sands, Ph.D.

Professor, Consumer and Family Studies Dept., San Francisco State University, CA

Lelia C. Mullis, Ed.D.

Adjunct Professor
Teacher Preparation Academy, University of Tennessee at Chattanooga
Dept. of Early Childhood Education, Cleveland State Community College,
Cleveland, TN

Wendy Bertoli, M.Ed.

Early Childhood Education Instructor
Lancaster County Career and Technology Center, Lancaster, PA

Finally, special thanks is given to Jeanne Schmidt for patience and efforts in preparing this manuscript.

Dedication

Partners in Play is dedicated to Kimberly Elizabeth and Lindsey Michelle Ensher, who were born prematurely more than a decade ago in Calcutta, India, and have grown into lovely, bright, caring, and energetic young women.

Special Contributors

Janet O'Flynn, MS, OTR/L, BCP; Masters degree student in Early Childhood Special Education, Syracuse University; Author of *Kelsie, Illustrations from the Field,* case study assessment included in the accompanying Online Companion™ that can be accessed at www.earlychilded.delmar.com.

Online Companion™ Supplement

Partners In Play is accompanied by an Online Companion™ that can be accessed at www.earlychilded.delmar.com. The Online Companion™ is your link to early childhood education on the web. The Online Companion™ to accompany *Partners In Play: Assessing Infants & Toddlers in Natural Contexts* contains useful features to help students and practitioners understand and use the *PIP* assessment. It includes a second case study using the *PIP* assessment complete with the actual assessment documents and worksheets. The Online Companion™ also contains PowerPoint® slides for each chapter and study questions. There is an instructional and assessment resources section that contains guidelines for family interviewing, and professional development resources. A sample course syllabus, author biographies, related web links, and a list of supplemental research books are just a few more resources included in the Online Companion™.

CHAPTER 1

Assessing Young Children Within the Family Context

After reading this chapter, you should be able to:

❖ Understand legislation defining eligibility of infants and toddlers for early intervention services.

❖ Understand key issues relating to the assessment of young children across diverse cultures.

❖ Understand some of the advantages of play-based assessment within natural contexts of community and home.

❖ Understand major benchmarks of the assessment process for families of infants and toddlers.

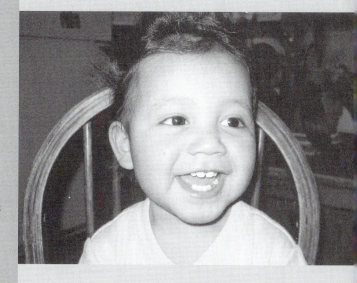

Meaningful Assessment of Infants and Toddlers

The passage and implementation of legislation on behalf of infants and toddlers over the past decade have brought about sweeping and much needed changes in the field of assessment in early childhood special education. Historically, the field has relied heavily on norm-referenced tests, the most widely used being *The Bayley Scales of Infant Development II (BSID-II)* (Bayley, 1993). Unfortunately, for young children at risk or those with established special needs within the first two years of life, such evaluations rarely yield the kind of information that is meaningful for future planning and program decision-making, often represent a dramatic mismatch in terms of the natural behaviors of infants and toddlers, and often fail to see young children within the context of natural environments and their families.

Recently *new visions for the developmental assessment of infants and young children* (Meisels & Fenichel, 1997) have moved toward assessing children within their own natural and more "authentic" environments (Bagnato, Neisworth, & Munson, 1997). Newer approaches now allow flexibility in administration format, materials, time, and involvement of primary caregivers that are more compatible with the styles and patterns of interaction of very young children. In so doing, these approaches afford increased possibilities for offering more genuine assessment information. Under typical circumstances, assessing infants and toddlers is an "imprecise" and undefined process. Flexible qualities of the evaluation environment become increasingly important with children who may have difficulties in communicating, attending, and focusing in structured situations with unfamiliar persons within prescribed periods of time. As described in Chapter 2, it is often necessary to adapt to diverse learning and temperament patterns and styles that challenge the most adept clinician. As noted by Ensher and Clark (1994),

> Time, follow-up, direct parent participation, and a range of natural settings are becoming routine in the course of evaluation, and the use of multiple criteria with a spectrum of behavioral and developmental measures is becoming common practice rather than the exception. Finally, professionals are learning that the real task of screening and assessment lies in the disclosure of competence (of both parents and children) rather than deficiency and that this goal is carried out most wisely with a realistic and unavoidable, but healthy, uncertainty. (p. 199)

Though goals of prediction and outcome, driven by the concerns of parents and pressing needs of educational programs, have often pervaded evaluations of young children, such objectives continue to elude our grasp. At best, with the benefits of newer approaches of criterion-, curriculum-, and play-based assessments, we now can make more meaningful and genuine determinations of particular special needs within short timeframes of a few months, with the understanding that the concept of risk and delay always is changing, especially with the benefits of early intervention and family involvement. For example, it is not unusual that infants and young children, referred for a suspected delay at one point in time, later are evaluated and may be found to be on-target developmentally in that domain of concern. That is the "miracle" of development and maturation in young children that continues to be extremely unpredictable long-term. As Ensher and Clark (1994) have stated,

> ...the concept of *levels of risk or vulnerability* is useful. Consistent with the Moving Risk Model, infants may progress up the ladder of programming, as necessary and appropriate to their needs and those of their families. Likewise, they move down the cascade of services, having had their early, most intense needs met, their primary disabilities addressed in normalizing educational programs, and secondary disabling conditions prevented altogether. Full development of this concept and cautious implementation on a widespread basis could resolve many problems of screening, identification, and diagnosis that continue to thwart efforts of early intervention. (p. 202)

Thus, frequent observation, confirmed by the invaluable notes of families who live daily with their young children, offers us the best promise for addressing and correcting assessment errors of the past on behalf of more effective programming.

Finally, discussion of meaningful, serial assessment of young children would not be complete without one further reference to the importance of setting. In the interest of saving time, expense, and convenience, evaluations of infants and toddlers, as well as three-to-five-year olds, often are carried out in "unfamiliar" places such as offices or schools. Such settings are far from natural environments for either families or their children under scrutiny. Frequent observations of children drive home this point when teams, alternatively having the advantage of home visiting first, later witness dramatically different patterns of behavior in more "clinical," stereotypic surroundings. All information is helpful; yet if teams wish to build on areas of strength, natural contexts need to be a central part of a meaningful evaluation scenario for the family and for the child. The importance of this standard of assessment likewise is strongly advocated in the 1997 Amendments to IDEA (McLean, Wolery, & Bailey, Jr., 2004).

Eligibility for Early Intervention

Quoting from the statutory language pertaining to eligibility definitions of IDEA, Part C, McLean, Wolery, and Bailey, Jr. (2004) state,

The term "infant or toddler with a disability":

(A)   means an individual under three years of age who needs early intervention services because the individual:

   (i)   is experiencing developmental delays, as measured by appropriate diagnostic instruments and procedures in one or more of the areas of cognitive development, physical development, communication development, social or emotional development, and adaptive development; or

       (ii) has a diagnosed physical or mental condition which has a high probability of resulting in developmental delay; and

(B)   may also include, at a state's discretion, at-risk infants and toddlers. The term "at-risk infant or toddler" means an individual under three years of age who would be at risk of experiencing a substantial developmental delay if early intervention services were not provided to the individual. (p. 4)

Given the definition above, states have been given a great deal of flexibility in terms of the criteria and ways in which they establish the basis of eligibility for early intervention services (Shackelford, 2005). Some states are guided by quantitative measures of developmental delay (McLean, Wolery, & Bailey, Jr., 2004); others such as New York State rely on percentages of delay in one or more developmental areas or domains; some states express the extent of delay in months; and still others use a combination of qualitative or quantitative measures along with informed clinical judgment. As we have noted above in our discussion of meaningful assessment, several authors over the past decade have argued strongly against the use of standardized or norm-referenced instruments which, at best, are "problematic" with very young children (McLean, Wolery, & Bailey, Jr., 2004). Shackelford's article (2005), included in Appendix D of this text, discusses criteria established by each of the 50 states relative to Part C of the IDEA Amendments of 1997. These respective criteria are of key importance in interpreting the developmental and behavioral patterns/profiles derived from the administration of assessments such as *PIP.* Moreover, we would like to emphasize that the initial assessment for establishing eligibility for early intervention is merely the first step in the evaluation process. Serial assessment is a critical part of the process, which follows hand-in-hand with the ongoing programming over time. Finally, as Ensher and Clark (1994) have stated, although criteria for both initial and continuing early intervention services appear to be "specific and clearly defined," many issues of ambiguity have a continuing impact on behavioral and developmental outcomes of children including cultural diversity, the process of child evaluation, and the nature of family assessment. We cannot emphasize enough the importance of "informed clinical opinion" in the identification and eligibility process where areas of delay and challenging needs very likely are overlapping, having an impact on other closely related developmental domains or in those situations where the behaviors of young children prohibit the use of formalized assessment strategies or diagnostic instruments. In such instances, parent report and careful observations of child play and behavior in natural environments are the only resource for sorting out the pieces of often complex diagnostic profiles. The federal regulations of Part C are sensitive to this issue of using "informed clinical opinion" with the evaluation of infants and toddlers in order to "safeguard against eligibility determinations based upon test scores alone" and to assure "consideration of both qualitative and quantitative information when addressing challenging questions regarding the development of an infant or toddler and the need for early intervention services" (McLean, Wolery, & Bailey, Jr., 2004, p. 10).

Assessing Young Children Across Diverse Cultures and Contexts

Changing Demographics/Changing Definitions

Discussion of assessing infants and toddlers would not be complete without consideration of the evaluation of young children across diverse cultures. Indeed, the United States is a country of rapidly changing demographics and ethnic populations (Hanson & Lynch, 2004a; 2004b; Lynch & Hanson, 2004). For example, Hanson and Lynch (2004a) have written:

> According to the U.S. Census Bureau, where one in eight Americans was a member of a race other than Caucasian at the turn of the last century, at the beginning of the 21st century, the ratio of people who were nonwhite to people who were white was one in four [Hobbs & Stoops, 2002]. According to the 2000 Census, nearly 89% of the population was born in the United States and 11% was foreign born.
>
> The breakdown of birth origin of the foreign born is as follows: Latin America, 51.7%; Asia, 26.4%; Europe, 15.8%; Africa, 2.8%; North America, 2.7%; and Oceania, .5%. According to the same census, in nearly 18% of U.S. homes, a language other than English was spoken.
>
> On April 1, 2000, during Census 2000, the population of the United States was 281,421,906. Of that number, more than 30% of individuals were of nonwhite, non-Anglo-European ancestry (with the breakdown being white, not Hispanic, 69.1%; Hispanic of any race, 12.5%; black or African American, 12.3%; Asian, 3.6%; American Indian and Alaska Native, .9%; Native Hawaiian and other Pacific Islander, 1%) [U.S. Bureau of the Census, 2000b]. pp. 6–7.

Slentz, Lewis, Fromme, Williams-Appleton, Milatchkov, and Shureen (1997, p. 5) noted the following additional factors that contribute to increasing numbers of culturally and linguistically diverse children in our schools today:

- Parents have brought their children to the United States for better educational, health care, and employment opportunities.
- Families have immigrated to escape war, political, and religious persecution.
- Family members have moved to the United States to reunite with others.
- Children are learning traditional beliefs, languages, customs, and world views as the foundation for early development.
- Youngsters in some communities grow up speaking English with distinct dialectical differences and with important variations in behavioral expectations.

Race is one of many aspects to be considered in terms of the evaluation of young children. Other factors include age, gender, geographic location, lifestyle, physical differences, and family belief systems. Moreover, Haarstad and Thomas (2003, p. 5) propose the following additional components with respect to cultural diversity:

- cognitive systems such as beliefs and values
- norms or rules regarding appropriate behaviors, sometimes called *codes of conduct*
- roles/expected behaviors of people, depending on gender, age, social positions, and other individual factors
- spiritual or religious institutions
- economic systems regulating how resources are shared among members
- political systems with identified leaders and rules to maintain social order
- language, for communication among members
- life styles including art, food, music, and dance produced by the group.

During the evaluation process, it is likewise important to remember that diversity exists within various ethnic groups. For example, Anderson, Capp, and Fix (as cited in Haarstad & Thomas, 2003) conducted a survey with immigrant families and found the following which run counter to a number of commonly held beliefs or myths about ethnically diverse families:

- Immigrant families are poorer, 52% below the federal poverty line, versus 37% of the native families.
- Among native families, 85% of their children are taken on outings several times per week versus 77% of immigrants' children.
- Among native families, 81% of their children are read to three or more times per week versus 70% of immigrant children.
- Children of immigrants are less likely to have parents volunteer at religious, school, or community functions (24% versus 40%).
- Among immigrant families, 7% of their children are in either fair or poor health compared to 2% of native children.
- Children of immigrants are no more likely to have behavioral problems than are children of natives. (Haarstad & Thomas, 2003, p. 4)

Current research offers multiple definitions of culture and cultural competence. Haarstad and Thomas (2003, p. 3) shared the following: The National Association of Social Workers (NASW) Board of Directors (2001) adopted this definition of culture: Culture is the *integrated pattern of human behaviors that includes thoughts, communications, actions, customs, beliefs, values, and institutions of social, ethnic, religious, or social group*. Similarly, Haarstad and Thomas (2003) quote the Child Welfare League of America [2002] in defining cultural competence as:

> The ability of individuals and systems to respond respectfully and effectively to people of all cultures, races, ethnic backgrounds, sexual orientations, and faiths or religions in a manner that recognizes, affirms, and values the worth of individuals, families, tribes, and communities, and protects the dignity of each. (p. 6)

Considerations Prior to Screening and Evaluation

Assessment of young American children can be challenging; however, when a child's roots come from another culture, additional pre-assessment knowledge of that culture is required. As emphasized above, it is critical that the assessment team understand the child within the context of the *family* as there are differences in the activities and expectations of children. Sorting out whether there are true delays or simply cultural differences involves spending time with the family and caregivers, involvement of an interpreter, and observation time in home, school, and daycare environments. For example, Lynch and Hanson (2004) have pointed out:

> Family priorities, children's opportunities to practice, and the families' culture all can influence when children attain developmental skills and milestones. In cultures in which individuation and independence are considered less important than interdependence, young children may demonstrate different developmental patterns. For example, in many Middle Eastern and Latino families, the emphasis is upon attachment and parent-child bonding [Sharifzadeh, 1998; Zuniga, 1998]; toddlers and preschoolers may not be pushed toward independence in eating, dressing, sleeping, or toilet training. As a result, screening instruments that rely on norms for Anglo-European children from middle-income homes may inappropriately identify some children as not meeting developmental expectations though these children come from families who hold different expectations for their children. . . . Although children from families who speak languages other than English often learn one or more languages, their initial vocabularies may be smaller in each language; they may mix grammar and syntax in their early years of language learning. In a screening assessment, these children's language may differ from the norm. (p. 88)

Further, Slentz et al. (1997, p. 11) stress that language and cognitive development cannot be separated. Cognitive delays likely will make language learning difficult in both a first and second language. Also, children who have not had an opportunity to achieve competence communicatively in their first language, while learning English, likely will demonstrate delays in academic learning. It is critical that the assessment teams understand the difference between language acquisition and a language disorder.

Slentz et al. (1997, p. 12) reported the following differences between language acquisition and language disorders:

Table 1-1 Differences between Language Acquisition and Language Disorders

Language Acquisition	Language Disorder
When children are learning English as a second language:	When children have a language impairment or <u>disorder:</u>
• It is typical for their skills in English vocabulary, pronunciation, grammar, and comprehension to be less well	• *Errors or limited skills in vocabulary, pronunciation, grammar, and comprehension interfere with*

(Continued)

Table 1-1 (*Continued*)

Language Acquisition	Language Disorder
developed than their peers who speak only English.	*communication in their first language (L1), compared to peers from the same language group.*
• They will acquire English in a predictable developmental sequence, similar to younger children who are beginning to learn English.	• *Their English skills are delayed in comparison to peers from the same language group who have been learning English for the same length of time.*
• Reduced opportunities to use their first language may result in loss of competence in L1 before becoming proficient in English.	• *Their communication is impaired in interactions with family members and others who speak the same language.*
• They may switch back and forth between L1 and English, using their most sophisticated skills in both languages within single utterances.	• *Skills in their first language will be limited, inappropriate, or confused in content, form, or use.*
• Results from assessments conducted in English are unlikely to reflect the child's true skills and abilities in most domains.	• *Assessments conducted in English will be unable to discriminate between language acquisition and language disorder.*

One cannot over-emphasize the importance of the role that knowledge of the culture and family play, along with the implications of learning a second language as a higher level of language and cognitive development.

The following guidelines for learning about culture are suggested by Slentz et al. (1997, p. 46). In particular, the assessment needs to include information about:

❖ family structure and composition including members of a family, key decision makers, the relationship of friends to the family, and how decisions are made within the family

❖ primary caregivers for the children including how much time is spent away from the family, environmental considerations such as housing or conflicts that may be having an impact on caregiving

❖ routines and practices including types of foods eaten, mealtime rules, and any beliefs associated with food preparation and handling

❖ family sleeping routines and practices including where the child sleeps at night

❖ patterns of daytime napping for the child, frequency of waking during the night, and family response to the child's waking at night

❖ family response to challenging behavior including perceptions of acceptable behavior, approaches to managing unacceptable child behavior, and strategies for calming the child

❖ family perceptions of child disability, health, medical needs, help-seeking, and early intervention language and communication styles of family and home visitors including the primary language spoken in the home, family proficiency in oral and written English, interpreter familiarity with culture and family region of origin, family comfort with an interpreter, and family styles of interaction and information sharing.

Pre-Assessment Phase

Slentz and colleagues (1997, p. 13) discuss assessment as either an improving or a disabling process for culturally diverse children. Accordingly, they present several potentially serious consequences without adequate consideration of cultural contexts:

❖ Without knowledge of the demands and standards of the home environment, the young child's behaviors may be negatively misinterpreted.

❖ Typical developmental competence in other languages and cultures may be mistakenly identified as delay or disability.

❖ Preschoolers may receive special education services instead of more appropriate bilingual or culturally relevant interventions.

❖ Children may be wrongly identified as having developmental delays or disabilities if the expectations of the primary culture are different than the mainstream developmental standards reflected in evaluation instruments.

❖ Self-esteem can suffer if children perceive that their languages and cultures are devalued, considered inferior, or a disadvantage to development.

❖ Children may lose contact with immediate family if parents interpret results of evaluation and assessment as an indictment of their efforts to socialize their children in their own life-ways.

❖ In the long term, educational, social, and vocational opportunities may be curtailed if children are labeled as having less potential for learning.

❖ Beneficial services may be overlooked if genuine disabilities/delays are masked or obscured by cultural differences.

Additional critical questions in the caregiver interview of the *PIP* assessment, which are part of the pre-referral process, include:

❖ whether an additional language is spoken in the home or caregiving environment in addition to English

❖ knowledge of the dominant language as well as the frequency of English spoken versus another language

❖ knowledge of the child's receptive and expressive abilities in both languages

❖ determination of whether one language or the other seems to be more successful with the child

❖ knowledge of the frequency of the child's participation in and out of the home social situations.

If a family member or caregiver is struggling with the English language, it is imperative that a trained interpreter be involved in *all* components of the process. This stage should entail an initial meeting where the team and translator can discuss roles and involvement, and review the overall assessment process. Often, during this initial contact, the translator can supply additional information regarding the culture and beliefs.

During the parent interview process, the interpreter should relay every comment made by both the examiner and parent/caregiver. No additional information or personal comments should be made. This is why it is particularly important not to have a family member or friend interpret.

Lastly, the parent conference requires the interpreter or culture guide to review all results obtained to assist with questions and to "debrief" with examiners as to the effectiveness of the assessment. Slentz and colleagues (1997, p. 21) offer several desired competencies of interpreters/translators.

Linguistic competencies. The interpreter/translator must be able to read, write, understand, and converse proficiently in both language 1 and language 2. He/she must be familiar enough with *both* languages to say things in different ways, understand idioms, adjust to colloquial and formal usage, and use the terminology of early childhood and assessment/evaluation. *Conversational use of language 2 is not adequate training.*

Cultural competencies. The interpreter/translator must also understand both mainstream American culture and the culture of the child and family well enough to explain cross-cultural variables, identify subgroups within the culture, and anticipate acceptable and expected conventions for interaction. *Adequate training includes knowledge of the family's culture and its variations.*

Ethical/professional considerations. The interpreter/translator must be able to maintain the same level of professional conduct expected of all team members, including requirements for confidentiality and neutrality, collaboration, and interpersonal communication. *The interpreter/translator role is different from that of an advocate.*

Other competencies desired for early childhood. The interpreter/translator must be familiar with assessment and evaluation procedures, specific test instruments and administration guidelines used, values and beliefs about child development and parenting in both cultures, and concepts involved in early childhood education services (eligibility, special services, prevention). *The interpreter/ translator must be able to clarify and explain beliefs and values about young children.*

The Evaluation-Interpretation Phase

Simply sitting down with a standardized instrument with children of diverse cultures obviously is not an answer. Once an evaluator has an in-depth understanding of the child's family and culture, observation in various settings is the next key step. Observation of play can be complex, even for children of the examiner's own culture. On the other hand, children of all cultures have one thing in common—they like to play!

Though cultures share some common playthings such as toy animals and balls, it is crucial that a variety of multi-social toys (dolls, puzzles, games, and books) be used in the assessment. Observation of children in a group setting such as a daycare or classroom also requires cultural knowledge. Despite the fact that the examiner may be familiar with the sequence of play schemes developmentally, these do not necessarily apply to a multi-social or multi-gender group—dependent on the "mix" of children.

Research on the effects of socioeconomic status on children's play skills is contradictory. Some studies have suggested that middle class children exhibit more constructive, associative, cooperative, and socio-dramatic play than do lower income children. This finding, however, was argued by other researchers that race and social class or culture and social class factors are variables that are difficult to sort out. Regardless, the examiner needs awareness of the potential impact on skill development.

Another critical element in the process is *professional* judgment. This is often necessary when assessing children, especially children with special needs and/or children from another culture. Professional judgment is more time consuming than simply using a standardized test, as it involves significant observation time and in-depth narratives justifying the decision of the examiner.

Slentz et al. (1997, p. 29) point out critical elements of professional judgment for English-as-a-second language children.

- ❖ *a rationale* for departing from the procedures and instruments commonly used to evaluate same-age peers with similar developmental concerns
- ❖ specification of alternative strategies used for evaluation
- ❖ *justification* for use of the alternative methods. Give compelling evidence that justifies the use of alternative methods and demonstrates that standardized data are not valid (e.g., research, recognized professional practices and procedures, clinical judgment, or behavioral observations)
- ❖ *a statement of results* in terms of the legal eligibility criteria
- ❖ *an explanation* of an identified disability or delay that specifically rules out cultural and linguistic factors as the cause of atypical cognitive and behavioral performance
- ❖ *an explanation* of ineligibility, giving evidence of the specific cultural and linguistic factors that explain academic and behavioral performance without identification of disability or delay.

With the above considerations in mind, the *PIP* assessment emphasizes the need for multiple methods for information gathering to include observations in multiple settings, records reviews, and interviews with family and caregivers/teachers.

Observations of a child's social and emotional skills or behavior require careful interpretation of a child from a different culture. A frequent criticism of norm-referenced instruments is that cultural biases and prejudices often are embedded in such measures. Further, Slentz and colleagues (1997, p. 8) point out that behavioral "differences" can indicate either a disability or delay. For example, a child who seems quiet and withdrawn may be demonstrating cultural values of respect, listening, and reflection. In certain cultures, it is not appropriate for children to make eye contact with adults, and "wait time" is considered "proper" to reflect cultural values of independence and self-reliance or perhaps a need for self-protection and self-sufficiency. Researchers concur that "culturally different" behaviors often are misinterpreted as emotional and/or behavioral disorders. Thus, children may be designated inappropriately as students with special needs. Again, the examiner and evaluation team must understand the culture and determine what the behavior means in the child's daily life. A nonjudgmental attitude, warm personality, and respect for the lives of others are critical personal characteristics.

In summary to this discussion of assessing across cultures, Lynch and Hanson (2004) have offered some sound advice:

> A final step in the assessment process is making decisions about intervention services. Decisions should be made collaboratively by family members and professionals, with each bringing his or her expertise to the table. However, it is not always easy. Professionals have to view family members as having knowledge and preferences that are important to the decision. Likewise, family members must view themselves as having expertise that is important to the decision-making process. Reaching this understanding is sometimes complicated by differences in language, communication style, and culture. . . . Perhaps the best way to determine what any family wants is to listen to what they say (or sometimes don't say). (p. 95)

A Process for Decision-Making in Partnership

Our discussion above on culture underscores the centrality of genuine partnership for decision-making between members of professional early education teams and families, which is a cornerstone of the Part C regulations of IDEA on behalf of Infants and Toddlers. The specifics of evaluations will vary from family to family and child to child. Overall, however, a template for gathering information during the initial evaluation process should include the following:

❖ a statement of why the child is being referred and areas of suspected or known concern, including the family's goals for the evaluation

❖ a record of the child's/family's medical, social, and developmental history

❖ assessment strategies used and described

❖ a careful record of child observations and evaluation results

❖ recommendations for early intervention services including priority areas of the family.

Initial Referral

Young children are referred for evaluation from several sources during the first two years of life. These may come from concerned parents or caregivers, from primary care physicians or pediatricians, from friends and relatives who are familiar with the child and family, or directly from neonatal intensive care units and developmental follow-up clinics. While these referrals can be made at any time, they often cluster at certain points during the first twenty-four months—i.e., throughout the first six to eight months when it is clear at birth or shortly thereafter that infants have noteworthy neuromotor difficulties or congenital/genetic conditions frequently associated with developmental delays or between twelve and eighteen months with presenting delays in speech/language or behavioral/interaction difficulties. Often too, related developmental areas are affected or implicated along with the primary areas of referral, that also will require closer observation and evaluation.

Social History of the Family and Child

Once team member roles are assigned and contact is made directly with the family, scheduling with the parents or primary caretakers is completed. Social history-taking forms can be sent to families prior to the first home visit along with releases for information from other agencies. This information always should be reviewed and confirmed in person during the first visit with the family. There is no substitute for face-to-face interaction, which initiates the relationship-building process with the family and child.

Parents or primary caregivers know their children best, and their information is a critical part of the assessment process. During the first meeting, families can make their needs and concerns known, offer their perspectives on developmental issues of their children, and fill in important information relative to numerous medical, social, financial, and other factors that are affecting their lives and those of their children. In addition, it is important to note that carrying out this first face-to-face discussion in the natural environment of the home is very different from, and hopefully less threatening than, meeting in school and/or clinical settings. Here parents have access to the normal course of play toys of their children, their other children if they are at home, and can make reference to their own daily, authentic contexts. Finally, it is at this time that the process of assessment and evaluation can be reviewed once again with families to answer questions that are still lingering.

Assessment Strategies Used and Described

In their text *Newborns at Risk* (1994), Ensher and Clark reference a number of guiding principles that should be considered in selecting strategies for the impending assessment. These involve responding to the following questions:

❖ Do strategies allow for a sufficient sampling of behavior and learning over time?

❖ Are strategies sensitive to cultural diversity, so that the strengths of children and families are heightened and problematic areas are identified?

❖ Can instruments and strategies be used in diverse settings?

❖ Do instruments and strategies allow for cross-confirmation of information obtained from work with the child and information obtained from primary caregivers?

❖ Are measures and strategies valid and reliable over time?

❖ Do measures and strategies address issues related to teaching the child?

❖ Do measures and strategies address issues connected to the child's everyday functioning and behavior at home and in the community?

❖ Do strategies and measures lead to a genuine breadth of understanding functional as well as developmental aspects of the child's learning and behavior? (p. 213)

In the total scheme of the assessment process, *PIP* would constitute one piece of the initial data-gathering process. With its flexibility of unstructured interaction and play observations, the instrument offers a genuine first step in later identifying areas of concern and noteworthy strength within the family and home environment. As we have noted above, the assessment may be the only effective approach to learning about the child's behavior and performance, if the child presents challenging behavior or other issues of impairment that prevent the use of more formal strategies. Therefore, it is important during the actual home visit and later in the body of the final report to describe in detail the toys and materials used for the play session because these may be a window to future plans for programming and early intervention.

Observations of the Child

Observations of a child admittedly offer merely a "snapshot" in time of child development and behavior. On the other hand, styles of learning, preferences for toys, length of attention, needed adaptations for assessment and learning, modes of communication, interactions with familiar and unfamiliar persons, needs for sensory input, among other dimensions, are all part of the clinical note-taking and observation process. As one team member works directly with the child, in an "arena" type of assessment, one or two other members of the team record. As we have emphasized elsewhere in this text, parents or primary caregivers likewise are central to the assessment process. Further, a careful recording of clinical observations is critical to this process. Numbers or ratings alone will not portray the full picture of qualities of responses that are so connected to the development of the intervention plan. Our discussion of Illustrations from the Field in Chapter 5 highlight the importance of such clinical observations that may not be captured by scores obtained during the assessment. In addition, it is essential that all of the observations be recorded at the time of the evaluation when the behaviors and performance of the child are fresh in mind.

From time to time, there may be discrepancies in terms of the recording of observations by different team members. These differences, as well as information from family members, can be discussed at a later time following the assessment.

Evaluation Results and Recommendations

The final phase of the initial evaluation process involves pulling together the evaluation results and formulating recommendations. The Child Assessment Team should conference with all disciplines present to review behavioral and developmental data for the child and information gathered from the family. At this time, differences in perspectives and clinical observations should be shared and discussed fully. Final results and recommendations that incorporate family priorities, however, should be considered tentative until the subsequent conference with the primary caregiver(s) or parents. It is extremely important that the final meeting with families yet remain a time of program formulation, and not merely a time to offer a "final stamp" of approval for families. This should be a time of sharing and development so that families are genuine partners in the process of decision-making. Following the development of mutually agreed upon goals, objectives, and strategies that are reflected in the Individual Family Service Plan (IFSP) for early intervention, a process for ongoing evaluation needs to be established. Ensher and Clark (1994) have described the process as follows:

> Once a child and family are receiving services, the final stage of maintaining an ongoing process for feedback and evaluation needs to be set in place. This mechanism subsequently provides an essential means for dialogue and exchange between family and professionals for the duration of programming and intervention and empowers caregivers to question, discuss, and bring about change in the implementation of services. (p. 210)

In Brief Review

In completing this chapter, the reader should remember several key concepts for future assessment of infants and toddlers and work with families:

❖ Within the wealth of their diversity, families know their children best. The information that they have to share is a key part of the evaluation process of their children that needs to be respected and valued.

❖ Behaviors of infants and young children today are extremely complex. As such, they will require primary reliance on informed clinical judgment, as well as other measures of development.

❖ Initial evaluations of infants and toddlers need to be based on serial assessments over time, in diverse settings, with multiple persons including families and primary caregivers.

❖ The diversity of families in the United States today is growing and requires that professionals become well acquainted with a variety of cultures and ethnic groups. In those instances where spoken and written English is not the primary language used in the home, interpreters will be necessary for carrying out effective evaluations.

❖ In final stages of the evaluation process, recommendations for children and their families must constitute an actualized partnership with direct input from parents or primary caregivers.

CHAPTER 2

Different Learning Styles: Individualizing Assessment Strategies

After reading this chapter, you should be able to:

❖ Understand some of the adaptations that may be necessary for assessing infants including changing child positions, modifying schedules, taking time for feeding, and changing the environment of the room.

❖ Understand some of the adaptations necessary for assessing toddlers including primary involvement of parents/primary caregivers, modifying number of toys and materials in the environment, modifying schedules to accommodate short attention spans, reorganization of environments to restrict movement, and different selections of toys and materials to accommodate child preferences and diverse cultures.

❖ Understand that some assessments of young children may involve observations only, with informed clinical judgment and parent history taking.

The goal of *Partners in Play* or any assessment of an infant or toddler is to elicit the child's best performance. There are four considerations when evaluating; i.e., the child, the family, the examiner/facilitator, and the environment (which includes people other than the examiner/facilitator), all of which will affect the outcome. All four of these considerations have some degree of changeability. The child's behavior changes during the day. In a trandisciplinary approach, there are different people who can serve as the examiner/facilitator, all of whom have different expertise and styles. Individual examiners/facilitators are capable of having a range in their styles or approaches to a child. The place where the assessment occurs can be set up differently, depending on the child. Where the caregiver(s) and the observers are seated can be changed. It is important to keep all of these factors in mind during the assessment.

The child needs to be in an optimal state at the beginning of the session, meaning that the child is alert and attentive. The child is not hungry, wet, or tired. These times will best be determined by talking with the parent/caregiver about the child's daily schedule, and can easily be done when interviewing the family.

Infants

Overall, infants are greatly affected by their immediate environment. The room where the infant is assessed needs to be at a comfortable temperature and not have light shining in the infant's eyes. Most infants are evaluated in their diapers or diaper and t-shirt. This is done so that the occupational therapist and physical therapist can better see how the infant moves, and also to ensure that the clothing is not affecting what the infant can do (e.g., denim offers resistance to an infant's movement, and a dress may become caught under an infant's knees as an infant tries to crawl). Most infants will not be bothered by less clothing. However, there may be an infant who does not like the added tactile input, when arms or legs are bare. In addition, there may be an infant who is more resistant to standing in bare feet when shoes are not worn. These responses may be evident by the infant's becoming more fussy or tense. In this instance, the clothing and shoes should be left on the infant, and clothing would be selected that does not hinder the movement of the infant. This is not to say that hypersensitivity to tactile input should not be addressed in therapy, but when evaluating, its effect should be minimized to acquire the best performance of the infant.

The infant may be resistant to certain positions. For example, they may not like being prone or sitting. Many babies initially do not like standing. The examiner/facilitator needs to be sensitive to these preferences and either save the least favorite position to the end, or do that position for short periods of time, on and off, during the evaluation.

The infant may be sensitive to the rate at which they are moved. Some infants startle very easily, and may interpret the startle reaction as an unpleasant feeling. These infants may need to have their positions changed more slowly so that the examiner/facilitator does not elicit a startle reaction. These sensitive infants may need to have their arms held in at their sides when placed in supine, so that their arms falling to the side do not startle them.

It is to be expected that an infant will fuss on and off during the assessment with *PIP*, especially if they are young. Fussing is not a bad thing. However, the examiner/facilitator does not want to upset the infant to a point where they cannot be calmed. The following list includes strategies for calming an infant that is becoming upset:

1. Swaddle or wrap the infant in a receiving blanket so that his/her arms and legs are held in against the body.
2. Pat the infant's back with a regular rhythm.
3. Gently jiggle the infant up and down or place the infant in a baby swing.
4. Rock the infant.
5. Stroke the infant's forehead or side of the face.
6. Repeat back to the infant sounds that he/she makes.
7. Talk or sing to the infant in a soothing tone.
8. Give the infant a pacifier.
9. Allow or encourage the infant to quiet self by sucking on his/her thumb or hand.
10. Check to see that the infant is not hungry.
11. Check to see that the infant's diaper is dry.
12. Check to see that the infant is not too hot or too cold.
13. Notice or ask how the parent/caregiver handles the infant and what the infant responds to positively.
14. Give the infant to the parent/caregiver to calm.

Some infants may have difficulty maintaining alertness during the administration of *PIP*. Some suggestions that may help include the following:

1. Try placing the infant in a more upright position.
2. Increase the volume, the amount of inflection, or the rate of speech in your voice.
3. Increase the lighting in the room.
4. Gently jiggle the infant up and down or place the infant in a baby swing.
5. Pick a toy that makes noise or has flashing colors.

While executing these techniques of calming or increasing the alertness of an infant, the examiner/facilitator can continue to administer the items in the assessment, depending on the state of the child.

Toddlers

Toddlers, likewise, are aware of their immediate and surrounding environment. Where the child is assessed, the set-up of the room, and the place where the other observers are located will be more critical to the toddler than to the infant. If some of the child's assessment is done sitting in a chair at the table, the chair should position the child so that his/her hips and knees are flexed at 90 degrees, the feet are flat on the floor, and the table is at chest height.

A few children will have definitive diagnoses. However for most, this is the critical time of discerning whether or not the child's development is within the typical range. If not, how do we then best define and address the child's needs? *Partners in Play* can do this, but during the assessment some adaptations may need to be made to acquire the best picture of the child. The following are some suggestions that address characteristics found in some children. These are not intended in any way, however, to offer a diagnosis for a child.

The Child with a Short Attention Span

Of primary importance is limiting the amount of stimuli in the room where the assessment takes place. Toys, colorful posters, or pictures within the child's visual field need to be minimized. Often the things that we think make the room inviting to children may present too much distraction for the child with a short attention span. If possible, have the observers watch through a one-way mirror, if in a clinical setting, or set back from the child and play facilitator. Noise not relevant to the evaluation situation should be minimized.

Prior to administering *PIP*, organize the toys the examiner/facilitator will need in such a manner that the examiner/facilitator can quickly present a new toy when the child's interest starts to wane. In the room where the assessment is taking place, give the child a home base. Home base is a chair at a table or a carpet square, where the child goes for sit-down activities. During the evaluation, alternate sitting tasks with moving tasks. If this approach still does not maintain the child's interest, then give the child short, frequent breaks during the assessment. Children sometimes perform better in more but shorter sessions.

The Child Who Is Hyperactive

All of the suggestions listed in the discussion above for *The Child with a Short Attention Span* apply to this child also. In addition, if the child sits on a ball or a T-stool where their hips and knees are flexed to 90 degrees, the child's attentiveness may improve and his/her tendency to move around the room may be reduced.

The Child Who Is Sensitive to Sensory Stimuli

Suggestions here typically overlap with other issues for a child, and are areas to be sensitive to for all children. The child who is sensitive to sensory stimuli may be distracted by outside noise, which includes even noise made by people in the room. The child may not like the quality of a sound, or the sound of the bell used in the item *Auditory Alerting to Bell* in the *PIP* assessment may even startle them. If this should happen, change the toy to an auditory toy that does not have an adverse effect on the child. In addition, the child may be sensitive to the amount and type of lighting in the room. The child may not like touching toys with certain textures or certain substances such as having food on their hands, soap bubbles touching their hands, or even having a soap bubble break on their skin. Though this may be unavoidable, the examiner/facilitator should minimize the occurrence if the child is adversely affected by these kinds of activities. It is very important for later programming to sort out these differences and dislikes.

In some sense, the opposite of being overly sensitive to sensory stimuli are children who do not respond to auditory input, who have receptive language issues. These behaviors are commonly found in children diagnosed with autism, as well as among less involved children. It is important for the examiner/facilitator to find out if a child does not respond to verbal requests or to the presentation of visual stimuli such as a toy. The items in *PIP* can help the team make these distinctions.

The following are some thoughts on the child who self-stimulates, for example flaps his/her hands in front of his/her face or repetitively manipulates an object in his/her hands. Sometimes if the examiner/facilitator is sensitive to the sensory issues mentioned above, the child may stop or reduce the amount of self-stimulating. On the other hand, sometimes regardless of what the examiner/facilitator does, the child still perceives the assessment situation as stressful and needs the self-stimulating behavior to remain calm. In still other instances, a child may be so turned inward that they just require this kind of self-focus or engagement. In any case, a general suggestion is that the examiner/facilitator should momentarily stop the self-stimulating if it hinders the child from giving an optimal performance in an activity. On the other hand, trying to stop entirely or greatly reduce the behavior may adversely affect the child's performance more than it helps it.

The Child Who Appears Uncoordinated

As a reminder, the child who appears awkward when doing motor tasks may just be going through an awkward stage or may end up with a specific diagnosis of Developmental Coordination Disorder, Pervasive Developmental Disorder, or even mild cerebral palsy. No matter what the diagnosis is or may be, it is important for the examiner/facilitator to separate motor difficulties from cognitive difficulties. The examiner/facilitator should not assume that just because a child does not know how to go about a new motor task that the child does not have age-appropriate cognitive skills.

Often the underlying factors for a child who appears uncoordinated are motor planning problems. These can be evident if a toddler appears to be typical when doing everyday tasks such as walking or climbing stairs, but seems awkward or does not know how to begin a novel motor task. If these observations are made, it sometimes helps if the examiner/facilitator allows the child a couple attempts at the task in *PIP* and then comes back to the same task at a later time in the assessment. Further, sometimes the performance of a child with this kind of difficulty deteriorates if he/she tries too many times or becomes very frustrated, which may adversely affect the rest of the evaluation.

The Child with Motor Impairments

This child may be the toddler with a diagnosis of cerebral palsy or spina bifida. It is to be recognized from the onset that there will be motor impairments. However, for the areas that are non-motor, the examiner/facilitator needs to access the child's level of skill, thus minimizing the effect of the motor deficit. The child will not have good hand function or good verbalizing or eating without a stable trunk. Even if the toddler has such difficulties to a minimal extent, the accuracy of pointing will be affected by the child's trunk stability. Trunk stability is affected by the legs. Even as the child who is not motorically involved needs to have his/her feet on the floor if sitting at a chair, even more does the child with motor deficits need to have the legs contribute to his/her base of support. This latter condition may mean placing the toddler in an adapted chair that has been fitted to the child. It also may mean sitting the child cross-legged on the floor with a second adult offering added trunk stability at the child's shoulders or hips. In the end, the examiner/facilitator is trying to maximize trunk stability and normalize the child's muscle tone.

In Brief Review

The brief discussion above offers merely a few examples of ways in which the play-based assessment, *PIP*, can be modified to accommodate a variety of behaviors and styles of learning in infants and young children. In addition, assessment teams should:

- ❖ feel free to add to modifications, as deemed necessary by parent report or their own firsthand observations of the child

- ❖ take written notes of any modifications made since these may be related to later programmatic and intervention decisions

- ❖ verify modifications made during the *PIP* assessment with changes made throughout other aspects of the evaluation process and in post-assessment conferencing with the family.

CHAPTER 3

Partners in Play: An Infant-Toddler Assessment for Natural Environments

After reading this chapter, you should be able to:

❖ Understand the parameters and components of the *PIP* assessment.

❖ Understand what needs to be done in preparation for the assessment.

❖ Understand the roles of various members of the assessment team.

❖ Understand the general guidelines for administering the *PIP* assessment, including the importance of building relationships with children and parents, roles of team members, and the evaluation process.

What Is the *PIP* Assessment?

Primary Developmental Areas Assessed

As discussed briefly in the Preface, *Partners in Play (PIP)* is a criterion-referenced, play-based assessment that offers opportunities in multiple formats for reporting parent information and observations of infants and toddlers in various contexts. Throughout both the parent report and observational sections of the instrument, five primary developmental areas are evaluated that offer a basis for validating informed clinical judgment by the assessment team. These areas include: Neuromotor skills (**NM**), Sensory-Perceptual skills (**SP**) that include adaptive behavior abilities, Cognitive abilities (**C**), Language and communication skills (**L**), and Social-Emotional behavior (**SE**). Note that these abbreviations are used throughout the record and scoring forms to denote the primary developmental area assessed by a given play activity/item. To obtain a sampling of the child's behavior and development across a variety of contexts, the *PIP* assessment is carried out by means of parent/caregiver report, two unstructured play periods, and a set of structured play-based activities. Following are descriptions of the five primary areas evaluated by *PIP*. Please refer to Appendix A for copies of the Caregiver and Developmental Assessment Record forms.

Neuromotor Domain (NM)

The Neuromotor Domain covers gross and fine motor abilities typically acquired between birth and three years of age. For infants, the focus includes skills and behaviors such as quality of movement, symmetry, and achievement of major milestones as seen in rolling, reaching, and sitting. For toddlers, items assess abilities such as walking, standing, transitions into and out of positions, activities with small toys, play with balls, and crossing midline.

Sensory-Perceptual Domain (SP)

The Sensory-Perceptual Domain involves the ability to take in information from the environment, using the senses, and subsequently to interpret and process that information. Early-developing skills and abilities include eating, drinking, responding to touch, visual tracking, and coordinating eye movement. For older children, undressing and dressing, playing with a bubble tumbler and bubbles, self-feeding with eating utensils, and maneuvering within the environment are evaluated. Clearly, several of these activities also sample self-help skills, or adaptive behavior. Such dual-purpose items are indicated with a double asterisk (**) throughout the Developmental Assessment Record form.

Cognitive Domain (C)

The Cognitive Domain refers to the development of thinking and problem-solving skills. For infants, items focus on attention to faces and designs, appropriate functional play with toys and persons, understanding of object permanence, object use, and comprehension of simple means-ends tasks. For toddlers, the focus of assessment shifts to more advanced behaviors such as symbolic play, social/cognitive games, problem-solving strategies, and understanding of cause-effect relationships.

Language Domain (L)

Prelinguistic abilities, communication, and early speech and language are all sampled in *PIP*. Infants and toddlers, particularly those with delays and special needs, are notably inconsistent in their linguistic behavior. Therefore, many of the same skills are sampled by either unstructured behavioral observation or by caregiver report—a design that adds breadth and validity to the results. Parents or primary caregivers can observe a young child's communication, language, and speech in far greater depth than can professionals, who can see the child only briefly and with whom the child may be reluctant to interact. Unstructured Caregiver-Child Play offers opportunities to observe strategies for communication, communicative intent, understanding of language and communication, vocalized turn taking, imitation skills, and joint referencing with the caregiver. In addition, structured activities are presented to evaluate responses to auditory stimuli and language behavior during early social games such as vocal play with puppets, pat-a-cake, and peek-a-boo.

Social and Emotional Behavior (SE)

The Social and Emotional Domain is measured almost exclusively by caregiver report and observations of unstructured play. Key observations include quality of interactions with familiar and unfamiliar persons, emotional stability, attentiveness, purposefulness during play, and attention-gaining behaviors. Finally during structured play, the child's abilities to adapt to various toys and materials, move from activity to activity, and attend are sampled.

The *PIP* assessment consists of the following components, all of which are described in the ensuing sections:

✣ Administration Guide

✣ Caregiver Record forms (containing the Initial Caregiver Interview and Caregiver Report of Child Development)

✣ Developmental Assessment Record forms (for recording the Unstructured Caregiver-Child Play, Unstructured Examiner-Child Play, and Structured Examiner-Child Interaction segments)

✣ forms for scoring the assessment

✣ suggested culturally sensitive toys and materials.

A Guide for Administration of the Assessment

Chapter 4 is the Guide for Administration containing instructions for administering *PIP*, including directions for the examiner/facilitator who interacts with the child and family and for the observers who assess behavior. General guidelines are provided for interviewing the primary caregiver and for setting up the unstructured play activities with the child. For each item in the Structured Examiner-Child Interaction part of the assessment, suggested toys and materials needed, guidelines for presenting the item/activity, directions for eliciting behaviors, and definitions for scoring are provided. Structured Examiner-Child Interaction is the only part of the *Partners in Play* assessment that requires specific administration procedures, because the other sections are designed for flexible and informal administration.

This guide also contains specific instructions for scoring and interpreting the results, in order to determine a child's eligibility for early intervention services. Appendices A and B contain all the worksheets, record forms, and tables needed for interpreting the evaluation results, and Appendix D lists state-by-state eligibility definitions under Part C of IDEA (Shackelford, 2005).

Caregiver and Developmental Assessment Record Forms

PIP has two record forms. The Caregiver Record contains forms for two caregiver interviews used to collect relevant information about the child and family. The Developmental Assessment Record forms are used for scoring the three parts that involve interaction with the child: Unstructured Caregiver-Child Play, Unstructured Examiner-Child Play, and Structured Examiner-Child Interaction. The Initial Caregiver Interview is completed by filling in background information relative to the child and family. The remaining forms follow a similar format. Each record form has a descriptive and quantitative checklist, designed to permit observers to record various aspects of a child's response quickly and efficiently. To record an item, the observer simply circles either the behaviors or skills seen or the appropriate rating of the child's performance. Age ranges are provided for every item as a guide for administration and observation. A few items require that the observer list specific examples of the child's behavior.

Caregiver Record Forms

The Initial Caregiver Interview is used to record a comprehensive birth and medical history, while the Caregiver Report of Child Development surveys the child's current developmental abilities in the five developmental domains (Neuromotor, Sensory-Perceptual, Cognitive, Language, and Social-Emotional).

Initial Caregiver Interview   The Initial Caregiver Interview is designed to assist service providers in gathering pertinent information about the child, family, and other people or circumstances that may be relevant to the child's development. This background information obtained from the caregivers during the first visit may be helpful as team members prepare for the later portions of the assessment. In this interview, information is historical and anecdotal; it does not contribute to the scoring of *PIP*.

Caregiver Report of Child Development   The second interview form, the Caregiver Report of Child Development, is used to sample information about the child's development and progress across key areas, as required by the Individual Family Service Plan (IFSP). Typically conducted during the first home or clinic/center visit, this interview focuses on the primary caregiver's observations of a range of child behaviors during daily care, family interactions, play, mealtimes, and other family routines. This section of the assessment constitutes more than 50% of the basis for determining eligibility for early intervention services. In the course of the interview, caregivers frequently volunteer additional information or examples of various behaviors. This information is not used in scoring, but observers are encouraged to make note of any information relevant to obtaining a complete picture of the child.

Developmental Assessment Record Forms

Two unstructured play segments—Unstructured Caregiver-Child Play and Unstructured Examiner-Child Play—comprise the first two periods of direct interaction with the child. In the first play period, one of the primary caregivers interacts with the child, and in the second a designated member of the evaluation team does. The same designated team member also interacts with the child later during the Structured Examiner-Child Interaction period. Observations from all three segments are recorded on the Developmental Assessment Record forms (included in Appendix A).

The Format of the Play Sessions

Unstructured Play

Each unstructured play period lasts up to 20 to 30 minutes and involves toys and materials selected by the primary caregiver for play prior to the team visit. (If the evaluation is conducted in a center or clinic, staff may select toys as well as having the caregiver bring clothing items, snacks, and perhaps a few favorite toys.) Specific administration instructions are not required for either of the two unstructured play sessions. Instead, each item taps standard developmental observations that team members record. Items are clustered on the forms by the method of observation used to assess the child's behavior, rather than by developmental domain. For example, in some parts of the assessment, an adult (caregiver or examiner) interacts directly with the child and the observers immediately record the child's behavior. Each item allows either a simple *yes/no* response or a *best-choice* selection, and the observer simply selects the *one* best choice from the checklist of descriptors. The results are therefore accurate and quickly attained. Each item belongs to only one domain, meaning that the observer is looking at a specific aspect of the child's behavior.

Structured Examiner-Child Play

The Structured Examiner-Child Interaction section of *PIP* is directed by the examiner/facilitator who has been selected to interact with the child. Although each item has specific administration instructions, the appointed individual should carry out the

Table 3-1 *Partners In Play* Assessment Components

Partners in Play Assessment Components	Corresponding *Partners in Play* Record Forms and Worksheets
Initial Caregiver Interview Background Information	Caregiver 1 Record Form: Initial Caregiver Interview
Caregiver Report of Child Development Caregiver Observations Interview	Caregiver 2 Record Form: Child Development. Scoring Worksheets 1 and 2
Unstructured Caregiver-Child Play Caregiver interacts with child	Developmental Assessment Record Form. Scoring Worksheets 1 and 2
Unstructured Examiner-Child Play Assessment team member interacts with child	Developmental Assessment Record Form. Scoring Worksheets 1 and 2
Structured Examiner-Child Interaction Assessment team member interacts with child	Developmental Assessment Record Form. Scoring Worksheet 1 and 2
	Summary Worksheet. Used with Scoring Worksheet 2 to determine the percentage of age-appropriate items passed

activities naturally and spontaneously, in order to elicit optimal responses and natural interactions. For this reason, no time limits are given for individual items or clusters of activities, and the items need not necessarily be presented in the order listed. This format allows the team flexibility in following the child's direction and interests. The items are clustered according to the suggested toys or play scenarios used. This gives the examiner opportunities to take out only one or two materials at a time and promotes a natural flow of interaction.

Suggested Culturally Sensitive Toys and Materials for Structured Play Activities

A variety of culturally sensitive toys and manipulatives are suggested for the Structured Examiner-Child play of *PIP*. Appropriate materials have been identified, based on our clinical experience of their (the toys) being attractive, durable, engaging, and age-appropriate for the target population. On the other hand, there still remains flexibility in administering the more structured portion of the assessment, should alternative materials of greater interest to the child need to be used. Accordingly, suggested toys and materials for the Structured Examiner-Child Developmental Assessment include the following toys:

+ bell with handle
+ round toy infant mirror
+ brightly colored vinyl checkerboard and schematic face
+ ethnically appropriate doll with diaper and shirt
+ plastic suspended red rings
+ tub buddies hand puppets
+ light baby blanket
+ three infant ring rattles
+ chime rattle with handle
+ toddler pull toy
+ pop-up pets box with four choice levers
+ shape sorter with blocks (with ball, square, and triangle shapes)

+ 8-inch ball
+ infant clutch ball
+ three small hardcover books
+ box of crayons
+ non-spill bubble tumbler with wand
+ baby bottle
+ comb and brush
+ dress-up vest or coat with fasteners including zipper, Velcro, buttons
+ problem-solving toy garage and cars
+ two opaque screens
+ small hand-held clear plastic container
+ toy construction hardhat

In addition, the caregiver should select certain toys and materials for the unstructured play period. The team should send or agree upon with the caregiver a list of materials to have prepared for the first or second home visit/evaluation session:

+ a variety of toys the child enjoys and plays with well
+ snacks and drinks for the child
+ cereal or small pieces of finger food (such as Cheerios)
+ one pair of the child's socks and shoes.

The examiner also will need the following items for the structured portion of the developmental assessment:

+ plain white drawing paper
+ a pair of his or her own socks and shoes (to demonstrate undressing and dressing skills).

The following picture includes a variety of toys and materials that would be appropriate for administering the structured play segment of the *PIP* assessment.

Considerations for Administering *Partners in Play*

Establishing rapport is critical to obtaining a sample of a child's typical behavior, so it is important that the child have an opportunity to interact and become familiar with team members prior to the Developmental Assessment portion of *PIP*. For this reason, schedule the Caregiver Interview components first so that the child can adjust to the unfamiliar team members' presence. With an infant of six to eight months or younger, the examiner/facilitator begins by talking with primary caregivers. Then, the examiner/facilitator gently talks with the baby and gradually engages him or her in play until rapport is established. (Another team member can be conducting the caregiver interviews during this time.) Young children, especially babies between eight and twelve months of age, may become anxious in the presence of strangers. Therefore, involve caregivers throughout the assessment process; they can sit nearby to comfort a shy child or may participate with the examiner/facilitator in direct play activities.

For children twelve months or older, allowing a period of warm-up and play is the best way to begin. Scheduling the caregiver interview for the first session and engaging the child in informal play following the interview is typically enough to overcome the child's hesitancy and anxiety. If necessary, several brief evaluation visits may be scheduled.

Building Relationships with Families

Public Laws 99–457, 102–119, and 105–17 recognize the centrality of families and caregivers in early intervention. Respect for the caregiver and family needs to pervade every dimension of the assessment process. Just as early interventionists seek to elicit the developmental and behavioral strengths of infants and toddlers, we also focus on and value the contributions of family members from widely divergent cultural, racial, educational, and financial backgrounds and living environments. We need to be sensitive to the many facets of caregivers' lives, including their work schedules, need for privacy, participation in recreational activities, outside pressures and stresses, their perceptions of special needs, and their perspectives on receiving help. Caring for young children, especially those with special needs, can be difficult and exhausting. Keeping these issues in mind will be critical toward building a positive rapport and relationships with caregivers and families. In addition, looking for opportunities for offering positive feedback to the family about the child's strengths and progress to date, especially during the initial identification/eligibility process, will go a long way toward building trust, rapport, and partnerships between the team and family members.

At best, having a group of strangers come to your home to determine whether your child has delays or areas of concern is uncomfortable and stressful. Whenever we are working in family homes, we must be sensitive to this dynamic and remember that we are guests in someone's home. Therefore, we need to offer the option that, should the family prefer, the initial evaluation be carried out in a setting outside the home, such as a hospital, clinic, or center. Here are some suggestions for making an in-home evaluation positive and successful:

1. Describe the assessment in simple terms so that the process of evaluation is clear.

2. Take the parent or caregiver step-by-step through various parts of the assessment prior to the first visit, explaining what will be done, over what period of time, and how the various activities will be completed.

3. Encourage parents or caregivers to ask questions along the way.

4. Take care to repeat explanations or information for families. Providing written information that families can review later also is very useful.

5. Show parents or caregivers genuine respect for the information and assistance that they deserve and bring to the assessment process.

6. Explain simply and clearly the results of the evaluation and the implications for early intervention programming.

7. Explain the next steps in the IFSP process and what services the child may receive in the future, if applicable.

8. Care should be taken so that the number of home visitors does not exceed three people. Otherwise, the team understandably will be overwhelming for both the family and the child being evaluated.

Finally, no assessment is culture free. While *Partners in Play* has been developed with sensitivity to cultural issues, language and communication are significant components in talking with the parent and interacting with the child. If English is not the family's primary language, make every effort to plan appropriate cultural guide accommodations, such as including someone who is familiar with the family's cultural/ethnic background and language in the evaluation process. In addition as discussed in Chapter 1, when visiting a family with a different ethnic/cultural background that is not shared by any of the team members, the team should take particular care to become familiar with the value systems and beliefs of those cultures that might have an impact on the interaction, evaluation, and future intervention process.

Building Relationships with Young Children

PIP is designed to obtain a sample record of a child's optimal current performance and typical behavior. Formal evaluations, unless carried out sensitively and carefully, may penalize an infant or toddler with even mild or subtle problems. Areas of special need often mask or hide the child's genuine areas of strength, unless the team has sufficient time to assess these concerns. Cross-referencing the information provided by the primary caregiver with observations during the evaluation is critical in determining whether the assessment team is obtaining an accurate representation of the child's developmental profile.

For infants and young children with significant suspected or identified delays, it may be obvious from informal observation that they meet established criteria to receive early intervention services, even prior to assessment with *PIP*. In such a case, it would be appropriate to administer items that may be significantly below the child's chronological or adjusted age but appear to correspond to his or her level of development. In such instances, it is very important to identify patterns of behavior and performance for the purposes of initial program planning and to write appropriate IFSP goals and objectives with the family. The caregiver report and unstructured and structured developmental format of *PIP*, together with clinical notes compiled during the evaluation, will aid the team in making these kinds of determinations.

Administration Time

The time required to administer *PIP* varies, depending upon the child's age, level of alertness, interest, and temperament during the evaluation. The following are general time frames for administering the assessment:

PIP Components	Administration Time (Minutes)
Both caregiver interviews	30–45 (first visit)
Unstructured Caregiver-Child Play	20–30 (second visit)
Unstructured Examiner-Child Play	20–30 (second or third visit)
Structured Examiner-Child Play	30–40 (second or third visit)

It is preferable to complete both the Unstructured Play and Structured Interaction components in a single visit. If the child's attention and endurance do not permit such a long session, try to complete the Unstructured Caregiver-Child and Unstructured Examiner-Child Play segments in one session. Schedule a third visit within five days to complete the evaluation. Particularly with infants 10 months or younger, be sensitive to cues of hunger and fatigue. We suggest that the caregiver have snacks available; the evaluation may be interrupted at any point if the child is hungry or thirsty. (Skill in eating and drinking are items included in the unstructured portion of the assessment; see items SP10, SP11, NM12, and NM13 in the Caregiver Record forms.) The assessment should proceed only when the infant or toddler is alert and attentive. If the child cannot be calmed with feeding, a brief period of rest, a change of position, or caregiver attention, the caregiver and team members may elect to discontinue the evaluation and resume at a later time.

Roles of Team Members in the Assessment

Procedures for administering *PIP* were developed to make the child's interactions with unfamiliar adults as consistent as possible. One professional (the examiner/ facilitator) works with the child, while other team members (observers) watch unobtrusively, fill out the record forms, and take clinical notes. Optionally, a third team member (the interviewer) may conduct the caregiver interviews, which allows the examiner/facilitator to be establishing rapport with the child during the first visit while the interviews are occurring. The role release inherent in the transdisciplinary assessment model requires that professionals become knowledgeable and experienced with evaluation across related disciplines. Thus, it is entirely appropriate for professionals in a number of different fields to administer *PIP*, once they have met the criteria and professional standards for formal testing. Professionals in nursing, pediatrics, special education, early childhood, psychology, communication disorders, and physical and occupational therapy may all be involved in administering and interpreting *PIP*.

Parents or Primary Caregivers

As we have emphasized several times throughout this book, the primary caregiver is an integral member of the assessment team. They are involved directly in offering information during the interview components and are the first individual(s) to interact with the child in unstructured play. While the examiner/facilitator interacts with the child during the remaining components of the assessment, parents or caregivers remain nearby and assist, as needed, with comforting the child and encouraging participation.

The Examiner/Play Facilitator

The evaluation team usually selects the examiner/facilitator (the person who interacts with the child) on the basis of expertise in the child's suspected areas of delay or concern. The examiner/facilitator should be thoroughly familiar with *PIP*, to avoid disrupting the assessment by too frequent reference to the specific instructions for administration.

Observers/Other Team Members

The observer or observers are responsible for recording and rating information obtained during all five components of the assessment. Having more than one discipline represented in the observation and recording process allows team members to offer a variety of perspectives, based on direct, firsthand data during the post-evaluation conference.

At the close of the assessment, all team members (including the interviewer, examiner/facilitator, and observers) should review and evaluate the child's performance on *PIP* in order to determine eligibility for early intervention according to criteria specified by the lead agency of the respective state. (Scoring worksheets are included in Appendices A and B as well as state-by-state eligibility criteria in Appendix D.) To the extent possible, the family should be involved in the final conferencing process.

The Evaluation Process

The evaluation process has three main stages:

1. pre-evaluation planning
2. evaluation activities (administering *PIP*)
3. post-assessment planning (reviewing and interpreting the results and formulating recommendations; child assessment team meeting and establishing goals).

Planning Before the Assessment

During the pre-evaluation meeting, team members review the reasons for the child's referral and any reports from hospitals or agencies that have had prior contact with the child and family. At this time, the team agrees who will be responsible for calling and later interviewing the family, interacting with the child, observing and scoring, and writing the evaluation report. Adequate planning ensures that the team's first visit with the family will be a coordinated, cooperative effort where members support the family, child, and each other. Additional calls may be necessary if the child has had prior services.

Prior to the visit, one team member should phone the family to explain the evaluation process and ask that the primary caregiver select a variety of toys and materials (including foods and drinks) and materials that the child enjoys and plays with well for use in the two unstructured play sessions. The caller also discusses the Unstructured Caregiver-Child Play portion of the evaluation, explaining the importance of watching the child interact with a familiar person. (If time permits, mailing a written copy of this information is helpful in ensuring the caregiver's understanding, especially if the family needs a cultural guide.) Team members subsequently should select a variety of materials that are similar to those suggested above, and that are culturally sensitive to the family and child for the more structured part of the play session. All toys and items need to be carefully washed and cleaned prior to the home visit. Finally, selected information on the caregiver forms may be completed prior to the first visit, if it is available on prior reports; however, this should be reviewed for accuracy at the time of the first visit.

PIP items and activities have been sequenced by developmental age ranges and to assure minimal changing of activities and manipulatives. To the extent possible, therefore, it is easiest to present the play activities in the order in which they appear on the record forms. However, the play assessment does allow flexibility of item presentation, based on the interviewer's and examiner's/facilitator's professional judgment.

Where to Begin and End the Assessment

In interviewing the caregiver, consult the age range given for each question. If the child's chronological age falls within the indicated range, the interviewer would normally ask a given question unless it is inappropriate for some reason; for example, the child is unable to perform the skill as a result of their delay or special need, and is clearly functioning below that level. It is critical to be sensitive in not asking questions that clearly are not developmentally appropriate, given the child's chronological age, adjusted age, or functioning level. As described below, questions not asked should be labeled NA (not appropriate) on the record form and the reason for not presenting the question noted.

On the developmental assessment, it is unnecessary to administer items that are clearly either above or below the child's current developmental level. The age ranges printed on the record forms indicate when certain behaviors are emerging or evident most of the time during the course of typical infant or toddler development. Use these age ranges for guidance in deciding where to begin the assessment, taking into account the child's actual or adjusted age, the caregiver's perception, and informal observations of the child. For the full-term infant or toddler suspected of developmental delays, start to administer items at least two months below the child's chronological age, probably more depending on readily apparent areas of difficulty. If the child was premature, use the child's adjusted or corrected age as explained below. Finally, if you are uncertain about the appropriate age range for starting the structured interaction activities, administer a sampling of item clusters as a firmer basis for making decisions. Any items not administered are not scored, as scatter skills are common in children with developmental delays and one cannot necessarily assume that a child has mastered all early-developing skills.

Thereafter, observe for/administer items up to the point where items are clearly beyond the child's appropriate developmental repertoire (as demonstrated with ratings of "not evident" or "rarely/never" on at least six consecutive items). Mark activities beyond the stopping point with "NA" (i.e., not appropriate) and indicate where the assessment was discontinued in the "Notes" section of the respective record form.

Determining Chronological and Adjusted Ages of the Child

Chronological age is determined by counting the number of months and days from the child's actual date of birth to the date of the first visit (e.g., 8 months, 16 days). Indicate the age in days and months on all record forms, but for the purposes of administration and scoring, round up or down to the nearest whole month. Corrected or adjusted age becomes important with children who were born prematurely because delays should be expected as a result of prematurity. To calculate adjusted age, assume a full-term gestation of 40 weeks and subtract the child's actual gestation from this figure. (For example, for an infant born at 26 weeks gestation, 40–26 = 14.) Therefore, subtract 14 weeks from the child's chronological age to arrive at an age that is adjusted for the effects of prematurity. When working with a premature child, be sure to discuss the concept of adjusted/corrected age with the parent or care-giver because this concept is important in formulating accurate developmental expec-tations and may affect eligibility for early intervention services.

Activities during the Evaluation

The *PIP* assessment may be administered in the family's home, in a clinic, or at an early intervention center. Minimize extraneous toys, materials, and noise to reduce distraction. Primary caregivers are an integral part of the assessment and should be present throughout, including during the examiner-child interaction periods. During the first visit, the examiner/play facilitator should make a record of the toys or mate-rials the caregiver has selected for unstructured play and should designate one group for Caregiver-Child Play and the other for Unstructured Examiner-Child Play. Changing materials between the two unstructured play sessions serves to maintain the child's interest and allows observation of how the child adjusts to transitions be-tween activities. It is best then to place these toys out of the child's sight during the interview segments of the evaluation.

Caregiver/Parent Interviews

The caregiver interviews may be conducted by the examiner or by a different team member. Because *PIP* is not standardized, the interviewer may choose to reword or explain questions if the caregiver or parent needs clarification. Typically, the inter-viewer would ask the open-ended question first (e.g., "What examples of problem solving have you seen when _____ is playing?"), to encourage descriptive answers. Then, if the parent does not spontaneously offer specific examples listed under that item (i.e., looks for objects dropped out of sight, plays with pull toys, finds items moved from one place to another, turns keys/tools to open doors, jars, or drawers), the interviewer can follow up by asking about these specific behaviors.

Unstructured Play

Specific directions for administration are not necessary for the unstructured play components of the assessment, because the items constitute observations of skills such as functional play, imitation, response to sounds, and babbling, which can easily be recorded during free play. To aid the observers, selected terms and blackline drawings are provided in Appendix C.

Once the interview components are completed, the examiner/facilitator carries out the remainder of the evaluation sitting on the floor near the caregiver and child, preferably on a carpeted or padded surface that is comfortable but that allows free movement for the child. The child may begin in any position that allows natural and spontaneous movement. If appropriate, adaptive equipment may be used to support and position the child. The unstructured play sessions continue for approximately 30 minutes each, or until sufficient information about the child has been gathered. Breaks for snacks, changing diapers, or other needs should be liberally offered, as necessary.

To begin the Unstructured Caregiver-Child Play segment, the designated toys are placed on the floor within the child's reach. The examiner/play facilitator asks the caregiver to begin by initiating play with one of the child's favorite toys, and then to move on to other play materials and objects, as determined by the child's interest. The caregiver is encouraged to interact as naturally as possible, as he or she would during normal daily play with the child, and to take breaks at any time to give the child a snack or provide for other needs.

For Unstructured Examiner/Facilitator-Child Play, the toys used in the previous segment are removed and the new set of toys presented to the child. While the parent or caregiver remains seated within the child's sight, the examiner/facilitator gains the child's attention and interest with one of the toys. The examiner interacts with the child in a nurturing, relaxed, and natural manner, following the child's lead, as befits a free-play assessment.

Structured Examiner/Facilitator Play

Toys and materials for the structured portion of the assessment should remain out of sight until needed. Several items in the Structured Examiner/Facilitator-Child Play component require some setup from time to time. Therefore, it is helpful to have a team member assist the examiner/facilitator by preparing materials and removing them when no longer needed. Item-by-item explanations of materials needed, administration procedures, and recording of responses for the structured interaction component are included in Chapter 4. Even though these activities have a structured administration procedure, the examiner/facilitator should carry them out as naturally and spontaneously as possible, in order to elicit optimal responses and authentic interactions. For items recorded as "not evident, emerging, developing," or "well developed," these ratings are based primarily on the consistency of the child's response. Thus, each of these items would be elicited up to four times, unless the child's behavior demonstrates unambiguously either mastery or inability to perform the item. No time limits are given for individual items or item clusters of activities, to allow the examiner/play facilitator flexibility in following the child's direction and interests. Based on good clinical judgment, the examiner/facilitator also may discontinue activities that are clearly developmentally inappropriate or that are excessively challenging to the child's comfort and frustration levels.

Suggested toys and materials are commonly available toddler toys, such as pull toys, dolls, and rattles. It may be that the caregiver provides some very similar toys for the unstructured play sessions, and the child may demonstrate some target skills during the free-play sessions. We recommend that all age-appropriate items still be administered, since the child's performance may vary across contexts or with unfamiliar materials.

Child Assessment Team Meeting Following Evaluation

The third part of the evaluation process entails compiling all of the family and child data, reviewing it, generating tentative recommendations with input from the family, and writing draft and final reports. If the child is eligible for early intervention, the team assists the family with setting up meeting dates to develop an IFSP and making contacts for referral to and entry into an appropriate program.

All members of the team should participate in the final review process in order to offer their input and perspectives. The administration of *PIP* very likely will be part of a total evaluation package, with other discipline-specific components that also have been given. All information relating to the child and family should be reviewed jointly by the psychologist, speech/language therapist, occupational therapist, physical therapist, and any other relevant team members. Specific types of information will be especially relevant in establishing eligibility and initial planning with the family for meaningful intervention programs. These data should include the following statements concerning the child: typical patterns of interacting with familiar and unfamiliar persons, both developmental and functional information, descriptions of the child's behavior in unstructured and more structured environments, the types of supports and assistance required, and information related to noteworthy preferences and instructional strategies (McLean, Wolery, & Bailey Jr., 2004). Following the review of all child information, concerns and priorities of the family again need to be considered prior to the establishing of specific goals to be incorporated into the Individual Family Service Plan (IFSP). As a reminder, it is very helpful if this preliminary process includes primary caregivers or parents in the discussion before the development of the IFSP in writing.

Establishing Goals and Meeting with the Family

Developing goals for the IFSP on the basis of the initial assessment should be viewed as a tentative blueprint, that is subject to ongoing review and change if or when a child enters a program. In addition to complying with state-specific policies and guidelines, goals described in the IFSP need to be developmental, functional for the child, and presented within the natural/cultural contexts of the family and anticipated program. In addition to the initial assessment results, *PIP* is an excellent authentic evaluation instrument that can be used for follow-up of developmental and behavioral progress throughout the first two years so that periodically (every six months), goals can be revised as appropriate. Finally, skills addressed in the goal-setting process for the child need to address: gross and fine motor (neuromotor) development, social and emotional behavior (including evaluation of sensory-motor regulation abilities), communication, cognitive development, and adaptive behavior.

Goals established in the IFSP need to be paired with realistic educational strategies for implementation on behalf of both the family and the educational staff who will be working with the child. This approach will go a long way toward assuring a closer collaboration among team members and between the educational staff and family. Various disciplines need to be mindful that while home visits are organized and carried out by professionals in the field, ultimately the family is the consistent consideration in the child's life and the "real teacher" in the implementation of the intervention program. The "power" and strength of the recommendations, over time, will reside not with the individual disciplines involved but in the partnership and follow-through by families.

In Brief Review

This chapter discussed the parameters of the *PIP* assessment, formats of the play sessions, considerations for administering *Partners in Play*, as well as phases of the evaluation process. Throughout the evaluation process, the following concepts are helpful to keep in mind:

❖ The team assessing a child needs to prepare for the evaluation in advance so that the roles of individuals are clear in terms of responsibilities.

❖ Multiple observers/recorders are helpful during the assessment.

❖ Results of the evaluation should be described and explained clearly to the family without professional jargon.

❖ The process of developing recommendations for the child needs to involve the family prior to finalizing goals and strategies for programming.

CHAPTER 4

A Manual for Observing, Recording, and Administering the *PIP* Assessment

After reading this chapter, you should be able to:

✧ Understand how to record responses to questions on the Caregiver Record forms.

✧ Understand how to record observations for the Unstructured Play sections of the *PIP* assessment.

✧ Understand how to administer items of the Structured Play section of *PIP* and record observations accordingly.

The Recording Format Described

While the examiner/facilitator and the interviewer are carrying out the evaluation, one or more team members serve as observers, filling out the record forms and noting pertinent behaviors or observations. All record forms should be completed at the time of the evaluation, *not* left to recall after the assessment. As noted in previous chapters, having more than one observer representing different disciplines is extremely helpful in obtaining the most complete picture of a child's development. In the case of multiple observers, each person records items individually; any consultation and resolution of recording discrepancies can take place during the post-assessment conference. The child's primary caregiver also may have useful input in confirming specific ratings and information following the evaluation.

PIP uses straightforward recording formats, as illustrated in Table 4-1. Individual items require supplying one of the following four types of information:

- Circle *any/all* (behaviors observed) and *sum*
- Circle the *one* most appropriate description of the frequency of a behavior:
    - Always requires assistance from another
    - Usually/often requires assistance from another
    - Sometimes/varies with situation
    - Rarely/never requires assistance
- Circle the *one* most appropriate rating of ability/skill level:
    - Not evident (never/rarely)—The behavior(s) or skills(s) are not observed at all or occur less than $1/_3$ of the time
    - Emerging (sometimes)—The behavior(s) or skill(s) occur approximately $1/_3$ to $1/_2$ of the time
    - Developing (usually/frequently)—The behavior(s) or skill(s) occur approximately $1/_2$ to $2/_3$ of the time.
    - Well developed (most of the time)—Behavior(s) or skill(s) occur more than $2/_3$ of the time; the child must produce the behavior spontaneously without physical prompts or models from the examiner (verbal encouragement is permitted)
- List or circle specific behaviors observed

The Caregiver Report of Child Development contains 47 items. Unstructured Caregiver-Child Play includes 13 items. Unstructured Examiner-Child Play and Structured Examiner-Child Interaction consist of 15 item clusters each. If a child demonstrates only certain skills or behaviors within an item cluster, then that performance observed should be recorded. Item activities not administered or questions not asked of the caregiver during the evaluation are labeled NA on the record form, and the reason for not presenting them noted. If more than one caregiver is present for the interview, the observers may wish to use separate recording forms to report each caregiver's responses. Alternatively, observers may write each caregiver's initials next

Table 4-1 Examples of Scored Items from Caregiver Report of Child Development and Unstructured Caregiver-Child 2

L42. What does _____ do with books?
   (7-36 months)

Circle Any/All and Sum	
Turns pages	(1)
Scans/looks at pictures	(1)
Points/pats	(1)
Vocalizes randomly	(1)
Imitates pictured sounds/ objects/living things	1
Verbalizes	1
Total	4

c. Shows appropriate functional play with toys/objects
   (17-36 months)

Circle One	
Not evident	1
Emerging	2
Developing	3
Well developed	(4)

C8. Play Strategies Observed
   a. Smiles/laughs at engaging routines
      (5-36 months)

Circle One	
Not evident	1
Emerging	2
Developing	3
Well developed	(4)

d. Represents two or more related events in play
   (17-36 months)

Circle One	
Not evident	1
Emerging	(2)
Developing	3
Well developed	4

b. Engages in games/gamelike play
   (5-36 months)

Circle One	
Not evident	1
Emerging	2
Developing	3
Well developed	(4)

e. Engages in symbolic play with toys/caregiver
   (23-36 months)

Circle One	
Not evident	(1)
Emerging	2
Developing	3
Well developed	4

to the responses he or she provided (particularly if the caregivers disagree about certain information).

Recording Unstructured Play Activities

Please refer to Appendix C for definitions and blackline drawings that will assist observers in recording behaviors accurately during the Unstructured Caregiver-Child Play and Unstructured Examiner-Child Play components of the *PIP* assessment. Complete administration and observation instructions for the Structured Examiner-Child Interaction component are included later in this chapter. The format as described above should be followed in recording observations for both segments of the unstructured play with the parent and with the examiner.

Prior to administration of the *PIP* assessment, team members should spend time practicing, observing, and recording sessions. This practice will give observers opportunities to develop a level of comfort so that they will be able to record effectively throughout the actual assessment session, without excessive reference to definitions and the blackline drawings in Appendix C. Familiarity with the assessment will greatly enhance the natural flow of administration and scoring. The observer also should note that each item typically includes several sub-items that are recorded at different child ages so that in actuality the observer may be rating and recording for only two of five sub-items. These sub-items are indicated with small letters (e.g., *a, b, c,* etc.). Each page of the record form also provides space for making notes to record child-specific behaviors for later reference. This observing and recording format is consistent throughout all items or activities of unstructured play. Finally, as described in Chapter 3, age ranges have been provided as a guide for the observer. These appear immediately above the scoring rubric for each item. In addition, capitalized letters that appear next to the item/activity number are abbreviations for each of the five primary developmental domains. These indicate the primary domain to which the item/activity belongs, that also should be used in the final count and scoring of the domains. The double asterisk (**) indicates that the skill is an Adaptive Behavior.

The following 13 items and item clusters are included in *Unstructured Caregiver-Child Play:*

L1. Strategies for Communication

a. Differential vocalization (1–6 months)

b. Vocal play (3–18 months)

c. Reduplicated babbling (9–18 months)

d. Variegated babbling (9–18 months)

e. Using gestures (9–36 months)

f. Jargon-like vocalizations (9–36 months)

g. Making requests (11–36 months)

h. Using single words (11–36 months)

      i. Putting two words together (11–36 months)

      j. Putting three or more words together (17–36 months)

      k. Initiating/engaging in dialogue/discourse (17–36 months)

L2. Communication of Needs/Intent

    a. Making basic needs known (1–36 months)

    b. Making social needs known (1–36 months)

L3. Child's Understanding of Language or Communication

    a. Responds to caregiver's vocal play (3–12 months)

    b. Responds to gestures (7–36 months)

    c. Responds to single-word requests/directions (9–36 months)

    d. Responds to 1-step direction (13–36 months)

    e. Responds to 2-step directions (23–36 months)

L4. Vocalized Turn-Taking

    a. Decreases/increases vocalizations in response to caregiver (1–6 months)

    b. Vocalizes across 1 turn (1–8 months)

    c. Vocalizes across 2 turns (3–18 months)

L5. Joint Referencing with Caregiver

    a. Attends to caregiver (1–18 months)

    b. Gains/directs attention of caregiver (3–18 months)

    c. Continues familiar routine with caregiver (5–24 months)

    d. Shows humor with caregiver (7–36 months)

SE6. Quality of Social Interaction with Caregiver

    a. Responds to smiling/soft talking (1–36 months)

    b. Goes to caregiver for comfort (1–36 months)

SE7. Emotional Stability

    a. Has periods of contentment during interaction with caregiver (1–36 months)

    b. Able to self-calm (1–36 months)

    c. Initiates interaction (7–36 months)

    d. Maintains interaction (9–36 months)

C8. Play Strategies Observed

    a. Smiles/laughs at engaging routines (5–36 months)

    b. Engages in games/game-like play (5–36 months)

    c. Shows appropriate functional play with toys/objects (17–36 months)

    d. Represents 2 or more related events in play (17–36 months)

    e. Engages in symbolic play with toys/caregiver (23–36 months)

SP9. Moving and Maneuvering in the Environment

    a. Rolls from stomach to back (3–12 months)

    b. Rolls from back to stomach (3–12 months)

    c. Creeps (5–12 months)

    d. Pulls up on people and furniture (7–16 months)

    e. Cruises around people and furniture (9–18 months)

    f. Walks (9–24 months)

    g. Runs (13–36 months)

SP10. Skill in Eating **

    a. Oral-motor response/appropriate gag reflex (1–6 months)

    b. Takes food appropriately into mouth (5–18 months)

    c. Lateralizes tongue with food (5–18 months)

    d. Swallows food (5–18 months)

    e. Chews (7–18 months)

SP11. Drinking **

    a. Uses continuous, organized sucking pattern with bottle/breast (1–6 months)

    b. Shows jaw, tongue, and lip control stable with cup/glass drinking (9–36 months)

    c. Drinks with little liquid lost (11–36 months)

NM12. Picking Up Finger Food/Self-Feeding **

    a. Brings finger food to mouth independently (9–18 months)

    b. Rakes to pick up food (9–18 months)

    c. Uses three-jaw chuck grasp (9–18 months)

    d. Uses index finger and thumb grasp (11–24 months)

SP13. Self-Feeding with Eating Utensils **

    a. Brings spoon to mouth (11–36 months)

    b. Puts spoonful of food in mouth independently (13–36 months)

    c. Uses pronated hand to hold spoon (13–36 months)

    d. Uses supinated hand to hold spoon (15–36 months)

The 15 following items/item clusters comprise the *Unstructured Examiner-Child Play* segment of the *PIP*.

SE14. Quality of Interaction with Unfamiliar Person(s)

    a. Responds to smiling/soft talking (1–36 months)

    b. Initiates interaction (7–36 months)

    c. Maintains interaction (9–36 months)

    d. Relates to two or more unfamiliar persons (9–36 months)

SE15. Attentiveness to Play Activities

    a. Attends to age-appropriate range of play events (1–36 months)

    b. Attends to play activities for age-appropriate periods of time (1–36 months)

L16. Response to Common Sounds in the Environment

    a. Responds to voices in same or different room (1–36 months)

    b. Responds to common sounds in the same or different room (1–36 months)

NM17. Quality of Movement

    a. Moves in and out of developmental positions (3–36 months)

    b. Uses graded, smooth movement (3–36 months)

NM18. Large Motor Milestones (without movement or maneuvering)

    a. Sits (5–36 months)

    b. Uses 4-point positions (7–36 months)

NM19. Hand Skills Observed

    a. Brings hands to midline (3–12 months)

    b. Reaches with right and left hands (3–12 months)

    c. Grasps with right and left hands (3–12 months)

    d. Transfers from hand to hand (5–12 months)

    e. Releases objects with right and left hands (5–12 months)

    f. Crosses midline with right and left hands (13–36 months)

NM20. Body Symmetry

    a. On back (1–6 months)

    b. On stomach (1–6 months)

    c. In sitting (5–18 months)

    d. In 4-point creeping (7–18 months)

    e. In standing/upright/walking (11–36 months)

NM21. Transitions into and out of Various Positions

    a. Moves out of sitting (9–24 months)

    b. Moves into sitting (9–24 months)

    c. Moves out of standing (13–36 months)

    d. Moves into standing (13–36 months)

SP22. Response to Touch

    a. Responds to personal, physical touch (1–36 months)

    b. Enjoys different textures (13–18 months)

    c. Walks on different surfaces (13–24 months)

SE23. Attention-Gaining Behaviors Observed

    a. Uses positive, nonverbal strategies to gain attention (5–36 months)

    b. Uses positive verbal strategies to gain attention (7–36 months)

NM24. Protective Responses Observed

    a. Uses forward propping (5–12 months)

    b. Uses lateral propping (5–12 months)

    c. Uses backward protective response/balance reaction (9–12 months)

C25. Purposeful Behavior in Play

    a. Uses play to practice familiar/known skills and routines (7–36 months)

    b. Uses play to acquire/try new skills/tasks (9–36 months)

L26. Intelligibility of Speech and Language

    a. Uses single prompted/imitated expressions that are understandable (11–36 months)

    b. Uses single spontaneous expressions (i.e., one word) that are understandable (11–36 months)

    c. Uses understandable multiword expressions (spontaneous or prompted) (11–36 months)

C27. Problem-Solving Skills Observed

    a. Solves problems without assistance (11–36 months)

    b. Solves age-appropriate problems (11–36 months)

L28. Imitation Skills Observed

    a. Uses gestures (5–36 months)

    b. Vowels (5–36 months)

    c. Reduplicated babbling (9–18 months)

    d. Variegated babbling (9–18 months)

    e. Blends (9–36 months)

    f. Single words (11–36 months)

    g. Two-word combinations (17–36 months)

    h. Three-word combinations (23–36 months)

Typically during a second or third visit, the Structured Examiner–Child Play activities are administered. Unlike the unstructured segments of the *PIP*, these items/activities have specific instructions for administration and scoring. Toys and materials are suggested for the administration of this part of the assessment. However, the evaluation team should feel free to select alternate toys and materials that are similar in nature, and that could be used to measure the same aspects of development. Accordingly, the observer should follow the instructions for administration and scoring that are provided in the following section.

Instructions for Administering and Observing Structured Examiner–Child Play Activities

The Structured Examiner/Facilitator-Child Interaction play activities are listed below. The following pages describe each in detail, and include suggested materials, administration procedures, recording instructions, and a copy of the actual activities from the scoring form. All of the materials referred to are listed and pictured in Chapter 3.

    L29. Response to Bell

    C30. Attention to Faces and Designs

  SP31. Tracking

    L32. Early Social Games

  NM33. Play with Rattles

    C34. Response to Hidden Objects

    C35. Early Understanding of Cause and Effect

    C36. Play with Blocks and Shape Sorter

  NM37. Play with Balls

    C38. Play with Pictures and Print

  SP39. Play with Bubble Tumbler

    C40. Advanced Play with Doll

    C41. Problem Solving

  SP42. Undressing and Dressing

  SE43. Adaptability

L29. Response to Bell

Items

a. Alerts/locates bell on right side
b. Alerts/locates bell on left side

Materials

❖ Bell with handle

Administration

With the child in any position, hold the bell out of the child's sight about 10 inches from the head. To assess alerting to and localization of the sound, ring the bell first on the right side. Then repeat on the left, making sure that the child is not looking at the bell when you ring it. Offer up to four trials on each side to determine consistency.

Guidelines for Recording

If the child's head or eyes turn to the side where the bell is rung, count this as a response. If the child does not turn to the sound, circle 1 (Not evident). If the child locates the sound on all three presentations on both sides, circle 4 (Responds consistently). Otherwise, circle 2 (Responds one time) or 3 (Responds inconsistently), whichever describes the child's behavior. If the child appears to locate the sound on one side but not the other, or consistently turns to the same side regardless of where the bell is presented, note this observation on the form.

a. Alerts/locates bell on right side
(1–36 months)

Circle One	
Not evident	1
Responds one time	2
Responds inconsistently	3
Responds consistently	4

b. Alerts/locates bell on left side
(1–36 months)

Circle One	
Not evident	1
Responds one time	2
Responds inconsistently	3
Responds consistently	4

C30. Attention to Faces and Designs

Items

a. Attends to human face
b. Attends to checkerboard
c. Attends to schematic face (includes social/communicative response)
d. Responds to real image in mirror (includes social/communicative response)
e. Early response to baby doll (e.g., holding, poking, touching, kissing)

Materials

- Schematic checkerboard and face
- Infant mirror
- Baby doll

Administration

This cluster addresses five visual attending activities. The child may be placed in any position, though supine or sitting is preferred. Administration time is flexible, with a recommended upper limit of 30 seconds for each activity. Refrain from talking to the child during these activities, so the child's interest is sustained visually not auditorally. With each attending activity, present the toy or your face approximately 12 inches from the child's face at midline. The items should be presented in developmental order, as listed on the record form. Administer each item up to four times, as needed to determine consistency.

Guidelines for Recording

For each cluster item, circle the one most appropriate evaluation response.

a. Attends to human face (1–6 months)

Circle One	
Not evident	1
Emerging	2
Developing	3
Well developed	4

b. Attends to checkerboard (1–6 months)

Circle One	
Not evident	1
Emerging	2
Developing	3
Well developed	4

c. Attends to schematic face (includes social/communicative response) (1–6 months)

Circle One	
Not evident	1
Emerging	2
Developing	3
Well developed	4

d. Responds to real image in mirror (includes social/communicative response) (3–18 months)

Circle One	
Not evident	1
Emerging	2
Developing	3
Well developed	4

e. Early response to baby doll (e.g., holding, poking, touching, kissing) (5–18 months)

Circle One	
Not evident	1
Emerging	2
Developing	3
Well developed	4

SP31. Tracking

Items

a. Tracks horizontally
b. Tracks in circle
c. Shows smooth eye movement
d. Shows coordinated eye movement

Materials

∴ Suspended red rings

Administration

Position the child in supine or in sitting position. To evaluate horizontal tracking, present the rings at midline, approximately 12 inches from the child's face. Once the child's attention is on the rings, move them slowly from left to right and back. This sequence may be repeated three times, as necessary, to determine consistency.

For circular tracking, present the rings slightly above the child's eyes, level with the top of his or her head. Once the child's attention is on the rings, move them in a clockwise circle approximately 8 inches in diameter and 12 inches from the child's face. This sequence also is repeated three times, as necessary to determine consistency.

Guidelines for Recording

For each item, circle the one most appropriate descriptor. Because the quality of the child's eye movements may be difficult to observe at a distance, the examiner may wish to indicate unobtrusively to the observers if issues of smooth or coordinated eye movement exist.

a. Tracks horizontally (1–36 months)

Circle One	
Not evident	1
Emerging	2
Developing	3
Well developed	4

b. Tracks in circle (1–36 months)

Circle One	
Not evident	1
Emerging	2
Developing	3
Well developed	4

c. Shows smooth eye movement (1–36 months)

Circle One	
Not evident	1
Emerging	2
Developing	3
Well developed	4

d. Shows coordinated eye movement (1–36 months)

Circle One	
Not evident	1
Emerging	2
Developing	3
Well developed	4

L32. Early Social Games

Items

   a. Engages in vocal play with puppet
   b. Plays peek-a-boo
   c. Plays pat-a-cake

Materials

   ❖ Puppet
   ❖ Doll blanket

Administration

This sequence of social games can be carried out in any position, though supine or sitting is preferred. Face the child for all games. The series begins with vocal play with the puppet. Present the puppet at midline about 12 inches from the child's face. Talk while moving the puppet to elicit vocalizations. Up to five opportunities may be offered before moving to peek-a-boo.

     For peek-a-boo, either make the puppet cover its eyes or place one corner of the doll blanket over the child's face. Then say "peek-a-boo" while uncovering the puppet's eyes or pulling the blanket off the child. If the child does not spontaneously cover his or her eyes, model and encourage this behavior. Attempt to engage the child in reciprocal play three or four times.

     Pat-a-cake may be played with or without the puppet, whichever seems most engaging for the child. Initiate the game by patting the child's hands, either with the puppet's or your hands, smiling, and perhaps giving a verbal prompt.

Guidelines for Recording

For each item, circle the one best descriptor. The child should actively vocalize in response to the puppet in item (a). For peek-a-boo, the child should pull off the blanket or uncover his or her eyes when the examiner says "peek-a-boo." For pat-a-cake, the child should imitate the examiner's hand movements. If the examiner offers any cues or models other than verbal prompts, note them on the recording form. To be rated as well developed, the child's behavior must be spontaneous, without physical prompts or models from the examiner.

a. Engages in vocal play with puppet (3–8 months)

Circle One	
Not evident	1
Emerging	2
Developing	3
Well developed	4

b. Plays peek-a-boo (3–12 months)

Circle One	
Not evident	1
Emerging	2
Developing	3
Well developed	4

c. Plays pat-a-cake (7–18 months)

Circle One	
Not evident	1
Emerging	2
Developing	3
Well developed	4

NM33. Play with Rattles

Items

a. Reaches for rattle
b. Grasps rattle
c. Transfers rattle hand-to-hand
d. Releases rattle

Materials

❖ Three ring rattles

Administration

With the child in any position, select one of the three rattles to present to the child. Suspend it approximately 12 inches from the child's body, at midline, and about arm height. Shake the rattle to attract the child's attention and move it within easy reach of the child, offering it. If the child does not spontaneously reach for and grasp the rattle, offer assistance by lightly stroking the top of the child's hand to elicit a grasp. Make a total of three attempts, if necessary, to encourage the child to reach for and grasp the rattle. If the child still does not respond, move to the next item cluster. Engage in play with the rattles long enough to observe reaching, grasping, transferring, and releasing. Presenting a second rattle to the child may elicit transferring or releasing the first rattle. Repeat the activity three times to determine consistency for recording purposes.

Guidelines for Recording

For each item, circle the one best descriptor of the child's behavior. Note whether the child reaches for and grasps the rattle with one or both hands. To receive credit for a well-developed release, the child should voluntarily release the rattle with either one or both hands. If the examiner offers any cues or models other than verbal prompts, note them on the recording form. To be rated as well developed, the child's behavior must be spontaneous, without physical prompts or models from the examiner.

a. Reaches for rattle
(3–12 months)

Circle One	
Not evident	1
Emerging	2
Developing	3
Well developed	4

b. Grasps rattle
(3–12 months)

Circle One	
Not evident	1
Emerging	2
Developing	3
Well developed	4

c. Transfers rattle hand-to-hand
(5–12 months)

Circle One	
Not evident	1
Emerging	2
Developing	3
Well developed	4

d. Releases rattle
(5–12 months)

Circle One	
Not evident	1
Emerging	2
Developing	3
Well developed	4

C34. Response to Hidden Objects

Items

a. Finds partially covered rattle
b. Finds completely covered rattle

Materials

✣ Chime rattle
✣ Doll blanket

Administration

If the child fails to reach for or grasp the rattle in the NM33 item cluster, the examiner may use professional judgment in determining whether this item is developmentally appropriate. If in doubt, always present the test item, as children may react differently depending on the context and their level of interest.

The child may be in any position except supine, though sitting is preferred. Show the rattle to the child and engage his or her interest in it. Then place it in front of the child within reach and partially cover the handle with the doll blanket. Encourage the child to find the rattle. Repeat the sequence two times by showing the rattle and partially covering again. Then present the rattle as before, but cover it completely with the doll blanket and encourage the child to find it. Present up to four opportunities to determine consistency of response.

Guidelines for Recording

Circle the one most appropriate descriptor of the child's response. The child needs only to uncover the rattle; grasping it is not required. If the examiner offers any cues or models other than verbal prompts, note them on the recording form. To be rated as well developed, the child's behavior must be spontaneous, without physical prompts or models from the examiner.

a. Finds partially covered rattle (5–12 months)

Circle One	
Not evident	1
Emerging	2
Developing	3
Well developed	4

b. Finds completely covered rattle (7–12 months)

Circle One	
Not evident	1
Emerging	2
Developing	3
Well developed	4

C35. Early Understanding of Cause and Effect

Items

   a. Plays with pull toy
   b. Plays with pop-up pets box

Materials

   ✛ Snoopy pull toy
   ✛ Pop-up pets box

Administration

The first item is best presented with the child standing, if developmentally appropriate. The pop-up box is best presented with the child in a supported or independent sitting position. The toys should be presented on a firm surface that allows for mobility and reaching.

For play with the pull toy, situate Snoopy in front of the infant or toddler with the dog a short distance away but the string stretched within easy reach of the child. First allow time for the child to reach and pull the string independently without demonstration, although verbal encouragement may be offered. If the child does not attempt to respond, demonstrate by pulling Snoopy once or twice, then again stretch the string within reach and wait for the child to retrieve it.

Next offer the pop-up toy with the doors to the box closed. Do not demonstrate initially, but encourage the child to find the animals, allowing the child to explore the various buttons and levers spontaneously. If the child does not successfully open at least one door independently, then demonstrate opening all the doors from left to right, keeping the toy turned toward the child. Then close the doors again and encourage the child to open them to see the animals or figures. If the child still is not successful in opening at least one door, provide a second demonstration of all the doors. If the child does not respond after the second demonstration, move on to the next item cluster.

Guidelines for Recording

Circle the one most appropriate descriptor of the child's behavior. Make a note if the child indicates an interest in the pop-up box but is unable to manipulate the levers due to physical limitations. The item cannot be credited, but the anecdotal evidence of cause-and-effect understanding may be considered in the post-assessment determination of eligibility. If the examiner offers any cues or models other than verbal prompts, note them on the recording form.

a. Plays with pull toy
(5–12 months)

Circle One	
No awareness evident	1
Shows interest in toy/ Holds string/ball only	2
Pulls without awareness	3
Pulls with awareness	4

b. Plays with pop-up pets box
(9–24 months)

Circle One	
No awareness evident	1
Opens 1 lever	2
Opens 2 levers	3
Opens 3 levers	4
Opens 4 levers	5

C36. Play with Blocks and Shape Sorter

Items

    a. Plays with blocks and shape sorter
    b. Visual discrimination skills

Materials

    ❖ Shape sorter with blocks

Administration

Place the shape sorter on the floor directly in front of the child with the lid off and the blocks inside. Observe how the child spontaneously plays with it. If the child does not do so spontaneously, encourage him or her to take out the blocks and put them back in the container.

    After a short period of play, take all the blocks out of the shape sorter and put the lid on it. Encourage the child to insert the blocks through the holes in the lid. You may name the shapes (beginning first with the circle, then the square and triangle) or give the blocks to the child, but refrain from pointing directly to the appropriate hole on the lid. If the child fails to insert at least one shape through the corresponding hole, then provide up to two demonstrations with the circle, allowing time for the child to respond after each prompt.

Guidelines for Recording

For (a) Plays with blocks and shape sorter, circle all behaviors the child demonstrates and sum. For (b)

Visual discrimination skills, circle the single best descriptor of the child's behavior. As before, if physical limitations appear to interfere with the child's ability to insert the blocks into the shape sorter, make a note of this, although the item cannot be credited. If the examiner offers any cues or models other than verbal prompts, note them on the recording form.

a. Plays with blocks and shape sorter (9–18 months)

Circle Any/All and Sum	
Holds	1
Bangs	1
Takes out container	1
Puts into container	1
Stacks	1
Total	

b. Visual discrimination skills (11–36 months)

Circle One	
Places 1 block near hole	1
Inserts 1 block through hole	2
Places 2–3 blocks near hole	3
Inserts 2–3 blocks through hole	4

NM37. Play with Balls

Items

a. Rolls ball with intent
b. Throws ball with intent
c. Catches ball with intent

Materials

✢ Infant clutch ball
✢ 8-inch ball

Administration

To assess ball-rolling ability, the child should be in supported or independent sitting. Sit facing the child and present the infant clutch ball. Roll the ball once toward the child, then wait for a response. If the child rolls the ball back to you, take turns rolling the ball back and forth. If the child does not respond, take the ball back and demonstrate rolling the ball toward the child three more times, allowing time for a response between each trial.

The throwing and catching items should be administered with the child in a supported or independent standing position. Determine whether standing, throwing, and catching are developmentally appropriate for the child before carrying out these activities. If so, sit on the floor facing the child. Give the child the 8-inch ball to hold and encourage him or her to throw it to you. If the child throws the ball when prompted, you may toss it gently back to assess catching ability and continue for two or more turns. If the child does not respond, take the ball and verbally prepare the child to catch it. Then toss it gently. Make four attempts to elicit throwing and catching before moving to the next item.

Guidelines for Recording

For each item, circle the one best descriptor of the child's behavior. "With intent" means that the child has the clearly observable purpose of throwing or catching the ball. If the child spontaneously engages in throw-and-catch turn-taking, this is a relevant developmental observation to include in the notes. If the examiner offers any cues or models other than verbal prompts, note them as well. To be rated as well developed, the child's behavior must be spontaneous, without physical prompts or models from the examiner.

a. Rolls ball with intent (7–12 months)

Circle One	
Not evident	1
Emerging	2
Developing	3
Well developed	4

b. Throws ball with intent (13–36 months)

Circle One	
Not evident	1
Emerging	2
Developing	3
Well developed	4

c. Catches ball with intent (15–36 months)

Circle One	
Not evident	1
Emerging	2
Developing	3
Well developed	4

C38. Play with Pictures and Print

Items

    a. Responds to books
    b. Responds to crayon and paper

Materials

    ❖ Three small hardcover books
    ❖ Large crayon
    ❖ Plain sheets of white paper (not in toy kit)

Administration

Both activities should be carried out with the child in independent or supported sitting. Select one of the small hardcover books. Sit beside the child and offer the book. Wait to see if the child responds by opening the book, turning pages, pointing, vocalizing, or naming pictures.

    If the child shows no interest in the book, present a different one. If the child still does not respond appropriately to the book, open it and model turning pages, pointing to pictures, and naming. Pause to allow the child to respond after each prompt.

    For the crayon activity, the child may sit on the floor, at a small table, or in a high chair. The child should have a firm surface for writing. Sit facing the child and place one colored crayon and one sheet of paper in front of him or her. Allow the child to draw and scribble spontaneously without prompting. Discontinue the activity if the child attempts to eat the crayon. If the child does not spontaneously begin drawing, encourage the child verbally to draw a picture. If necessary, offer up to three demonstrations of drawing a circle on the paper, pausing after each one to allow the child to imitate.

    To assess imitation of designs, provide a fresh sheet of paper. Begin by drawing a vertical line and encourage the child to draw the same thing you did. Provide three trials. Then, on a fresh sheet of paper, repeat with horizontal lines, followed by a closed single circle (also on a different sheet of paper). Be sure to allow plenty of time for the child to imitate you after each demonstration.

Guidelines for Recording

For both items, circle all behaviors the child demonstrates and sum. Examples of appropriate imitation of the circle and vertical and horizontal lines for "Imitates at least one design" are provided in Figure 4-1. Note that the child need imitate only one design to receive credit. If item (b) is terminated because the child attempts to eat the crayon, be certain to note this on the recording form. If the examiner offers any cues or models other than verbal prompts, note them as well.

a. Responds to books
(7–36 months)

Circle Any/All and Sum	
Shifts eye gaze/scans/ studies	1
Turns pages	1
Points to pictures	1
Vocalizes/verbalizes in reponse to pictures	1
Total	

b. Responds to crayon and paper
(9–36 months)

Circle Any/All and Sum	
Reaches for/holds crayon	1
Marks paper by banging	1
Makes strokes/circular lines	1
Imitates at least one design	1
Total	

Figure 4-1 Criteria for Imitation of Designs, Item C38b

a. Vertical lines

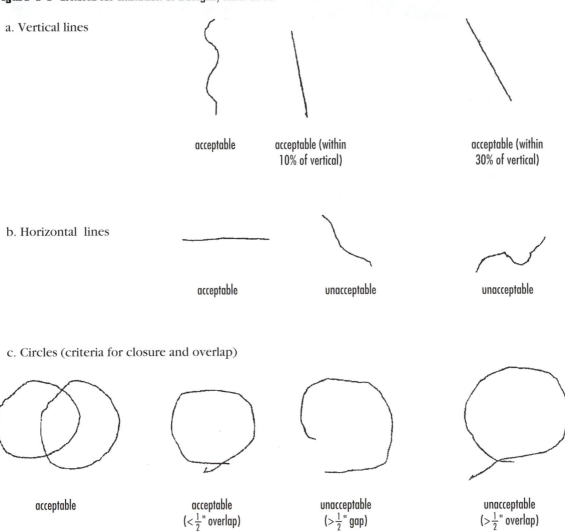

acceptable   acceptable (within 10% of vertical)   acceptable (within 30% of vertical)

b. Horizontal lines

acceptable   unacceptable   unacceptable

c. Circles (criteria for closure and overlap)

acceptable   acceptable ($<\frac{1}{2}$" overlap)   unacceptable ($>\frac{1}{2}$" gap)   unacceptable ($>\frac{1}{2}$" overlap)

SP39. Play with Bubble Tumbler

Items

a. Uses wand
b. Blows bubbles

Materials

❖ Non-spill bubble tumbler

Administration

Decide whether the activity is developmentally appropriate for the child. If so, position the child in a seated or standing position. Offer the tumbler to the child with the wand in place, encouraging the child to take the wand and blow bubbles. If the child does not respond by taking out the wand and attempting to blow, give a demonstration and return the tumbler to the child with the wand in place as before. Give up to three demonstrations, if necessary, to elicit a response. You may assist with stabilizing the tumbler if the child has difficulty withdrawing the wand. Discontinue the activity if the toddler puts the wand in his or her mouth or attempts to throw the tumbler.

Guidelines for Recording

For both items of this cluster, circle all behaviors observed. If the activity is discontinued because the child's use of the tumbler is inappropriate, be certain to note this on the recording form. If the examiner offers any cues or models other than verbal prompts, note them as well.

a. Uses wand
(13–36 months)

Circle Any/All and Sum	
Reaches for/holds wand	1
Puts wand into container	1
Takes wand out of container	1
Brings wand near mouth	1
Total	

b. Blows bubbles
(13–36 months)

Circle Any/All and Sum	
Puckers mouth	1
Imitates blowing with or without wand	1
Brings wand near mouth, then blows	1
Blows through wand/ produces bubbles	1
Total	

C40. Advanced Play with Doll

Items

a. Single play scenarios (e.g., covers baby, feeds, rocks, dresses, undresses)
b. Related play scenarios (feeds/rocks, feeds/changes diaper, sings to baby/puts to bed)

Materials

✣ Appropriate ethnic baby doll
✣ Comb and brush
✣ Doll blanket
✣ Baby bottle
✣ Infant mirror

Administration

Seat the child on the floor, facing or next to you. Give the child the doll and spread the other items within the child's reach. Allow the child to play spontaneously with the doll, and watch for feeding, covering the baby, and other appropriate play routines. If the child does not respond with any individual or related play scenarios, demonstrate and verbally comment on activities such as feeding the doll, putting her to bed, singing to her, or changing her diaper. Give the doll back to the child and wait for a response, encouraging the child to play with the doll. Repeat these models up to three times, as needed. If the child does demonstrate the skill, elicit sufficient repetitions to determine consistency of response.

Guidelines for Recording

For both items, circle the one descriptor that best fits the child's behavior. If the examiner offers any cues or models other than verbal prompts, note them on the recording form. To be rated as well developed, the child's behavior must be spontaneous, without physical prompts or models from the examiner.

a. Single play scenarios (e.g., covers baby, feeds, rocks, dresses, undresses) (13–36 months)

Circle One	
Not evident	1
Emerging	2
Developing	3
Well developed	4

b. Related play scenarios (feeds/rocks, feeds/changes diaper, sings to baby/puts to bed) (17–36 months)

Circle One	
Not evident	1
Emerging	2
Developing	3
Well developed	4

C41. Problem Solving

Items

a. Seeks food behind one screen
b. Seeks food behind one of two screens
c. Seeks food inside clear container
d. Plays with toy garage

Materials

✣ Cheerios or similar finger food (not in-cluded in kit)
✣ Two opaque screens
✣ Clear plastic container
✣ Toy garage and cars

Administration

All four items are best administered with the child sitting on the floor and you sitting facing the child. Before beginning the activities, confirm with the primary caregiver that the child can eat the selected finger food safely. If not, present only item (d) Plays with Toy Garage, if that activity is develop-mentally appropriate.

Begin by showing the child a piece or two of the finger food and allowing him or her to eat it. Then balance one screen against the toy kit, and without the child watching, hide a piece of food behind the shield. Encourage the child to find the food, giving verbal prompts if the child does not respond. If the child makes no attempt to seek the food, give the child another piece to eat and repeat the prompt. If there still is no response, allow the child to watch you hiding the food behind the screen. These cues may be repeated once if the child still fails to respond.

If the child was successful with the first activ-ity, balance two screens against the toy kit bag. Hide a piece of food behind *one of the screens,* again without allowing the child to see. Verbally encour-age the child to find the food, as before. If the child fails to retrieve the food, allow him or her to watch you hiding it again behind the same screen.

Next remove the screens, and place three or four pieces of food into the clear plastic container. Hand the container to the child, and wait to see whether the child explores ways to retrieve the food, such as turning the container upside down. If the child is not successful in getting the food out, model how to empty the container, then give it back to the child with one piece of food inside. Repeat the model one more time if the child remains unsuccessful.

Item (d) in this cluster of activities involves a complex problem-solving toy, a toy garage with color-coded keys, doors, and cars that require color-matching ability. Decide whether this activity is developmentally appropriate, and skip it if it is above the child's level.

To carry out this play activity, place the garage in front of the child with all the doors closed and give the set of keys to the child. Allow time for

C41. Problem Solving (Continued)

exploration and play, encouraging the child to try to open the garage doors with the keys. If the child is not successful in opening any of the doors after a reasonable period, demonstrate with the blue key—inserting it, turning it, opening the garage door, and pushing the corresponding button to eject the car. Meanwhile talk about what you are doing.

Then close the door, return the keys to the child, and encourage an attempt to open the door. If the child has not retrieved a car by the close of the activity, you may open one of the doors and allow the child time to play with the toy, especially if the child is frustrated at not being able to retrieve the cars.

Guidelines for Recording

For items (a), (b), and (c), circle the single best descriptor of the child's performance. For item (d), circle all behaviors the child demonstrates and sum. If the child successfully finds the food in items (a)-(c) but cannot pick it up, credit the item. If poor fine motor skills appear to interfere with the child's playing successfully with the garage, note this on the recording form, but do not credit any items not actually observed. If the examiner provides physical prompts or models, note them on the form as well. To be rated as well developed, the child's behavior must be spontaneous, without physical prompts or models from the examiner.

a. Seeks food behind one screen (13–36 months)

Circle One	
Not evident	1
Emerging	2
Developing	3
Well developed	4

b. Seeks food behind one of two screens (13–36 months)

Circle One	
Not evident	1
Emerging	2
Developing	3
Well developed	4

c. Seeks food inside clear container (13–36 months)

Circle One	
Not evident	1
Emerging	2
Developing	3
Well developed	4

d. Plays with toy garage (17–36 months)

Circle Any/All and Sum	
Attempts to insert key	1
Inserts key	1
Turns key	1
Opens door	1
Ejects car	1
Total	

SP42. Undressing and Dressing

Items

    a. Takes off socks
    b. Puts on socks
    c. Takes off shoes
    d. Puts on toy hard hat
    e. Puts on vest
    f. Opens and closes vest fasteners

Materials

    ✣ Child's socks (caregiver provided)
    ✣ Child's shoes (caregiver provided)
    ✣ Toy hardhat
    ✣ Vest or child coat with fasteners

Administration

This sequence of dressing and undressing activities comprises six sets of tasks. The series begins with the easiest activity, taking off and putting on socks and shoes. Assure in advance that the caregiver has taken out pairs of the child's socks and shoes and has them at hand. Also put a pair of socks on your own feet, if you are not already wearing them. All the undressing and dressing activities should be carried out with the child seated opposite you. The child should begin the series in stocking feet.

Begin by taking off one of your own socks, then ask the child to do the same. This undressing activity may be presented as a game, similar to "do what I do." If the child does not respond, take off your other sock, then once again encourage the child to do the same. If the child is still unsuccessful, assist by pulling one sock partially off the child's foot so it is on only the toes. Then encourage the child to take the sock the rest of the way off.

The second activity involves putting on socks. Follow the same series of cues, first putting on one of your own socks and encouraging the child to do the same. Repeat with a second sock, if necessary. If there still is no response, put the sock partway on the child's foot and encourage him or her to finish the task.

The third activity is more difficult: taking off shoes. Once again, begin with your own and the child's shoes on and unfastened. Follow the procedure described for previous items, demonstrating with one of your own shoes and encouraging the child to do the same. Repeat with the other shoe, if necessary. Then if there still is no response, pull the shoe partway off.

The fourth activity involves play with a toy hard hat. Give the hat to the child and encourage him or her to put it on. You may offer several verbal prompts if the child does not respond readily. If the child still does not show any interest, demonstrate placing the hat on your own head. Then return the hat to the child and encourage him or her once again to put it on.

The last two activities entail play with a vest or coat with multiple fasteners. Hold out one armhole of the vest near the child's arm and encourage him or her to put the vest on. If the child does not respond after several verbal prompts, demonstrate slipping an armhole partway on your own arm. Again hold the armhole out near the child's arm and encourage the child to attempt putting it on. If the child still is reluctant, move to the last activity.

SP42. Undressing and Dressing (Continued)

For the last activity, place the vest on a firm surface, such as the floor, in front of the child. If necessary, you may provide stabilization, as the child attempts to unfasten or fasten the various openers. To present these tasks in a game-like manner, allow the child to watch you hide a small toy inside one of the pockets. Present the fasteners in the order as follows. Velcro, buttons, snaps, and zipper. A dressing frame may also be used.

Prompt the child to open and then close each fastener. Provide a demonstration if the child does not respond to two or three verbal requests. Have the child open each fastener three or four times to determine consistency of response.

Guidelines for Recording

For all activities in this cluster, circle the single best description of the child's behavior. For items (a), (b), (c), and (d) the examiner demonstrates putting on and taking off shoes and socks, putting on vest or coat. To earn a rating of well developed, the child must respond successfully after a single demonstration, with no further prompts or models other than verbal encouragement. For item (f): Uses vest fasteners, the child must independently open at least three of the four fasteners and close one fastener to be credited with developing the skill. To meet the criteria for well developed, the child must open all four fasteners and close at least two.

a. Takes off socks
(9–36 months)

Circle One	
Not evident	1
Emerging	2
Developing	3
Well developed	4

b. Puts on socks
(13–36 months)

Circle One	
Not evident	1
Emerging	2
Developing	3
Well developed	4

c. Takes off shoes
(13–36 months)

Circle One	
Not evident	1
Emerging	2
Developing	3
Well developed	4

d. Puts on toy hard hat
(13–36 months)

Circle One	
Not evident	1
Emerging	2
Developing	3
Well developed	4

e. Puts on vest
(13–36 months)

Circle One	
Not evident	1
Emerging	2
Developing	3
Well developed	4

f. Opens and closes vest fasteners
(15–36 months)

Circle One	
Not evident	1
Emerging	2
Developing	3
Well developed	4

SE 43. Adaptability

Items

a. Makes transitions with interest
b. Attends during structured play

Administration

There are no specific administration procedures for this cluster. The team should evaluate these two items, based on the child's behavior throughout the entire structured play session.

Guidelines for Recording

Adaptability is defined as the child's ability to change to a different activity and become engaged in it following sustained interest and attention to a previous activity. For each item, circle the single descriptor that best fits the child's performance.

a. Makes transitions with interest (11–36 months)

Circle One	
Never/rarely	1
Sometimes	2
Usually/frequently	3
Most of the time/always	4

b. Attends during structured play (11–36 months)

Circle One	
Never/rarely	1
Sometimes	2
Usually/frequently	3
Most of the time/always	4

In Brief Review

This chapter described instructions for observing, recording, and administering the *PIP* assessment. The following reminders will be helpful for students and team members to keep in mind:

 ❖ Practicing the *PIP* before the assessment will be helpful so that all team members are familiar with the instructions for administering, scoring, and interpreting results of the evaluation.

 ❖ *PIP* should be given only when the child is alert and calm in temperament. As a result, a minimum of two sessions will be necessary for the assessment.

 ❖ Recording all data at the time of the assessment is essential so that key information is not left out or forgotten.

 ❖ While the instructions for the Structured Examiner-Child Play are written with specific suggested toys and materials cited, similar alternate toys can be used for this segment of the assessment. Accordingly, it is helpful if these alternate materials have parallel parts or components that can be adapted to the scoring rubric for respective individual items.

CHAPTER 5

Interpreting the *PIP* Assessment

After reading this chapter, you should be able to:

❖ Understand the system for scoring the *PIP* assessment.

❖ Understand some guidelines for interpreting the assessment.

❖ Understand the *PIP* assessment of two young children who qualified for early intervention services (one is presented in the Online Companion for this text at website-Delmar).

Guidelines for Interpretation

The process of interpreting the *PIP* evaluation results begins by asking the child's primary caregiver(s) to confirm that the child's performance during the assessment is representative of his or her natural, daily performance.

PIP has been developed with a simple but flexible system for scoring and interpretation that can be adapted easily to the varied criteria for establishing eligibility for early intervention services from state to state (see State and Jurisdictional Eligibility Definitions for Infants and Toddlers with Disabilities under IDEA, in Appendix D). Each item of *PIP* is recorded in a checklist format, where the best response is indicated or behaviors observed are summed to derive a score for each item. To facilitate the interpretation process, either during the evaluation or afterwards, circle in red any items that have scores of "3" or above, which is the criterion for passing. (A score of "3" corresponds to behavior ratings of "developing," "usually or frequently observed," or demonstration of at least three behaviors in a developmental sequence.)

In making final decisions relative to eligibility for early intervention services, we would like to emphasize the following:

- ❖ Numbers alone rarely reflect the full picture of a child's behavior and performance. Clinical observations play a critical part in the decision-making process.

- ❖ The pace of development is unequal across the early months and years of life; therefore, it is essential to use a serial assessment approach with periodic re-evaluations of all the primary developmental domains. A child may not qualify for services on first assessment, but on re-evaluation six or eight months later demonstrate a sufficient delay to qualify at that point.

- ❖ Broad age ranges for administration are given for many of the *PIP* items. With experience in using the assessment, however, team members will become more sensitive to the quality of behavior and skills that are typical at various ages, and can use this information to make beneficial decisions with respect to a child's need for services.

- ❖ The assessment is designed to reveal how a child performs in various contexts; namely, with familiar versus unfamiliar adults and in unstructured versus relatively structured situations. Such information, though not considered in scoring, is valuable later in writing goals and developing plans for programming.

- ❖ No assessment is entirely culture free. Cultural considerations are always important in the final interpretation process.

Keeping these considerations in mind, the final phases of scoring and interpreting *PIP* are as follows:

1. Scoring Worksheet 1 (Appendix B) is an optional worksheet that provides a more concise record of the child's performance than the record forms. It may be filled out for placement in the child's permanent record, if desired.

2. For all four sections of the assessment (i.e., Caregiver Report of Child Development, Unstructured Caregiver-Child Play, Unstructured

Examiner-Child Play, and Structured Examiner-Child Interaction), compile all the items passed with a score of "3" or above and mark them with a + on Scoring Worksheet 2. Note that this worksheet groups items by developmental domain, rather than in order of administration.

3. Next, total the number of items that the child passed in each developmental domain (i.e., Language, Cognitive, Social-Emotional, Neuromotor, and Sensory-Perceptual) for each component of the assessment. Transfer these numbers to the top table on the Summary Worksheet (Appendix B), then add these subtotals to derive a total score for each domain. Adaptive behavior (the items indicated with **) is not scored separately because it overlaps with several developmental domains. However, the team may wish to review the adaptive behavior items passed to gain a sense of the child's skill in this area.

4. To calculate the percentage of age-appropriate items the child passed in each domain, consult the Index of Item Totals by Month (Appendix B). Determine the child's chronological or adjusted age and round to the nearest full month. (Use the chronological age for children born at full-term, and adjusted age for those born prematurely, as described on page (#TK: To be filled in at proofread—it's in Chapter 3, ms pg. 78, Head 3.) Look up the expected total for each developmental area on the Index of Item Totals by Month and divide the number of items the child actually passed by this number to determine the percentage of age-appropriate items passed in each domain. Enter these percentages on the Summary Worksheet.

One final note that needs to be kept in mind in calculating the Item Totals: Unlike other assessments perhaps used by professionals, items throughout this instrument are not considered to be cumulative; i.e., children are not given credit for items below their age levels or ages of administration. Instead, Item Totals are figured on the basis of *only* those questions asked of families and on the basis of those child skills observed after unstructured or structured play. This was a conscious decision made by the author team, based on the fact that young children with special needs often have splinter abilities and gaps in their development. In other words, one cannot assume uniform and chronological achievement of certain skills in the event that a child does have disabilities and delays.

5. The percentages on the Summary Worksheet can be compared against your state's criteria for early intervention eligibility (a complete list of state eligibility definitions under Part C of IDEA is provided in Appendix D for your reference). In addition, as is clear from the listings in Appendix D, many states permit the use of clinical judgment in making determinations of eligibility—a position we strongly support. The use of sound clinical judgment is particularly critical in the evaluation of infants and young children, who are frequently difficult to assess and variable in their performance.

Interpretation of evaluation results does not end with the identification of percentages or degrees of delay. Consider the following several additional factors in deciding what services will most benefit a particular child and family:

❖ Primary developmental areas and item clusters where the child manifests particularly strong performance. Infants and toddlers who qualify for early intervention services rarely manifest isolated or unrelated areas of delay.

More typically assessment reveals patterns of problematic development that are fairly consistent across contexts and situations. The organization of *PIP* facilitates the analysis of patterns, problem-solving styles, and other key dimensions of responding across a variety of activities and tasks, which become clear from examining Scoring Worksheets 1 and 2.

❖ Areas of development and behavior where caregiver reports corroborate behavioral observations. Even without any formal assessment, most parents and primary caregivers know reasonably well what their children can and cannot do. Their day-to-day experiences of playing and interacting with their child are an invaluable resource for early intervention professionals to tap. *PIP* has been designed so that numerous behaviors asked about in the caregiver report component are cross-referenced with skills sampled in the developmental assessment, serving as a reliability check for behavior noted within the evaluation period.

❖ Areas where growth is apparent versus those where delays persist. *PIP* can be readministered periodically to track a child's development over several months or even years. Such information can be extremely helpful in monitoring the effectiveness of intervention strategies and in identifying ongoing programming needs.

❖ Learning styles and quality of responses. Valuable information may be revealed by noting the ways in which a particular child goes about solving problems, communicating, moving, or orienting within the environment. For instance, a child may be able to come to a standing position only by locking his or her knees, rather than by moving easily through a developmentally appropriate kneel-stand position. Similarly, infant and toddler temperaments and frustration levels during challenging activities may offer important clues about cognitive and/or sensory regulatory development.

❖ Considerations of the family's cultural context. We have said this before, but with the rapidly expanding diversity of cultures that now characterizes the United States (Hanson & Lynch, 2004a; 2004b), early intervention teams continually need to be sensitive to instances where a family's attitudes, beliefs, customs, values, languages, and behaviors may differ from their own and from mainstream American culture. Parental perceptions of a child's needs, the amount and type of information that parents reveal to the team, how they respond to the assessment and early intervention experiences, as well as their systems of communication and child rearing all may affect the team's interactions with the family, the data gathered during the evaluation, how the child develops, and the delivery of services. Early interventionists no longer can or should expect all children and families to conform to a uniform set of standards and value systems. Sensitivity to such issues is critical in light of the fact that cultural differences too often have been misinterpreted as evidence of disability in the child or an unwillingness of caregivers to cooperate.

❖ The child's background and medical/environmental history. Information obtained in a formal evaluation always must be considered against the backdrop of the child's history. Interpretations of a child's progress and prognosis may be greatly affected by knowledge of his or her previous medical treatments, length of hospitalization, or unusual circumstances such as extended residence in a Third World country.

❖ Genuine respect for caregivers' priorities for their children, families, and lives.

PIP highlights the importance of the child's primary caregiver(s) and their goals for the child and desires for services. Through consultation with the family, it is important to determine their main priorities and concerns and make those the cornerstone of the IFSP and any subsequent programming.

Illustration from the Field

The following Illustration from the Field is a report that was written by a team of professionals, representing the disciplines of early childhood special education, communication sciences and disorders, and occupational therapy. The evaluation was carried out in the home of the child, with the family present during the assessments. This report is offered as an example of the kinds of information that can be derived, using the *PIP* assessment. This report was written about a 20-month old, Kyle; a second report can be found in the Online Companion™ www.earlychilded.delmar.com and was written about a 33-month old, Kelsie. The names of the children and all identifying information have been changed on behalf of confidentiality issues.

Kyle

Child's Name:	Kyle
Date of Birth:	October 1, 2003
Chronological Age:	20 months
Adjusted Age:	18 months
Parents:	Denise and Robert Jones
Address:	Any Street
	Any City, State, USA
Telephone:	XXX
Dates of Evaluation:	
Initial Home Visit:	June 1, 2005
Second Home Visit:	June 8, 2005
Conference:	June 24, 2005

Gebbie Clinics Psychoeducational Team:

Gail Ensher, Ed.D. (Clinical Supervisor for Team)
Carol Reinson, Ph.D., OTR/L
Deborah Bryden, MS, SLP

Reason for Referral

Kyle's parents requested that Dr. James Smith, Kyle's primary pediatrician, refer Kyle for a core evaluation to determine eligibility for early intervention services and to make specific recommendations for his developmental needs. The Jones family has recently moved to the Syracuse, NY area from Georgia, where Kyle had previously received early intervention services. The family is particularly concerned with Kyle's persistent feeding problems, language development, and motor delays.

Initial Home Visit—Parent Interview

The Gebbie Clinics Psychoeducational Team at Syracuse University met with Kyle and his mother, Denise, in their home on June 1, 2005 for their initial parent interview. The evaluation was conducted over two home visits, each lasting between one to two hours. Kyle lives with his mother, Denise (28 years old), his father, Robert (27 years old), and his sister, Jessica (5 years old). They recently moved to Syracuse, New York, from Georgia, where Mr. Jones was a manufacturing supervisor. He now is currently employed with a local subsidiary and the family has relocated to the Syracuse, NY area.

During the initial visit, Kyle seemed reluctant to have his mother leave the room; thus, all team members sat with Kyle and Denise in the living room observing Kyle's interactions with familiar and unfamiliar toys. The team subsequently divided roles; one person conducted an interview with Denise to gain further background information, one person carried out an initial informal play session with Kyle, and one person recorded the observations.

Denise's first pregnancy was full-term without complications, resulting in a healthy baby girl. However, during the 18th week of her second pregnancy, it was discovered that she had placenta previa and that the placenta also was enlarged. She was hospitalized at 24 weeks because she began to hemorrhage and was advised either to stay in the hospital until the birth of her child or to remain on complete bed rest at home. Denise decided to go home, and her mother stayed with the family to provide assistance and support. Labor began at 32 weeks, and Denise was rushed to the hospital. Her contractions were medically stopped; however, her placenta abrupted, and Kyle was delivered by emergency Caesarean section. Prior to the surgery, Denise was given steroids to stimulate development of Kyle's lungs. Complications arose during the surgery as a result of the enlarged placenta, and two perpendicular incisions were made in order to locate and deliver Kyle. At this time, Denise lost a great deal of blood, she was weak, and recovery was long.

Denise stated that she believes that the complications of the second pregnancy possibly were caused by the medications that her husband was required to take when conducting business overseas. The injections that he received were given prior to the conception of their child.

Kyle was delivered at a general hospital, weighing 1901 grams (4 lbs., 3 oz). His Apgar scores were unknown by his mother. At delivery, Kyle was in respiratory distress, and the hospital personnel subsequently transported him to a Neonatal Intensive Care Unit (NICU) in a large metropolitan hospital. It was approximately five hours before he entered the NICU. According to his mother, Kyle continued to experience respiratory distress with retractions during this time.

Kyle remained in the NICU for six weeks. While at the hospital, he was treated for respiratory complications, was placed on a ventilator for two weeks and required six chest tubes because of his lungs collapsing. Kyle also required resuscitation several times while he was on the ventilator with repeated episodes of apnea.

The family visited Kyle in-hospital on a daily basis; however, Denise could not hold him for the first two weeks until he was off the ventilator. She indicated that she was pleased with the care that her son received in the hospital and with the instruction that the hospital staff offered their family. Before Kyle left the hospital, his parents were trained in resuscitation and CPR, as well as feeding techniques with Kyle. At the time of discharge, the baby had difficulty sucking and was experiencing reflux problems with projectile vomiting. He left the hospital with an apnea monitor, which the family used for three months. During Kyle's first week transitioning to home, he experienced one significant episode of bradycardia. The apnea monitor went off, his parents startled him by "flicking" his foot, and he began to breath on his own again. Kyle was assigned a public health nurse who visited once per week to monitor his weight gain. This service continued for six weeks after his discharge from the hospital.

When it became apparent that Kyle was manifesting delays, he was evaluated by the NICU Developmental Follow-up Program and assigned a physical therapist from a local county agency. During the course of therapy, this individual worked on acquisition of major neuromotor milestones such as rolling over, creeping, and walking. Initially, Kyle received services twice per month; however, as he progressed, his therapy was reduced to once per month. Kyle also received in-home educational services. According to Denise, the educator visited the home only sporadically as a result of scheduling difficulties. Denise stated that she was not pleased with this service. She felt that the educator did not provide enough information on how she and her husband could assist their son.

Kyle at 14 months had surgery to correct strabismus of both eyes. He is presently receiving follow-up care by Dr. Muller, an ophthalmologist in Syracuse, NY. Currently, Kyle is experiencing frequent ear infections, and has had various antibiotics for the condition. However, the infections have persisted, and prior to this evaluation he had an ear infection for which he took a 30-day course of antibiotics. In addition, Kyle recently had a serious cold for which he was treated with Albuterol and a nebulizer.

Kyle's present weight is 20 pounds, 13 ounces. He is 31 inches long. Kyle eats mashed food from a spoon. He does not eat any solid food such as Cheerios, though recently he successfully ate a small piece of a French fry. He still has a tendency to gag, cough, and spit up food while eating. Though he has taken Tagamet in the past, he currently is no longer on medication for reflux. Kyle's feeding problems have been a constant concern for his mother, and she feels they have not been seriously addressed by his physician or therapists. Kyle does not seem to enjoy mealtime.

In addition to the reflux problems, Denise stated that she has to give Kyle liquids to wash down food because he has a tendency to hold a large amount of food in his mouth to avoid choking. He is allergic to milk and milk products; therefore, he drinks Pediasure and lactose-free milk which he still takes from a bottle. In order for him to drink, the bottle must be placed in his hands. He also needs to be encouraged not to throw the bottle when he is finished. Denise indicated that Kyle does not attempt to finger feed himself (though this hesitation may be related to his not yet eating chunkier foods), hold a spoon, or drink independently from a cup. Kyle eats three meals a day with two to three snacks. His slow weight gain continues to be a concern for Denise.

Kyle sleeps on his back through the night without waking. He averages about eight to ten hours per night and takes a two-hour nap during the day. He has a night-time routine that includes brushing his teeth, putting on his pajamas, saying prayers, then going to sleep. At times, he cries for a few minutes but then falls to sleep soon thereafter.

Kyle has achieved several important developmental milestones over the past year. These include sitting at 8 months, standing alone at 12 months, walking at 16 months, saying approximately three words (Da-Da, Ma-Ma, and no-no), and using jargon when attempting to communicate with others. Presently, Kyle assists with dressing and undressing by holding up his arms and pulling out his arms from his sleeves. He enjoys bath-time. Denise stated that recently Kyle was told it was bath-time, and he walked towards the bathroom for the first time. Kyle also can crawl upstairs unassisted, but requires assistance stepping downstairs.

According to his mother, Kyle does not yet communicate his needs with words or gestures. He indicates his discontent usually by screaming; e.g., when he becomes frustrated with his sister. Denise reported that he does not have to indicate most wants or needs because family members anticipate them for him. She does recognize that she should encourage him to indicate his needs on his own. She was especially pleased that one day recently, however, Kyle went to the door, appearing to wait for her to take him outside.

Kyle does not seem to have any problems transferring from one activity to another and will play alone for approximately five to ten minutes. He prefers to play with adults versus other children. He enjoys games of peek-a-boo and chase with family members. At this time, Kyle's interactions with people consist primarily of his relationships with his parents and his sister. He does attend a church child care for a duration of one and a half hours per week. Again in this situation, he usually plays with the adults in the room or alone. Denise stated that he separates well from her and is good-natured while at church child care.

Denise expressed concerns about the variety of Kyle's play. He enjoys toys that make noise, that involve parent interaction, and at such times plays appropriately. However, he has a strong tendency to repeatedly bang and throw toys. She is also concerned about Kyle's strong preference for "W"-sitting while playing.

His mother noted that Kyle's primary means of communication is babbling with voice inflection. He uses all vowel sounds during jargon and the following consonants: /d/, /m/, /n/, and /j/. As indicated above, he reportedly says *Da-Da*, *Ma-Ma*, and *no-no*. He smiles, laughs, cries, and screams to express himself. Denise stated that he understands "no-no," their names, his name, and the name of the family bird. Yet, he does not seem to follow one-step directions at this time. Denise also stated that he does not point or use gestures to communicate (such as waving "bye-bye"), and he does not imitate sounds.

In terms of services for Kyle and new information for the family, Denise expressed interest in a play group for Kyle, as well as help with his feeding and speech and language development. She and her husband would like to meet other parents their own age and secure quality babysitting services.

Initial Home Visit—Play Session

During the initial home visit, Kyle displayed a quiet affect and required intense stimulation and reinforcement to evoke any kind of response. By the end of the session, which lasted approximately one hour, he interacted with team members more readily and became more animated. Activities were presented approximately every five to ten minutes and included toys such as a wind-up bunny, stacking rings, blocks and container, a telephone, paper and crayon, a book, and a toy with a spinning component.

Cognitive Development

Kyle engaged in active play throughout the session, as demonstrated by a limited repertoire of behaviors, including repetitive motor movements such as banging, hitting, and throwing. He attended to each activity for approximately one to two minutes. However, initially there were several instances when his attention appeared interrupted and his eyes drifted upward. When presented with a wind-up bunny, Kyle swiped at it as it moved across the table. He exhibited this behavior several times, when presented with the toy in the same manner before repeatedly picking up the object and throwing it without directionality.

Kyle performed well with three of his familiar toys. Each had a spinning component, which he aggressively swiped with gross arm movements and his right hand. Near the end of the session, Kyle isolated his right index finger and dialed a play phone independently after several visual demonstrations, as well as two hand-over-hand assists. After several attempts, he performed this skill with increasing proficiency.

It should be noted that Kyle needed both verbal and physical support, direction, and reinforcement to maintain attention in activities. In addition, he interrupted his play frequently to play with the hair of the team members, an activity that offered him tactile input that seemed extremely pleasurable.

Social-Emotional Development

Kyle was rather shy and took some time to interact with the team members. At the beginning of the session, he stood next to his mother sitting on the couch and intently observed the unfamiliar adults. He scanned the room frequently and pulled away at first, when the examiner/play facilitator attempted to engage him in play by touching him softly. He did, however, welcome a second attempt by a team member to touch him again and appeared to enjoy the exchange. He smiled slightly at team members, as he became more comfortable and eventually interacted quite readily by the end of the session. Kyle frequently looked at his mother, using her as a base of security, as he became involved in the various play activities off-and-on during the initial visit. Although Kyle was reticent at the beginning of the session, he eventually became pleasantly social, demonstrating imitative behavior including clapping and blinking during a game of peek-a-boo.

Language Development

During the initial visit, Kyle engaged in a limited repertoire of vocalizations. Kyle was observed initially making some loud squeals and whines. Occasional vocalizations consisted of consonant-vowel (CV) sounds, combined into open syllables. These combinations included "mmm," "ag gee," "ah dee," "ah git," and "ah git goo." His consonants vocalizations varied in front and back positions. He did not demonstrate reduplicated babbling, nor did he appear to vocalize for communicative intent. Kyle often exhibited slight tongue protrusion at rest, predominantly to the right side.

Kyle was able to convey pleasure with a laugh or a slight smile, and he surveyed team members during the play session, though he rarely made or maintained eye contact.

Neuromotor Development

Kyle was slow to initiate walking or creeping. His gait had a very wide base of support, and he seemed to prefer cruising. When walking, he held his hands in a high-guard, waist-level position. His arm movement was gross and used primarily for clapping and throwing objects. He did not demonstrate a controlled, volitional grasp release.

At the beginning of the session, it was noted that Kyle displayed less adaptive or inappropriate neuromotor positions. For instance, he sometimes stood with his toes pointed inward. During play, he demonstrated a strong preference for "W"-sitting so that his position required frequent changing by his mother and team members. It also was noted that when Kyle sat with his legs in front of him, his back remained rounded, and at times he leaned against an examiner's leg for trunk support. He was able to play without difficulty in these two latter positions. In addition, Kyle demonstrated side-sitting, frequently propping himself with his left hand. Kyle also used a wide upper extremity base of support with his hands open, while creeping.

When reaching for toys, Kyle evidenced gross arm extension and typically held objects with a radial palmar grasp. When manipulating toys such as blocks, he frequently banged these against his free hand (bringing both hands to midline). However, he did not readily transfer toys from hand to hand, and relied on using a throwing motion. It was evident that he had difficulty with an active, controlled release, even when the examiner attempted to inhibit his throwing behavior and substitute wrist tenodesis to facilitate finger extension during passive release; e.g., with a stacking ring.

The status of Kyle's ocular motor control was uncertain. During the first session, Kyle maintained little eye contact with team members and appeared to have difficulty focusing on toys. His eyes appeared to be asymmetrical and, as mentioned previously, occasionally drifted upward, thus coinciding with a lack of attending behaviors. It was apparent too that Kyle's ocular motor control was not well developed or refined, as evidenced by his slow eye movement and inability to sustain his gaze.

Sensory-Perceptual Development

With regard to sensory input, Kyle demonstrated strong preferences for soft touch. He frequently interrupted his play to stroke the examiner's long hair and enjoyed touching the hair of team members throughout the session. His mother indicated that he likes playing with hair and loves his bath. He also appeared to enjoy having his cheeks and hands lightly stroked and his hair gently brushed.

Kyle displayed some self-stimulatory types behavior. He often clapped his hands repeatedly directly in front of his eyes. When presented with several objects, including a crayon, a pen, and a ring, he would frequently bang the object and his free hand together repeatedly. When the examiner/play facilitator presented a book to Kyle, he hit the cover and pages several times, without attending to the pictures. Moreover, he appeared to obtain pleasurable sensory input from banging toys in his hands and hitting those that were too large to hold.

Second Home Visit—Play Session

Neuromotor Development

Gross motor development　Kyle was progressively more interactive during the course of the assessment sessions, but generally stayed within a small radius of space. He was able to maneuver himself in his environment without bumping into or knocking over objects. He walked alone with a wide-based, immature gait, with his arms at waist level. He seemed to prefer stabilizing himself while upright by holding onto people or tables. Kyle's speed of movement was generally moderate; however, with the support of the sides, he was able to run around a playpen on one occasion. During this singular "comfortable" activity, his vocalizations increased and were more complex. He once was observed moving into a standing position, using a plantigrade maneuver with two straight legs, with his hands pushing off the floor.

Kyle sometimes played with toys on the floor while demonstrating ring-sitting and side-sitting, but most frequently assumed a "W"-sitting position. His mother and the team members frequently repositioned him from the "W-" position to one with his legs extended. He did not object to being repositioned. Kyle's transitions from standing to sitting and from creeping on knees to sitting consistently resulted in this "W-"position. It was discovered, however, that he could reposition himself in response to his feet being tickled. Kyle sat on his coccyx with a rounded back and, on one occasion, made use of the examiner's leg for additional back support.

Overall, Kyle's balance responses appeared to be adequate. For example, when the examiner/play facilitator tipped him backwards from a sitting position, he curled forward and then extended his arms backwards to catch himself from falling. When tipped to the right or the left from a sitting position, he also demonstrated appropriate arm extension. Held in the air and rocked from side to side, Kyle demonstrated good head righting responses.

Fine motor development   Kyle's fine motor functioning appears to be an area of concern. For example, when playing with a pop-up toy that required depression of keys, Kyle used gross maneuvers with an open hand to bat at the keys, without isolating any one key. In this instance, it was not possible to ascertain whether his relative difficulty was the result of a cognitive or a motor dysfunction. Moreover, when blocks in a container were presented to Kyle, he grasped a block from inside the shape-sorter and removed it by trapping the block with his fingers and dragging it along the inside of the container. While manipulating the blocks, he demonstrated a radial palmar grasp with thumb flexion. During the beginning of the session, he grasped only after hand contact; later he initiated grasping on his own. Presented with one block, he maintained it in one hand; presented with another block, he held one in each hand. On the other hand, when offered a third, he looked perplexed and did not act upon the new stimuli.

As with all objects that Kyle grasped, he banged them together, bringing both hands to midline. He released objects primarily by flinging them. Even after repeated opportunities, he did not demonstrate an ability to release blocks into a container. Following several trials specifically structured to facilitate Kyle's basic release skills, however, he did evidence an emerging skill of dropping an object with volitional intent.

When Kyle was not engaged in an activity, frequently his thumbs were tucked in a cortical position. He occasionally postured or crossed his fingers on the same hand when at rest. Though he sometimes demonstrated more control with his right hand, right/left differences were subtle and inconclusive.

When presented with a book, Kyle (in contrast to the first session in which he batted at the book) scanned the pages, isolated his index finger to point at pictures, looked from one page to the next, and closed the book. These behaviors were facilitated with repeated trials, short and concrete verbal cues, modeling of appropriate responses, and verbal encouragement. When presented with a pull toy, Kyle visually tracked the Snoopy dog. He pulled grossly on the string, but was not successful. The string was later adapted for easier grasping; however, on subsequent trials he reverted to clapping his hands or throwing the adapted string. He visually traced the movement of bubbles, but turned his face away if they came close to his head. When this response was noted, the examiner/play facilitator blew the bubbles toward the floor and Kyle tracked them until they burst. Overall, Kyle's ability to direct his gaze to activities at hand improved during the course of subsequent visits.

Language Development

At the team's request, Kyle was fed by his mother a pureed consistency with very soft chunks. On this occasion, Kyle closed his mouth around the spoon before his mother withdrew it. He appeared to have good lip closure, as no food escaped after it was introduced into his mouth; however, he did not appear to remove food from the spoon with his lips. His tongue and jaw were at rest in anticipation of food. Once the food was placed in his mouth, he appeared to have a continuous, well-organized, rhythmic pattern of sucking (up and down), and did not exhibit a phasic bite reflex.

While it still contained food, Kyle frequently opened his mouth for several seconds. In part, this tendency may have been prompted by his considerable nasal congestion on the particular day of evaluation. During the course of feeding, his mother alternated liquid (in a bottle) with the puree because he tended to hold a good portion of food in his mouth without initiating a swallow. Initially, Kyle required that his hands be placed around his bottle, but subsequently he was able to hold the bottle independently and suck without dribbling. Kyle also occasionally nibbled at his lower lip. He demonstrated tongue lateralization only to the right side (but not to the left).

Kyle did not imitate any oral-motor movements made by the team members. He did not imitate blowing bubbles or any vocalizations. He did, however, respond by taking turns when the examiner/play facilitator imitated his verbal output. With successive visits, he became increasingly more verbal. In total, he demonstrated reduplicated and variegated babbling, contrast between front and back sounds, voiced and voiceless sounds, nasal, velars, stops, and affricates. His babbling included "tut tut tut," "chuh cheh cha cha," "da ga," "she chee," and "eh," with fluctuating intonation when he was frustrated. His most frequent vocalizations were "a dee," "a gee," and "da da da." Finally, as noted above, he giggled a lot when tickled. Kyle increased his verbal output when he seemed more relaxed with the team members and had the option to hold onto something for balance and stability.

Sensory-Perceptual Development

During the second play session, Kyle's attention span increased to the point where a single object or activity held his interest for up to eight minutes. After his initial reticence to being touched by an unfamiliar person, Kyle seemed to relish this contact. He responded to and interacted with team members more positively with subsequent visits and never objected to being touched or repositioned. He generally was agreeable to hand-over-hand assistance during activities, except when one team member attempted to inhibit his throwing of objects. Kyle seemed to enjoy having his cheeks, hands, and hair stroked softly. As noted earlier, he also demonstrated a strong attraction to hair, both visually and tactually. In general, all indications suggested that he greatly enjoyed repeated sensory input during the course of any activity, and that this might be an excellent modality for working with Kyle at home and in program.

In terms of his localization to auditory and tactile stimuli, Kyle turned to the sound of his mother's voice coming from another room, to a ringing bell in the same room, and to air puffs directed behind his ear. Though his response to an air puff was not consistently immediate, he displayed no adverse reactions.

Cognitive Development

Kyle demonstrated object permanence several times with a wind-up bunny hidden under a blanket. When his face was covered several times with a blanket by the examiner/play facilitator, he consistently pulled off the blanket and smiled. He engaged in turn-taking when the examiner imitated his utterances. He also showed communicative intent that he wanted the examiner to wipe his runny nose, when he facially gestured and looked directly at the examiner. Kyle was shown a cause and effect pop-up toy where the levers had to be manipulated in order to make animals appear. When the examiner/play facilitator demonstrated the action, Kyle pushed the animals back down and randomly banged at the closed lids. However, it was not clear whether he was unable to solve the problem of making the animals pop up because of inadequate hand skills or not understanding the cause-effect relationship. As mentioned previously, Kyle attended appropriately to a book by pointing at the pictures with his index finger, looking from one picture to another, and closing the cover of the book. He sustained attention to the book with the help of the examiner/play facilitator for a period of eight minutes.

Kyle demonstrated an emerging comprehension of cause-effect relationships with a pull toy. For example, he tracked the movement of the Snoopy dog attached to a string and made one attempt to pull the string. On the other hand, his problems with grasp and release could have had a direct effect on his performance of this activity. In addition, he shook his head from side to side, a behavior that seemed to be an attempt to imitate the spring action of the dog's tail. In another activity, the play facilitator presented an arch/spiral maze to Kyle, where beads needed to be pushed from side to side. He responded by spinning or swiping at the beads in place without pushing them directly through the maze. In a doll play sequence of activity, Kyle studied the baby, then touched its face, hair, and fingers. After the examiner kissed the doll, Kyle brought the doll to his mouth, but did not pucker. Following the examiner's demonstration, Kyle took a brush, banged it in his hands, but did not brush the baby's hair, even after several hand-over-hand, physical cues. When presented the baby's bottle, Kyle grasped it, put it in his mouth, and began to suck.

In terms of undressing skills, the examiner/play facilitator pulled off Kyle's sock half-way. Kyle then grasped the sock, but did not pull it off the rest of the way.

Social-Emotional Development

During much of the initial play session, Kyle often had a dazed appearance. His behavior may have been the result of overstimulation by the presence of new and unfamiliar people in his home. As mentioned before, with each subsequent visit, however, he appeared more "at home" with team members and, as he relaxed and enjoyed himself, demonstrated higher-level skills. He generally did not have trouble separating from his mother, given adequate transitioning time, though he seemed comforted by hearing the sound of her voice. He rarely initiated interactions with team members, yet appeared to enjoy such interactions once prompted. During early sessions, he needed a great deal of reinforcement/support to continue activities; during later visits, he responded with smiles and giggles to various social interactions such as playing pat-a-cake and clapping on cue. Finally, it was obvious that he enjoyed playing with his mother in social interactive games.

Summary

Kyle is a toddler born at 32 weeks gestation with an extremely complicated medical history. He was referred for a core evaluation to determine eligibility for early intervention services and to make specific recommendations for his developmental needs. The family recently moved to the Syracuse, NY area. At the time of the move, Kyle had been receiving early intervention services with an infant education specialist and physical therapist. The present referral was made in order to activate early intervention services at this time. The Psychoeducational Team met with Kyle and his mother, Denise, for a total of two home visits. A final conference and IFSP meeting was held with both parents during a third subsequent visit. At this time, a Family Service Coordinator and the early intervention team from the local county were in attendance.

Kyle is an adorable, sweet 20-month-old toddler (adjusted age 18 months) with a very gentle personality and mild temperament. He is a child who is extremely affectionate with and bonded to his mother. Given an initial period of time to warm up with various Psychoeducational Team members, he related easily, and was more interactive and responsive to toys and structured activities. With each successive visit, Kyle became increasingly vocal, demonstrating a greater variety and complexity of play schemas. He especially enjoyed any situation and activity that involved sensory and tactile opportunities, such as lightly stroking his cheek or his gently touching the hair of his mother or of various team members. This particular preference or desire was repeatedly observed on every visit that was made to the family home.

A particular strength for Kyle at this time is the loving attention and strong commitment that he receives from his family. His mother, Denise is extremely invested in immediately securing those services that will most benefit her child's development. She asked questions directly of team members, asked for specific suggestions, and in fact has made telephone calls to the neonatologist who was in charge of Kyle's care while in the hospital.

Over the course of the two-visit period, Kyle presented as a child who appeared to significantly benefit from individual, structured intervention strategies to teach him alternate play behaviors. He was patient and responsive to the team's requests.

However, despite Kyle's aforementioned strengths, he is a toddler who evidences significant need in all developmental areas, especially neuromotor (hand skills), speech/language/feeding, and cognitive development. In particular, though Kyle did receive early intervention services in Georgia for his neuromotor delays, this domain continues to be an area of need. Kyle has reached several major milestones such as sitting independently and walking. On the other hand, he continues to display atypical patterns of neuromotor behavior such as a strong preference for "W"-sitting, a rounded back when sitting, and a wide-based gait in a 4-point position and while walking. Though he is walking independently, he often does require people and furniture for additional stability and support. Most noteworthy is the fact that Kyle has a strong preference for throwing objects. The team believes this tendency is the result of difficulties in executing an active, volitional release. His relative difficulty with specific hand skills also is complicated by his continued lack of thumb opposition (cortical) on both hands. In light of his level of functioning at this time, these neuromotor difficulties continue to impact heavily on his ability to interact with toys and educational materials. He demonstrates a lag in cognitive development, which may be negatively impacted by his lack of hand skills during play activities. His play repertoires are very limited at this time.

The area of speech/language development is a second major concern. The team concurs with Denise that feeding continues to remain problematic. Kyle still shows evidence of a strong gag reflex, thus severely limiting the textures and types of foods he can consume. As a result, he currently is restricted to a diet of pureed/baby food. These feeding difficulties, in Denise's judgment, have had a major impact on Kyle's ability to gain weight. As also recognized by his mother, Kyle's variety and complexity of expressive and receptive language are extremely limited at this time. His language sample basically consisted of vocalizations with reduplicated and variegated babbling and a range of articulation placements; however, the team noted no evidence of Kyle's appropriate use of "protowords" or real words in context. He demonstrated turn-taking when prompted by the examiner/play facilitator, but never independently initiated that kind of reciprocal vocal play. In addition, he did not display any joint referencing abilities, as observed by the team members. It also should be noted that Kyle has had a history of repeated ear infections since birth, and these may have contributed to the language delays noted above. In conclusion, the team has assessed Kyle in the area of speech/language development to be functioning within an age range of eight to ten months.

Finally, given Kyle's limited repertoire of play behaviors, the Psychoeducational Team believes that Kyle's cognitive development constitutes another area that needs to be addressed in his early intervention services. He clearly demonstrated awareness of object permanence; however, his understanding of basic cause/effect relationships at best appears to be just emerging. Presented with a range of toys such as blocks, cup and spoon, rattles, and other small toys, Kyle often resorted to basic banging and throwing behaviors, which are inappropriate for a child of his age. He did respond well to early social games such as peek-a-boo and pat-a-cake, where he revealed an emerging sense of anticipation in these play schemas. His mother, too, reported that recently he has responded occasionally to familiar daily routines such as going into the bathroom for a bath and going outdoors. Overall, based on the two home visits made by the Psychoeducational Team, we estimate Kyle's cognitive functioning also to be approximately eight to ten months of age. A particular concern in addition to this cognitive delay is Kyle's tendency to resort to self-stimulatory behaviors such as the clapping of his hands when it is clearly not goal-directed or purposeful behavior.

Based upon the evaluation and summary above, the Gebbie Clinics Psychoeducational Team recommends the following:

1. As soon as possible, Kyle should be referred to a comprehensive early intervention program to address delays in the areas of neuromotor, speech/language/feeding, and cognitive development. These services should be intense with regular, weekly visits by a collaborative team including an early intervention teacher, speech/language therapist, physical therapist, and occupational therapist.

2. Given the family's strong commitment to and investment in this child, the parents should be actively involved in the daily programming for Kyle. It would be extremely helpful if Kyle were referred to a program that included the benefit of parent support groups.

3. In light of Kyle's history of chronic ear infections, he needs to be monitored regularly by his pediatrician for this condition, which may relate to his speech/language delays.

4. Given Kyle's remarkable medical history, it is advisable that sometime in the near future he be seen by a pediatric neurologist to rule out major central nervous system (CNS) dysfunction.

5. Presently Kyle is being followed by Dr. Muller, an ophthalmologist. It is important that Kyle's visual status continue to be monitored.

6. Because of Kyle's speech/language delays, a complete audiological evaluation should be conducted by a licensed audiologist.

7. Specific intervention for Kyle's feeding difficulties should be implemented as soon as programming services are initiated. These may be carried out by Kyle's parents under the guidance of a qualified speech/language therapist and a qualified occupational therapist specially trained in feeding techniques.

8. The Psychoeducational Team has included an appendix containing suggestions for specific activities that Kyle's parents can carry out within the context of their daily caregiving and play with their son at home.

9. In response to Denise's request for resource materials, the Psychoeducational Team has suggested several books about enhancing child development.

Caregiver 1 Record Form: Parent Interview

Evaluation date: _6_ / _1_ / _05_   Interviewer's name: _Gebbie Clinics Psychoeducational Team_
                 _6_ / _8_ / _05_

Child's name: ___Kyle___ _____ ___Jones___ _____ Sex: __male__

                First   Middle   Last   M/F

DOB: _10_ / _1_ / _03_   Chronological age: _20_ months ____ days   Adjusted age: _18_ months ____ days

Race: ___X X___   Ethnicity: ___X X___

What language(s) are commonly spoken in the child's home? _English_

PRIMARY CAREGIVERS

Full name: ___Robert Jones___   Relationship to child: __father__   DOB: ___/___/_78_

Full name: ___Denise Jones___   Relationship to child: __mother__   DOB: ___/___/_77_

Home phone: ___X X___   Work phone: ___X X___   Other: _____

Home address: ___X X___   City: __X X__   State: _X_ Zip code: __X X__

Work address: ___X X___   City: __X X__   State: _X_ Zip code: __X X__

Education: ___Both parents = AAS (2 year) Degree___

Child lives with caregiver(s): __X__ Full time _____ Part time _____ No

SIBLINGS

1. First Name _Jessica_ MI ___ Last _Jones_ M/F _F_ Age _5_ Race _X_ At Home? (Y) N

2. First Name _____ MI ___ Last _____ M/F ___ Age ___ Race ___ At Home? Y N

3. First Name _____ MI ___ Last _____ M/F ___ Age ___ Race ___ At Home? Y N

4. First Name _____ MI ___ Last _____ M/F ___ Age ___ Race ___ At Home? Y N

5. First Name _____ MI ___ Last _____ M/F ___ Age ___ Race ___ At Home? Y N

HEALTH SERVICE PROVIDERS

Primary Care Physician: _Dr. James Smith_   Phone: ( ) _X_ - _X_ Fax: _X_ - _X_

Other Physicians Currently Providing Medical Care

Name: ___Dr. Muller___ Phone: ( ) ___X___ - ___X___ Fax: ___X___ - ___X___ Specialty: ___opthal.___

Name: _____ Phone: ( ) _____ - _____ Fax: _____ - _____ Specialty: _____

Name: _____ Phone: ( ) _____ - _____ Fax: _____ - _____ Specialty: _____

Public Health Nurse (if assigned):

Name: ___unknown___ Phone: ( ) _____ - _____ Fax: _____ - _____

AGENCIES PRESENTLY SERVING THE CHILD AND FAMILY

Name of Agency	Contact Person	Phone Number

PREVIOUS HEALTH-RELATED AND INTERVENTION SERVICES

Date	Services Received	Service Provider
C.A. 14 months	eye surgery	unknown

FAMILY HISTORY OF PREMATURITY OR DEVELOPMENT PROBLEMS

Please describe below: ___None reported___

_____

_____

_____

_____

_____

Medical History of Child and Mother

PERINATAL HISTORY

1. Describe the frequency and nature of your visits to health care professionals during pregnancy with your child.

_____
_____
_____
_____

1st trimester:

    Regular visits—no complications.
_____
_____
_____
_____

2nd trimester:

    Visits scheduled every two weeks.
_____
_____
_____
_____

3rd trimester:

    Hospitalization and bed rest at home.
    Labor began at 32 weeks.
_____
_____
_____

2. Describe any significant medical problems during pregnancy with your child.

Date	Problem	Outcome
18th week	placenta previa	
	enlarged placenta	
24th week	hemorrhaging, bed rest at home	

3. Describe any significant medical problems during any other pregnancy.

First pregnancy was full-term without complications.

4. Describe any family problems that occurred during pregnancy with your child.

None reported.

5. Describe any use of drugs, tobacco, other toxins, or medications (prescription and nonprescription) during pregnancy with your child.

Father – Rx and injections for overseas travel

– Prior to conception

6. Describe any maternal hospitalizations during pregnancy with your child.

Dates	Description of Problem
24th week	hemorrhaging – placenta abrupted

DELIVERY AND BIRTH

7. Describe your child's birth: _32nd week of gestation._
_____Emergency cesarean section._____

8. Setting of birth (e.g., hospital, home): _hospital_____
_____

9. Type of delivery (e.g., vaginal, (cesarean): _____
_____

10. Term at birth: _X_ Pre-term ____ Full-term ____ Post-term

   Gestational age: __32__ weeks   Birth weight: ___1901___ grams

11. Apgar score(s): 1 minute: _____   5 minutes: _____ unknown

12. Describe any medical problems you or your baby had at birth. ___Child-respiratory distress_____
_____

13. If your baby was placed in a special nursery, give length of stay after birth.

   Level I: Neonatal newborn nursery   Dates _____

   Level II: Neonatal intensive care nursery   Dates _____

   Level III: Neonatal intensive care/regional nursery   Dates _Oct. 1 – Nov. 14 (6 weeks)_

   _____Child on ventilator for two weeks_____

14. Length of your hospitalization after delivery: _____
   _five days_____

INFANT CARE IMMEDIATELY AFTER DELIVERY

15. Describe the ease of visiting/caring for your baby during the hospital stay. _____
   _____Parental visits on a daily basis._____
   _____Parents could not hold infant for first two weeks while on ventilator._____

16. Describe your level of satisfaction with healthcare professionals during the hospital stay. _____
   _____Mother was pleased with care received during NICU stay._____
   _____Instruction and training for home care was good._____

Additional Comments:_Complications during NICU stay:_____
_____– child on ventilator two weeks_____
_____– required a chest tube secondary to collapsing lungs_____
_____– repeated episodes of apnea_____
_____– required resuscitation several times_____
_____

HOSPITAL DISCHARGE

17. Describe any special arrangements healthcare providers made on discharge from the hospital.

Instructions and training in resuscitation, CPR, and feeding

18. Describe the adequacy of information you received about how to care for your baby at home.

mother reported she was pleased

19. List any special services/programming arranged at the time of discharge.

–Public health nurse - one time/week to monitor weight

–PT - two times/month (later one time/month) and in-home ed. gain

20. Describe any problems experienced in caring for the baby immediately following discharge.

(1) Significant episode of bradycardia

21. List any services not offered/received at the time of discharge that might have been helpful.

CHILD'S HEALTH HISTORY

22. Describe any problems you experienced in caring for your baby/child or any major illnesses your baby/child had.

Type of Problem	Frequency
bradycardia	(1)
reflux	
sucking difficulty	on-going
frequent ear infections	
milk and milk product allergy	
strabismus (bilateral) corrected @ 14 months	

23. List dates of hospitalization(s) and reason(s) (including emergency room visits).

Date	Reason for Hospitalization	Outcome
__ / __ / __	eye surgery to correct strabismus	OK
__ / __ / __		
__ / __ / __		
__ / __ / __		

24. List any specialists seen.

Name	Specialty	Reason Seen	Dates
Dr. Muller	ophthalmologist		

25. List all medications taken in the past.

Medication	Reason Prescribed	Date
antibiotics	ear infections	__ / __ / __
albuterol	congestion	__ / __ / __
tagament	reflux	__ / __ / __
		__ / __ / __
		__ / __ / __

CHILD'S CURRENT HEALTH

Weight: __20__ pounds __13__ ounces   Length/height: _____ feet __31__ inches

Head circumference, if known _____

26. Describe your child's present general health.

      slow weight gain

      feeding difficulties

      motor delays

      delays in language development

27. List all known allergies.

      milk and milk products

28. List all current medications.

Medication	Reason Prescribed	Date	
antibiotics	ear infections	__ / __ / __	
albuterol	congestion	__ / __ / __	
tagament	reflux	__ / __ / __	on-going as needed
		__ / __ / __	
		__ / __ / __	

CHILD/FAMILY DEVELOPMENT AND ENVIRONMENT

29. List any medical/developmental problems family members experienced and any services they received.

Family Member	Problem	Services	Dates
Robert	Ø		
Denise	Ø		
Jessica	Ø		

30. List any circumstances in the family or environment that may have affected your baby or child.

move from Georgia to Syracuse, NY

In Georgia

31. Describe any childcare you have received and your level of satisfaction with the provider.

Child Provider/Setting	Frequency/Occasion (days per week)	Duration Per Day	History/Length of Care	Satisfaction with Care
PT	two times/month			OK
Public nurse	one time/week		6 weeks	OK
In-home teacher	sporadic			dissatisfied

32. List any present child/family service or support needs that are not being met.

Discussed with parent:

Comprehensive EI program

EI special education teacher

Speech/language pathologist

OT

PT   Recommended *audiological evaluation

*neurological evaluation

Caregiver 2 Record Form: Child Development

Evaluation date: June 1, 2005

Child's name: Kyle Jones

DOB: 10 / 1 / 03   Chronological age: 20 months 0 days   Adjusted age: 18 months 0 days

Address: Any Street

Any City, State USA

Caregiver interviewed: Denise   Relationship to child: mother

Caregiver's phone: Home: X X X   Work: X X X   Other: X X X

Team member conducting interview: Gail Ensher, EdD

Date of report: June 15, 2005

Social-Emotional Development

SE1. How frequently does _____ attend to people?
(1–36 months)

Circle One	
Rarely/never	1
Sometimes	2
Usually	③
Most of the time/always	4

SE2. How frequently does _____ attend to toys or activities?
(1–36 months)

Circle One	
Rarely/never	1
Sometimes	②
Usually	3
Most of the time/always	4

SE3. How often does _____ become distressed or fussy during the day?
(1–36 months)

Circle One	
Most of the time/always	1
Usually	2
Sometimes	③
Rarely/never	4

SE4. Can you calm _____ when he/she becomes distressed?
(1–36 months)

Circle One	
Rarely/never	1
Sometimes	2
Usually	③
Most of the time/always	4

SE5. Is _____ unusually sensitive to specific situations or things in your home, such as sound, light, or different textures?
(1–36 months)

Circle One	
Most of the time/always	1
Usually	2
Sometimes	③
Rarely/never	4

SE6. How well does _____ communicate his/her needs and emotions?
(1–36 months)

Circle One	
Communicates little	①
Communication varies with need or situation/sometimes	2
Usually communicates well	3
Most of the time/always communicates well	4

SE7. How well is _____ able to adapt to new situations?
(1–36 months)

Circle One	
Always requires assistance from another	①
Usually/often requires assistance from another	2
Sometimes/varies with situation	3
Rarely/never requires assistance	4

SE8. How well does _____ show or express emotions with people?
(3–36 months)

Circle One	
Rarely/never	1
Sometimes	②
Usually	3
Most of the time/always	4

SE9. Does _____ respond to the emotions or feelings of other people?
(5–36 months)

Circle One	
Rarely/never	①
Sometimes	2
Usually	3
Most of the time/always	4

Notes:
shy
_____
_____

Cognitive Development

C10. What types of toys does _____
particularly enjoy?
(3–36 months)

Circle Any/All and Sum	
Large motor (e.g., balls)	(1)
Small motor (e.g., rattles, blocks, puzzles, beads)	(1)
Sensory (e.g., Koosh balls, light- or sound-producing toys)	(1)
Problem solving/cause-effect (e.g., busy boxes, pop-up boxes)	1
Pretend play (e.g., stuffed animals, dolls, dishes)	1
Total	3

C11. What qualities does _____
demonstrate in playing games with your
family?
(3–36 months)

Circle Any/All and Sum	
Social/interactive (e.g., peek-a-boo, pat-a-cake, this little piggy)	(1)
Language (e.g., gestural, vocal play, turn taking)	1
Problem solving (e.g., hide and seek, hiding games)	1
Large motor (e.g., chase)	(1)
Games with simple routines (e.g., bedtime or bath-time routines)	(1)
Total	3

C12. Who does _____ like to play with?
(3–36 months)

Circle Any/All and Sum	
Primary caregivers	(1)
Siblings	1

Extended family	1
Adults/children outside the home	1
Pets	1
Total	1

C13. How well does _____ initiate play with
others?
(5–36 months)

Circle One	
Always requires assistance from another	(1)
Usually/often requires assistance from another	2
Sometimes/varies with situation	3
Rarely/never requires assistance	4

C14. What examples of problem solving
have you seen when _____ is
playing?
(7–36 months)

Circle Any/All and Sum	
Looks for objects dropped out of sight	(1)
Plays with pull toys	1
Finds items moved from one place to another	1
Turns keys/tools to open doors/opens jars or drawers	1
Total	1

C15. What examples of cause-and-effect
understanding have you seen in
_____'s play?
(7–36 months)

Circle Any/All and Sum	
Turns on TV/VCR/radio/stereo with/without remote	1

Uses one object to reach another	1
Turns on light switch	1
Turns on mechanical toy (e.g., tape recorder)	1
Uses pull toys	1
Total	

C16. How does _____ explore his/her
environment?
(7–36 months)

Circle Any/All and Sum	
Creeps to investigate	(1)
Looks inside or under covers/zippered bags	1
Plays with feely boxes	1
Visually searches/scans immediate surroundings	(1)
Total	2

C17. What examples of pretend play have
you seen?
(13–36 months)

Circle Any/All and Sum	
Pretends that one object is another (e.g., pretending a box is an oven)	1
Pretends to be another person (e.g., mommy)	1
Acts out a familiar routine	1
Acts out a sequence of routines with dolls/stuffed animals	1
Total	

Notes:
Prefers to play with adults
mostly bangs or throws
throw toys
enjoys playing outdoors

Neuromotor Development

NM18. What early positions does _____ use?
(1–12 months)

Circle Any/All and Sum	
Back	1
Stomach	1
Sitting	1
Standing	1
Total	

NM19. What hand skills does _____ have?
(5–12 months)   *Still an area of concern*

Circle Any/All and Sum	
Brings hands to midline/ does finger plays	①
Grasps objects	①
Transfers objects from hand to hand	1
Releases/lets go of objects	1
Total	2

(+ − and − markings noted beside items)

NM20. In what positions do you see _____ bearing weight?
(5–18 months)

Circle Any/All and Sum	
On stomach	1
In sitting (e.g., supporting weight with hands in front or to the side)	1
In independent sitting	①
In 4-point position	①
In independent sitting	①
Total	3

NM21. What positions does _____ move out of?
(5–36 months)

Circle Any/All and Sum	
Lying on back	①
Lying on stomach	①
Sitting	①
Creeping	①
Squatting	1
Standing	①
Total	5

NM22. What positions does _____ move into?
(5–36 months)

Circle Any/All and Sum	
To back	1
To stomach	1
Sitting	①
Creeping	①
Squatting	1
Standing	①
Total	3

NM23. How often does _____ need help eating?
(5–36 months)

Circle One	
Always requires assistance from another	①
Usually/often requires assistance from another	2
Sometimes/varies with situation	3
Rarely/never requires assistance	4

NM24. What are _____'s eating habits like (e.g., eating a variety of foods)?
(5–36 months)

Circle One	
Rarely/never eats well	①
Sometimes eats well	2
Usually/often eats well	3
Most of the time/always eats well	4

NM25. How do you feed _____?
(5–36 months)

Circle Any/All and Sum	
Bottle/breast feeds	①
Takes food from spoon	①
Uses fingers	1
Uses trainer or regular cup/glass	1
Total	2

NM26. How does _____ move from place to place?
(9–36 months)

Circle Any/All and Sum	
Rolls	1
Belly creeps	1
4-point creeps	①
Cruises along furniture/ people	①
Steps/walks	①
Total	3

mostly watches

NM27. What large movement games does _____ enjoy?
(9–36 months)

Circle Any/All and Sum	
Playing ball (e.g., rolls, throws, catches, kicks)	1
Tumbling	1
Rough-and-tumble (e.g., being tossed in the air and caught)	1
Jumping	1
Total	

Notes:

Feeding is an area of concern- weight gain?

"w"-sits   wide-gait

Prefers cruising and hold on for support

?balance

Sensory-Perceptual Development

SP28. How does _____ react to being held and cuddled?
(1–36 months)

Circle One	
Rarely/never enjoys	1
Sometimes enjoys	2
Usually/often enjoys	③
Most of the time/always enjoys	4

SP29. What sensory experiences does _____ enjoy?
(1–36 months)

Circle Any/All and Sum	
Taking a bath	①
Cuddling/being covered with a blanket	1
Being held closely by a person	①
Touching a person	①
Being rocked/patted	1
Having hair combed/brushed	1
Total	3

SP30. How well is _____ able to follow your face and objects visually?
(1–36 months) ❓

Circle Any/All and Sum	
Tracks left to right	1
Tracks right to left	1
Tracks up and down	1
Tracks in a circle	1
Has smooth and coordinated eye movements	1
Total	

– Has had visual problems, per parent

SP31. What manipulative toys/materials does _____ enjoy playing with?
(5–36 months)

Circle Any/All and Sum	
Rattles	①
Blocks	①
Shape sorters	1
Fit-together toys (e.g., puzzles)	1
Modeling clay/paints/food	1
Total	2

SP32. How does _____ help with dressing and undressing?
(11–36 months)

Circle Any/All and Sum	
Takes off shoes/socks	1
Takes off 1 or 2 pieces of clothing	1
Puts on 1 or 2 pieces of clothing	1
Puts on socks/shoes	1
Does/undoes simple fasteners	1
Total	

SP33. Can you give examples of how _____ knows where his/her body is in space?
(7–36 months) ⊕−

Circle Any/All and Sum	
Goes under tables	1
Climbs on chairs/furniture	1
Goes up and down stairs/turns self around	1
Creeps around furniture and people	1
Changes direction in movement	1
Total	

SP34. What does _____ do with pencil (or crayon) and paper activities?
(11–36 months) ❓

Circle Any/All and Sum	
Holds pencil/crayon	1
Bangs pencil/crayon on paper	*not tried* 1
Scribbles	1
Imitates simple lines/figures	1
Draws simple pictures	1
Total	

Notes:

Not independent.

Assists by putting arms in

correct position.

very limited

play repertoire

Walks around playpen

? stereotypic self-stimulation

Communication and Language Development

L35. What range of sounds does _____ respond to at home?
(1–36 months)

Circle Any/All and Sum	
Voices in same or different room	①
Telephone ringing	①
Doorbell	①
TV/stereo/radio	1
Vacuum cleaner	1
Objects dropping/startles/ locates	1
Total	3

L36. What single sounds have you heard _____ say? *(Area of concern)*
(1–8 months)

Circle Any/All and Sum (1 or more per set = 1 point)	
ⓐⓔ i *all vowels*	1
ⓞⓤ y	1
b, c, ⓓ *d, m,*	1
ⓜ g, ⓗ *h, j*	1
r, s, t	1
ⓙ l, f	1
Total	

L37. How does _____ communicate with you and other people?
(3–36 months)

Circle Any/All and Sum	
Cries/whines	①
Points/gestures	1
Looks/scans	①
Vocalizes	①
Verbalizes	1
Total	3

L38. What names of people does _____ recognize?
(5–36 months)

Circle Any/All and Sum	
Own name ?	①
Mommy	①
Daddy	①
Names of siblings (List): *Jessica*	①
Others: *family bird*	①
Total	5

L39. What words (other than names) does _____ understand? (List)
(5–36 months)

Circle Any/All and Sum (1 or more per set = 1 point)	
People:	1
Action words:	1
Body parts:	1
Animals:	1
Foods/food related:	1
Total	

L40. What nonverbal or verbal expressions does _____ imitate?
(5–36 months)

Circle Any/All and Sum	
Gestures (e.g., hi, bye, throwing kisses)	1
Single sounds (e.g., a, e, i, o, u, d, m)	1
Sound combinations (e.g., oh, ba, da)	1
Sound sequences (e.g., oh-oh, mama, dada, mada)	1
Total	

Notes:

⊕⊖ Language
− appears to
be emerging.

Area of concern

L41. What sound combinations does _____ say?
(7–36 months)

Circle Any/All and Sum *(1 or more per set = 1 point)*	
ba, (ma,) (da)	①
mama, dada (reduplicated babbling)	①
baga, tada, magada (variegated babbling)	①
Please note others:	1
Total	3

L42. What does _____ do with books?
(7–36 months)

Circle Any/All and Sum	
Turns pages	1
Scans/looks at pictures	①
Points/pats	①
Vocalizes randomly	1
Imitates pictured sounds/ objects/living things	1
Verbalizes	1
Total	2

L43. What requests or directions does _____ understand?
(9–36 months)

Circle Any/All and Sum	
No-no	①
Come	1
Look/see	1
1-step (give examples):	1
2-step (give examples):	1
Total	1

L44. What does _____ do if you or someone else does not understand him/her?
(11–36 months)

Circle One	
Becomes frustrated	①
Cries/whines	2
Leads you to desired object/place/person	3
Gestures	4
Increases vocalizations	5
Repeats requests	6
Total	

L45. About how many words does _____ say?
(13–36 months)

Circle One	
1–5 words	①
6–10 words	2
11–25 words	3
26–50 words	4
Up to 100 words	5
Up to 200 words	6
300 words or more	7

} da-da
ma-ma
no-no

L46. What words does _____ say? (List)
(13–36 months)

Circle Any/All and Sum *(1 or more per set = 1 point)*	
People: *da-da ma-ma*	①
Action words:	1
Body parts:	1
Animals:	1
Foods/eating:	1
Modifiers (e.g., all gone, big, mine): *No-No*	①
Total	2

L47. How many words does _____ put together?
(17–36 months) ⊖

Circle One	
2 words	1
3 words	2
4 words	3
5 words	4
More than 5 words	5

Notes:
↑ *just started to babble*
_____
_____
_____
_____
_____

Partners in Play Developmental Assessment Record Form

Evaluation date: _June 8, 2005_

Name of child: _Kyle Jones_

Chronological age: _20_ months _0_ weeks   Adjusted age: _20_ months ____ weeks

Address: _Any Street_

_____ Any City, State   USA_

Telephone # of Caregiver(s): (Home): _XXX_

(Work): _XXX_

Alternate Telephone #: _XXX_

Name and Relationship to Child: _Denise (mother)_

Date(s) of Evaluation: _June 1 & June 8, 2005_

Team Members Working with Child: _Carol Reinson, Phd, OTR/L_

_____

Team Members Observing Child: _Deborah Bryden, MS, SLP_

_____

Team Members Recording Information: _Gail Ensher, EdD_

_____

Date of Report: _June 15, 2005_

_____

Unstructured Caregiver-Child Play

L1. Strategies for Communication

a. Differential vocalization
(1 month – 6 months)

Circle One	
Not evident	1
Emerging	2
Developing	3
Well developed	4

b. Vocal play
(3 months – 18 months)

Circle One	
Not evident	1
Emerging	2
Developing	③
Well developed	4

c. Reduplicated babbling
(9 months – 18 months)

Circle One	
Not evident	1
Emerging	2
Developing	③
Well developed	4

d. Variegated babbling
(9 months – 18 months)

Circle One	
Not evident	1
Emerging	②
Developing	3
Well developed	4

e. Using gestures
(9 months – 36 months)

Circle One	
Not evident	①
Emerging	2
Developing	3
Well developed	4

→ doesn't use gestures

f. Jargon-like vocalizations
(9 months – 36 months)

Circle One	
Not evident	1
Emerging	②
Developing	3
Well developed	4

g. Making requests
(11 months – 36 months)

Circle One	
Not evident	①
Emerging	2
Developing	3
Well developed	4

h. Using single words
(11 months – 36 months)

Circle One	
Not evident	①
Emerging	2
Developing	3
Well developed	4

i. Putting 2 words together
(11 months – 36 months)

Circle One	
Not evident	①
Emerging	2
Developing	3
Well developed	4

j. Putting 3 or more words together
(11 months – 36 months)

Circle One	
Not evident	①
Emerging	2
Developing	3
Well developed	4

k. Initiating/engaging in dialogue/discourse
(17 months – 36 months)

Circle One	
Not evident	①
Emerging	2
Developing	3
Well developed	4

L2. Communication of Needs/Intent

a. Making basic needs known (e.g., fatigue, hunger, change of position)
(1 month – 36 months)

Circle One	
Never/rarely	1
Sometimes	2
Usually/frequently	③
Most of the time/always	4

b. Making social needs known (e.g., desire to be picked up, to engage in play)
(1 month – 36 months)

Circle One	
Never/rarely	1
Sometimes	②
Usually/frequently	3
Most of the time/always	4

Notes:

Language output increases
when Kyle is in supportive
positions.

– difficulty combining motor
and language

L3. Child's Understanding of Language or Communication

a. Responds to caregiver's vocal play
(3 months – 12 months)

Circle One	
Not evident	1
Emerging	2
Developing	3
Well developed	4

?

b. Responds to gestures (e.g., being beckoned to come)
(7 months – 36 months)

Circle One	
Not evident	(1)
Emerging	2
Developing	3
Well developed	4

c. Responds to single-word requests/directions
(9 months – 36 months)

Circle One	
Not evident	(1)
Emerging	2
Developing	3
Well developed	4

d. Responds to 1-step directions
(13 months – 36 months)

Circle One	
Not evident	(1)
Emerging	2
Developing	3
Well developed	4

e. Responds to 2-step directions
(23 months – 36 months)

Circle One	
Not evident	1
Emerging	2
Developing	3
Well developed	4

L4. Vocalized Turn-Taking

a. Decreases/increases vocalizations in response to caregiver
(1 month – 6 months)

Circle One	
Not evident	1
Emerging	2
Developing	3
Well developed	4

?

b. Vocalizes across 1 turn
(1 month – 8 months)

Circle One	
Not evident	1
Emerging	2
Developing	3
Well developed	4

?

c. Vocalizes across 2 turns
(3 months – 18 months)

Circle One	
Not evident	(1)
Emerging	2
Developing	3
Well developed	4

L5. Joint Referencing with Caregiver

a. Attends to caregiver
(1 month – 18 months)

Circle One	
Not evident	1
Emerging	2
Developing	(3)
Well developed	4

b. Gains/directs attention of caregiver
(3 months – 18 months)

Circle One	
Not evident	1
Emerging	(2)
Developing	3
Well developed	4

c. Continues familiar routine with caregiver
(5 months – 24 months)

Circle One	
Not evident	1
Emerging	(2)
Developing	3
Well developed	4

d. Shows humor with caregiver
(7 months – 36 months)

Circle One	
Not evident	1
Emerging	(2)
Developing	3
Well developed	4

Notes:

_____
_____
_____
_____
_____
_____
_____

SE6. Quality of Social Interaction with Caregiver

a. Responds to smiling/soft talking
   (1 month – 36 months)

Circle One	
Never/rarely	1
Sometimes	2
Usually/frequently	③
Most of the time/always	4

b. Goes to caregiver for comfort
   (1 month – 36 months)

Circle One	
Never/rarely	1
Sometimes	2
Usually/frequently	③
Most of the time/always	4

SE7. Emotional Stability

a. Has periods of contentment during interaction with caregiver
   (1 month – 36 months)

Circle One	
Not evident	1
Emerging	2
Developing	③
Well developed	4

b. Able to self-calm
   (1 month – 36 months)

Circle One	
Not evident	①
Emerging	2
Developing	3
Well developed	4

c. Initiates interaction
   (7 months – 36 months)

Circle One	
Not evident	①
Emerging	2
Developing	3
Well developed	4

d. Maintains interaction
   (9 months – 36 months)

Circle One	
Not evident	1
Emerging	②
Developing	3
Well developed	4

C8. Play Strategies Observed

a. Smiles/laughes at engaging routines
   (5 months – 36 months)

Circle One	
Not evident	1
Emerging	2
Developing	③
Well developed	4

b. Engages in games/game-like play
   (5 months – 36 months)

Circle One	
Not evident	1
Emerging	②
Developing	3
Well developed	4

c. Shows appropriate functional play with toys/objects
   (17 months – 36 months)

Circle One	
Not evident	①
Emerging	2
Developing	3
Well developed	4

d. Represents 2 or more related events in play
   (17 months – 36 months)

Circle One	
Not evident	①
Emerging	2
Developing	3
Well developed	4

e. Engages in symbolic play with toys/caregiver
   (23 months – 36 months)

Circle One	
Not evident	1
Emerging	2
Developing	3
Well developed	4

Notes:
- sensory seeking behaviors, (e.g. strokes hair)
- Doesn't initiate
- Appears content and bonded with mother
- ↑bangs and throws toys repeatedly.

SP9. Moving and Maneuvering in the Environment

a. Rolls from stomach to back
(3 months – 12 months)   *OK*

Circle One	
Not evident	1
Emerging	2
Developing	3
Well developed	4

b. Rolls from back to stomach
(3 months – 12 months)   *OK*

Circle One	
Not evident	1
Emerging	2
Developing	3
Well developed	4

c. Creeps
(5 months – 12 months)   *OK*

Circle One	
Not evident	1
Emerging	2
Developing	3
Well developed	4

d. Pulls up on people and furniture
(7 months – 16 months)   *OK wide-stance plantigrade*

Circle One	
Not evident	1
Emerging	2
Developing	3
Well developed	4

e. Cruises around people and furniture
(9 months – 18 months)

Circle One	
Not evident	1
Emerging	2
Developing	(3)
Well developed	4

f. Walks
(9 months – 24 months)

Circle One	
Not evident	1
Emerging	2
Developing	(3)
Well developed	4

g. Runs
(13 months – 36 months)

Circle One	
Not evident	1
Emerging	2
Developing	(3)
Well developed	4

Notes:

Preferred mode is cruising
around couch and ↑holds on
for support
_____

SP10. **Skill in Eating

a. Oral-motor response/appropriate gag reflex   ↑hypes gag
(1 month – 6 months)

Circle One	
Never/rarely	1
Sometimes	2
Usually/frequently	3
Most of the time/always	4

b. Takes food appropriately into mouth
(5 months – 18 months)

Circle One	
Not evident	1
Emerging	2
Developing	(3)
Well developed	4

c. Lateralizes tongue with food
(5 months – 18 months)

Circle One	
Not evident	1
Emerging	2
Developing	(3)
Well developed	4

d. Swallows food
(5 months – 18 months)

Circle One	
Not evident	1
Emerging	2
Developing	(3)
Well developed	4

actual feeding in 2nd visit

e. Chews
(7 months – 18 months)

Circle One	
Not evident	(1)
Emerging	2
Developing	3
Well developed	4

Notes:
_____
_____
_____
_____
_____
_____

SP11. **Drinking

a. Uses continuous, organized sucking pattern with bottle/breast (1 month – 6 months) OK

Circle One	
Not evident	1
Emerging	2
Developing	3
Well developed	4

b. Shows jaw, tongue, and lip control stable with cup/glass drinking (9 months – 36 months)

Circle One	
Never/rarely	(1)
Sometimes	2
Usually/frequently	3
Most of the time/always	4

c. Drinks with little liquid lost (11 months – 36 months)

Circle One	
Never/rarely	(1)
Sometimes	2
Usually/frequently	3
Most of the time/always	4

NM 12. **Picking Up Finger Food/ Self-Feeding

a. Brings finger food to mouth independently (9 months – 18 months)

Circle One	
Not evident	(1)
Emerging	2
Developing	3
Well developed	4

b. Rakes to pick up food (9 months – 18 months)

Circle One	
Not evident	1
Emerging	(2)
Developing	3
Well developed	4

c. Uses three-jaw chuck grasp (9 months – 18 months)

Circle One	
Not evident	1
Emerging	(2)
Developing	3
Well developed	4

d. Uses index finger and thumb grasp (11 months – 24 months)

Circle One	
Not evident	1
Emerging	2
Developing	3
Well developed	4

SP13. **Self-Feeding with Eating Utensils

a. Brings spoon to mouth (11 months – 36 months)

Circle One	
Not evident	(1)
Emerging	2
Developing	3
Well developed	4

b. Puts spoonful of food in mouth independently (13 months – 36 months)

Circle One	
Not evident	(1)
Emerging	2
Developing	3
Well developed	4

c. Uses pronated hand to hold spoon (13 months – 36 months)

Circle One	
Not evident	(1)
Emerging	2
Developing	3
Well developed	4

d. Uses supinated hand to hold spoon (15 months – 36 months)

Circle One	
Not evident	(1)
Emerging	2
Developing	3
Well developed	4

Notes:
- *Feeding is an area of concern.
- Does not enjoy trying chunkier foods.
- weight gain?
- allergies

Unstructured Examiner-Child Play

SE14. Quality of Interaction with Unfamiliar Person/s
a. Responds to smiling/soft talking
(1 month – 36 months)

Shy

Circle One	
Never/rarely	1
Sometimes	(2)
Usually/frequently	3
Most of the time/always	4

b. Initiates interaction
(7 months – 36 months)

Circle One	
Never/rarely	(1)
Sometimes	2
Usually/frequently	3
Most of the time/always	4

c. Maintains interaction
(9 months – 36 months)

Circle One	
Never/rarely	1
Sometimes	(2)
Usually/frequently	3
Most of the time/always	4

d. Relates to 2 or more unfamiliar persons
(9 months – 36 months)

Circle One	
Never/rarely	1
Sometimes	(2)
Usually/frequently	3
Most of the time/always	4

SE15. Attentiveness to Play Activities
a. Attends to age-appropriate range of play events
(1 month – 36 months)

Circle One	
Never/rarely	1
Sometimes	(2)
Usually/frequently	3
Most of the time/always	4

b. Attends to play activities for age-appropriate periods of time
(1 month – 36 months)

Circle One	
Most of the time/always requires assistance from another	(1)
Usually/often requires assistance from another	2
Varies with situation	3
Rarely/never requires assistance	4

L16. Response to Common Sounds in the Environment
a. Responds to voices in same or different room
(1 month – 36 months)

Circle One	
Never/rarely	1
Sometimes	2
Usually/frequently	(3)
Most of the time/always	4

b. Responds to common sounds in same or different rooms (e.g., telephone, television)
(1 month – 36 months)

Circle One	
Never/rarely	1
Sometimes	2
Usually/frequently	(3)
Most of the time/always	4

? *Typically 1–2 minute attention span*

8 minute maximum

unwilling and/or unable

NM17. Quality of Movement
a. Moves in and out of developmental positions
(3 months – 36 months)

Circle One	
Never/rarely	1
Sometimes	2
Usually/frequently	(3)
Most of the time/always	4

b. Uses graded, smooth movement
(3 months – 36 months)

Circle One	
Not evident	1
Emerging	2
Developing	(3)
Well developed	4

Notes:
- *used own familiar toys*
- *needs hand–over–hand and is OK with it.*
- *sensory–seeking*

NM18. Large Motor Milestones (without movement or maneuvering)

a. Sits
   (5 months – 36 months)

Circle One	
Not evident	1
Emerging	2
Developing	③
Well developed	4

b. Uses 4-point positions
   (7 months – 36 months)

Circle One	
Not evident	1
Emerging	2
Developing	③
Well developed	4

NM19. Hand Skills Observed

a. Brings hands to midline
   (3 months – 12 months)

Circle One	
Not evident	1
Emerging	2
Developing	3
Well developed	4

OK

b. Reaches with right and left hands
   (3 months – 12 months)

Circle One	
Not evident	1
Emerging	2
Developing	3
Well developed	4

OK

c. Grasps with right and left hands (Hand preference noted)
   (3 months – 12 months) +–

Circle One	
Not evident	1
Emerging	2
Developing	3
Well developed	4

d. Transfers from hand to hand
   (5 months – 12 months) +–

Circle One	
Not evident	1
Emerging	2
Developing	3
Well developed	4

e. Releases objects with right and left hands
   (5 months – 12 months) –

Circle One	
Not evident	1
Emerging	2
Developing	3
Well developed	4

f. Crosses midline with right and left hands
   (13 months – 36 months)

Circle One	
Not evident	1
Emerging	2
Developing	③
Well developed	4

Notes:
- *? quality of motor patterns*
- *? volitional release*
- *traps object versus mature grasp pattern*

_____

Hand skills are
area of concern
– may need supportive
↑positioning

NM20. Body Symmetry

a. On back
   (1 month – 6 months)

Circle One	
Not evident	1
Emerging	2
Developing	3
Well developed	4

b. On stomach
   (1 month – 6 months)

Circle One	
Not evident	1
Emerging	2
Developing	3
Well developed	4

c. In sitting
   (5 months – 18 months)

Circle One	
Not evident	1
Emerging	2
Developing	③
Well developed	4

d. In 4-point creeping
   (7 months – 18 months)

Circle One	
Not evident	1
Emerging	2
Developing	③
Well developed	4

e. In standing/upright/walking
   (11 months – 36 months)

Circle One	
Not evident	1
Emerging	2
Developing	③
Well developed	4

NM21. Transitions into and out of Various Positions
a. Moves out of sitting
(9 months – 24 months)

Circle One	
Not evident	1
Emerging	2
Developing	(3)
Well developed	4

b. Moves into sitting
(9 months – 24 months)

Circle One	
Not evident	1
Emerging	2
Developing	(3)
Well developed	4

c. Moves out of standing
(13 months – 36 months)

Circle One	
Not evident	1
Emerging	2
Developing	(3)
Well developed	4

d. Moves into standing
(13 months – 36 months)

Circle One	
Not evident	1
Emerging	2
Developing	(3)
Well developed	4

SP22. Response to Touch
a. Responds to personal, physical touch (e.g., hugging)
(1 month – 36 months)

Circle One	
Never/rarely	1
Sometimes	(2)
Usually	3
Most of the time/always	4

b. Enjoys different textures
(13 months – 18 months)

Circle One	
Never/rarely	1
Sometimes	2
Usually	(3)
Most of the time/always	4

c. Walks on different surfaces
(13 months – 24 months)

Circle One	
Never/rarely	1
Sometimes	2
Usually	(3)
Most of the time/always	4

SE23. Attention-Gaining Behaviors Observed
a. Uses positive, nonverbal strategies to gain attention (e.g., eye gaze, reaching for, tugging)
(5 months – 36 months)

Circle One	
Not evident	1
Emerging	(2)
Developing	3
Well developed	4

b. Uses positive verbal strategies to gain attention
(7 months – 36 months)

Circle One	
Not evident	1
Emerging	(2)
Developing	3
Well developed	4

NM24. Protective Responses Observed
a. Uses forward propping
(5 months – 12 months) OK

Circle One	
Never/rarely	1
Sometimes	2
Usually/frequently	3
Most of the time/always	4

b. Uses lateral propping
(5 months – 12 months) OK

Circle One	
Not evident	1
Emerging	2
Developing	3
Well developed	4

c. Uses backward equilibrium/balance reaction
(9 months – 12 months) OK

Circle One	
Not evident	1
Emerging	2
Developing	3
Well developed	4

Notes:
Try:
sensory
diet/tactile modality
approaches

C25. Purposeful Behavior in Play

a. Uses play to practice familiar/known skills and routines
(7 months – 36 months)

Circle One	
Not evident	1
Emerging	②
Developing	3
Well developed	4

b. Uses play to acquire/try new skills/tasks
(9 months – 36 months)

Circle One	
Not evident	1
Emerging	②
Developing	3
Well developed	4

L26. Intelligibility of Speech and Language

a. Uses single prompted/imitated expressions that are understandable (e.g., bye-bye)
(11 months – 36 months)

Circle One	
About 10% or less of the time	①
About 25% of the time	2
About 50% of the time	3
About 75% or more of the time	4

b. Uses single spontaneous expressions (i.e., 1 word) that are understandable
(11 months – 36 months)

Circle One	
About 10% or less of the time	①
About 25% of the time	2
About 50% of the time	3
About 75% or more of the time	4

c. Uses understandable multiword expressions (spontaneous or prompted)
(11 months – 36 months)

Circle One	
About 10% or less of the time	①
About 25% of the time	2
About 50% of the time	3
About 75% or more of the time	4

C27. Problem-Solving Skills Observed

a. Solves problems without assistance ?
(e.g., prompting, demonstration, hand-over-hand)
(11 months – 36 months)

Circle One	
Never/rarely	①
Sometimes	2
Usually/frequently	3
Most of the time/always	4

b. Solves age-appropriate problems
(11 months – 36 months)

Circle One	
Never/rarely	①
Sometimes	2
Usually/frequently	3
Most of the time/always	4

L28. Imitation Skills Observed

a. Uses gestures
(5 months – 36 months)

Circle One	
Not evident	1
Emerging	②
Developing	3
Well developed	4

b. Vowels
(5 months – 36 months)

Circle One	
Not evident	1
Emerging	②
Developing	3
Well developed	4

c. Reduplicated babbling
(9 months – 18 months)

Circle One	
Not evident	1
Emerging	②
Usually	3
Well developed	4

d. Variegated babbling
(9 months – 18 months)

Circle One	
Not evident	1
Emerging	②
Developing	3
Well developed	4

e. Blends
(9 months – 36 months)

Circle One	
Not evident	1
Emerging	②
Developing	3
Well developed	4

f. Single words
(11 months – 36 months)

Circle One	
Not evident	①
Emerging	2
Developing	3
Well developed	4

g. Two-word combinations
(17 months – 36 months)

Circle One	
Not evident	①
Emerging	2
Developing	3
Well developed	4

h. Three-word combinations
(23 months – 36 months)

Circle One	
Not evident	1
Emerging	2
Developing	3
Well developed	4

Structured Examiner-Child Play

L29. Response to Bell
a. Alerts/locates bell on right side
(1 month – 36 months)

Circle One	
Not evident	1
Responds 1 time	2
Responds inconsistently	3
Responds consistently	(4)

b. Alerts/locates bell on left side
(1 month – 36 months)

Circle One	
Not evident	1
Responds 1 time	2
Responds inconsistently	3
Responds consistently	(4)

C30. Attention to Faces and Designs
a. Attends to human face
(1 month – 6 months)　OK

Circle One	
Not evident	1
Emerging	2
Developing	3
Well developed	4

b. Attends to checkerboard
(1 month – 6 months)　OK

Circle One	
Not evident	1
Emerging	2
Developing	3
Well developed	4

c. Attends to schematic face (e.g., includes social/communicative response)
(1 month – 6 months)　OK

Circle One	
Never/rarely	1
Emerging	2
Developing	3
Well developed	4

d. Responds to real image in mirror (e.g., includes social/communicative response)
(3 months – 18 months)

Circle One	
Not evident	1
Emerging	2
Developing	(3)
Well developed	4

e. Shows early responses to baby doll (e.g., holding, poking, touching, kissing)
(5 months – 18 months)

Circle One	
Not evident	1
Emerging	(2)
Developing	3
Well developed	4

SP31. Tracking
a. Tracks horizontally
(1 month – 36 months)

Circle One	
Not evident	1
Emerging	2
Developing	(3)
Well developed	4

b. Tracks in circle
(1 month – 36 months)

Circle One	
Not evident	1
Emerging	2
Developing	(3)
Well developed	4

c. Shows smooth eye movement
(1 month – 36 months)

Circle One	
Not evident	1
Emerging	2
Developing	(3)
Well developed	4

d. Shows coordinated eye movement
(1 month – 36 months)

Circle One	
Not evident	1
Emerging	2
Developing	(3)
Well developed	4

L32. Early Social Games
a. Engages in vocal play with toy puppet
(3 months – 8 months)

Circle One	
Not evident	1
Emerging	2
Developing	3
Well developed	4

b. Plays Peek-a-Boo
(3 months – 12 months)　OK　(+ –)

Circle One	
Not evident	1
Emerging	2
Developing	3
Well developed	4

c. Plays Pat-a-Cake
(7 months – 18 months)　?

Circle One	
Not evident	(1)
Emerging	2
Developing	3
Well developed	4

Notes:
- Play behaviors are limited.
- needs a lot of prompts.
_____
_____
_____

NM33. Play with Rattles
a. Reaches for rattles
   (3 months – 12 months)

Circle One	
Not evident	1
Emerging	2
Developing	3
Well developed	4

b. Grasps rattles
   (3 months – 12 months)

Circle One	
Not evident	1
Emerging	2
Developing	3
Well developed	4

c. Transfers rattles
   (5 months – 12 months)

Circle One	
Not evident	1
Emerging	2
Developing	3
Well developed	4

d. Releases rattles
   (5 months – 12 months)

Circle One	
Not evident	1
Emerging	2
Developing	3
Well developed	4

C34. Response to Hidden Objects
a. Finds partially covered rattle
   (5 months – 12 months)   OK

Circle One	
Not evident	1
Emerging	2
Developing	3
Well developed	4

b. Finds completely covered rattle
   (7 months – 12 months)   (+ −)

Circle One	
Not evident	1
Emerging	2
Developing	3
Well developed	4

C35. Early Understanding of Cause and Effect
a. Plays with pull toy
   (5 months – 12 months)   adapted? 1 attempt

Circle One	
No awareness evident	1
Holds string/ball only	2
Pulls without awareness	3
Pulls with awareness	4

b. Plays with pop-up pets box
   (9 months – 24 months)   (?)

Circle One	
No awareness evident	①
Opens 1 lever	2
Opens 2 levers	3
Opens 3 levers	4
Opens 4 levers	5

C36. Play with Blocks and Shape Sorter
a. Plays with blocks and shape sorter
   (9 months – 18 months)

Circle Any/All and Sum	
Holds	①
Bangs	①
Takes out of container	①
Puts into container	1
Stacks	1
Total	3

Notes:

Hand Skills—

• impact on cognitive?

• with assistance >toy showed

  potential for learning and practice

b. Displays visual discrimination with
   shape sorter
   (11 months – 36 months)

Circle One	
Places 1 block near hole	①
Inserts 1 block through hole	2
Inserts 2 or 3 blocks near holes	3
Inserts 2 or 3 blocks through holes	4

NM37. Play with Balls
a. Rolls with intent
   (7 months – 12 months)

Circle One	
Not evident	①*
Emerging	2
Developing	3
Well developed	4

b. Throws ball with intent
   (13 months – 36 months)

Circle One	
Not evident	①
Emerging	2
Usually	3
Well developed	4

c. Catches ball with intent
   (15 months – 36 months)

Circle One	
Not evident	①
Emerging	2
Usually	3
Well developed	4

C38. Play with Pictures and Print
a. Responds to books
   (7 months – 36 months)

Circle Any/All and Sum	
Shifts eye gaze/scans/ studies	①
Turns pages	①
Points to pictures	①
Vocalizes/verbalizes in response to pictures	1
Total	3

closed book (handwritten note)

b. Responds to crayon and paper
   (9 months – 36 months)

Circle Any/All and Sum	
Reaches for/holds crayon	①
Marks paper by banging	1
Makes strokes/circular lines	1
Imitates design/designs	1
Total	1

SP39. Play with Bubble Tumbler
a. Uses wand
   (13 months – 36 months)   *watched*

Circle Any/All and Sum	
Reaches for/holds wand	1
Puts wand into container	1
Takes wand out of container	1
Brings wand near mouth	1
Total	

b. Blows bubbles
   (13 months – 36 months)   *watched*

Circle Any/All and Sum	
Puckers mouth	1
Imitates blowing with or without wand	1
Brings wand near mouth, then blows	1
Blows through wand/ produces bubbles	1
Total	

C40. Advanced Doll Play
a. Displays single play scenarios (e.g., covering baby, feeding, rocking, dressing, undressing)
   (13 months – 36 months)   *kiss?*

Circle One	
Not evident	1
Emerging	②
Developing	3
Well developed	4

b. Displays related play scenarios (e.g., feeds/rocks, feeds/changes diaper, sings to baby/puts to bed)
   (17 months – 36 months)

Circle One	
Not evident	①
Emerging	2
Developing	3
Well developed	4

C41. Problem-Solving
a. Seeks food/object behind one screen
   (13 months – 36 months)

Circle One	
Not evident	1
Emerging	②
Developing	3
Well developed	4

b. Seeks food/object behind two screens
   (13 months – 36 months)

Circle One	
Not evident	①
Emerging	2
Developing	3
Well developed	4

c. Seeks food inside clear container
   (13 months – 36 months)

Circle One	
Not evident	①
Emerging	2
Developing	3
Well developed	4

d. Plays with toy garage
   (17 months – 36 months)   *not tested*

Circle Any/All and Sum	
Attempts key	1
Inserts key	1
Turns key	1
Opens door	1
Exits car	1
Total	

Notes:

_____

_____

_____

_____

_____

SP42. Undressing and Dressing
a. Takes off socks
   (9 months – 36 months)

Circle One	
Not evident	①
Emerging	2
Developing	3
Well developed	4

b. Puts on socks
   (13 months – 36 months)

Circle One	
Not evident	①
Emerging	2
Developing	3
Well developed	4

c. Takes off shoes
   (13 months – 36 months)

Circle One	
Not evident	①
Emerging	2
Developing	3
Well developed	4

d. Puts on toy hard hat
   (13 months – 36 months)

Circle One	
Not evident	①
Emerging	2
Developing	3
Well developed	4

e. Puts on vest
   (13 months – 36 months)

Circle One	
Not evident	①
Emerging	2
Developing	3
Well developed	4

f. Opens and closes vest fasteners
   (15 months – 36 months)

Circle One	
Not evident	①
Emerging	2
Developing	3
Well developed	4

SE43. Adaptability
a. Makes transitions with interest
   (11 months – 36 months)

Circle One	
Never/rarely	1
Sometimes	2
Usually/frequently	③
Most of the time/always	4

b. Attends during structured play
   (11 months – 36 months)

Circle One	
Never/rarely	1
Sometimes	2
Usually/frequently	③
Most of the time/always	4

Notes:

Sweet kid!

_____

_____

_____

_____

Partners in Play Scoring Worksheet 1

Child's name: ___Kyle Jones___   Evaluation date: ___20 months___

Chronological/adjusted age: ___18___ months

Photocopy and complete this worksheet to provide a permanent record of the child's performance.

Caregiver Report of Child Development

SOCIAL-EMOTIONAL SKILLS

Interview Question	Age Range	Score
1. How frequently does _____ attend to people?	1–36 months	3
2. How frequently does _____ attend to toys or activities?	1–36 months	2
3. How often does _____ become distressed or fussy during the day?	1–36 months	3
4. Can you calm _____ when he/she becomes distressed?	1–36 months	3
5. Is _____ unusually sensitive to specific situations or things in your home, such as sound, light, or different textures?	1–36 months	3
6. How well does _____ communicate his/her needs and emotions?	1–36 months	1
7. How well is _____ able to adapt to new situations?	1–36 months	1
8. How well does _____ show or express emotions with people?	3–36 months	2
9. Does _____ respond to the emotions or feelings of other people?	5–36 months	1

COGNITIVE SKILLS

Interview Question	Age Range	Score
10. What types of toys does _____ particularly enjoy?	3–36 months	3
11. What qualities does _____ demonstrate in playing games with your family?	3–36 months	3
12. Who does _____ like to play with?	3–36 months	1
13. How well does _____ initiate play with others?	5–36 months	1
14. What examples of problem solving have you seen when _____ is playing?	7–36 months	1
15. What examples of cause-and-effect understanding have you seen in _____'s play?	7–36 months	
16. How does _____ explore his/her environment?	7–36 months	2
17. What examples of pretend play have you seen?	13–36 months	

NEUROMOTOR SKILLS

Interview Question	Age Range	Score
18. What early positions does _____ use?	1–12 months	
19. What hand skills does _____ have?	5–12 months	2
20. In what positions do you see _____ bearing weight?	5–18 months	3
21. What positions does _____ move out of?	5–36 months	5
22. What positions does _____ move into?	5–36 months	3
23. How often does _____ need help eating?	5–36 months	1
24. What are _____'s eating habits like?	5–36 months	
25. How do you feed _____?	5–36 months	2
26. How does _____ move from place to place?	9–36 months	3
27. What large movement games does _____ enjoy?	9–36 months	

SENSORY-PERCEPTUAL SKILLS

Interview Question	Age Range	Score
28. How does _____ react to being held and cuddled?	1–36 months	3
29. What sensory experiences does _____ enjoy?	1–36 months	3
30. How well is _____ able to follow your face and objects visually?	1–36 months	
31. What manipulative toys/materials does _____ enjoy playing with?	5–36 months	2
32. How does _____ help with dressing and undressing?	11–36 months	
33. Can you give examples of how _____ knows where his/her body is in space?	7–36 months	
34. What does _____ do with pencil/crayon and paper activities?	11–36 months	

+−

LANGUAGE SKILLS

Interview Question	Age Range	Score
35. What range of sounds does _____ respond to at home?	1–36 months	3
36. What single sounds have you heard _____ say?	1–8 months	
37. How does _____ communicate with you and other people?	3–36 months	3
38. What names of people does _____ recognize?	5–36 months	5
39. What words (other than names) does _____ understand?	5–36 months	
40. What nonverbal or verbal expressions does _____ imitate?	5–36 months	
41. What sound combinations does _____ say?	7–36 months	3
42. What does _____ do with books?	7–36 months	2
43. What requests or directions does _____ understand?	9–36 months	1
44. What does _____ do if you or someone else does not understand him/her?	11–36 months	2
45. About how many words does _____ say?	13–36 months	1
46. What words does _____ say?	13–36 months	2
47. How many words does _____ put together?	17–36 months	

Unstructured Caregiver-Child Play

L1. STRATEGIES FOR COMMUNICATION

Observation	Age Range	Score
a. Differential vocalization	1–6 months	
b. Vocal play	3–18 months	3
c. Reduplicated babbling	9–18 months	2
d. Variegated babbling	9–18 months	2
e. Gestures	9–36 months	1
f. Jargon-like vocalizations	9–36 months	2
g. Makes requests	11–36 months	1
h. Uses single words	11–36 months	1
i. Puts two words together	11–36 months	1
j. Puts three or more words together	17–36 months	1
k. Initiates/engages in dialogue/discourse	17–36 months	1

L2. COMMUNICATION OF NEEDS/INTENT

Observation	Age Range	Score
a. Makes basic needs known	1–36 months	3
b. Makes social needs known	1–36 months	2

L3. UNDERSTANDING OF LANGUAGE OR COMMUNICATION

Observation	Age Range	Score
a. Responds to caregiver's vocal play	3–12 months	
b. Responds to gestures	7–36 months	1
c. Responds to single-word requests/directions	9–36 months	1
d. Responds to 1-step directions	13–36 months	1
e. Responds to 2-step directions	23–36 months	

L4. VOCALIZED TURN-TAKING

Observation	Age Range	Score
a. Decreases/increases vocalizations in response to caregiver	1–6 months	
b. Vocalizes across one turn	1–8 months	
c. Vocalizes across two turns	3–18 months	1

L5. JOINT REFERENCING WITH CAREGIVER

Observation	Age Range	Score
a. Attends to caregiver	1–18 months	3
b. Gains/directs attention of caregiver	3–18 months	2
c. Continues familiar routine with caregiver	5–24 months	2
d. Shows humor with caregiver	7–36 months	2

SE6. QUALITY OF SOCIAL INTERACTION WITH CAREGIVER

Observation	Age Range	Score
a. Responds to smiling/soft talking	1–36 months	3
b. Goes to caregiver for comfort	1–36 months	3

SE7. EMOTIONAL STABILITY

Observation	Age Range	Score
a. Has periods of contentment during interaction with caregiver	1–36 months	3
b. Able to self-calm	1–36 months	1
c. Initiates interaction	7–36 months	1
d. Maintains interaction	9–36 months	2

C8. PLAY STRATEGIES OBSERVED

Observation	Age Range	Score
a. Smiles/laughs at engaging routines	5–36 months	3
b. Engages in games/gamelike play	5–36 months	2
c. Shows appropriate functional play with toys/objects	17–36 months	1
d. Represents two or more related events in play	17–36 months	
e. Engages in symbolic play with toys/caregiver	23–36 months	1

SP9. MOVING AND MANEUVERING IN THE ENVIRONMENT

Observation	Age Range	Score
a. Rolls from stomach to back	3–12 months	
b. Rolls from back to stomach	3–12 months	
c. Creeps	5–12 months	
d. Pulls up on people and furniture	7–16 months	
e. Cruises around people and furniture	9–18 months	3
f. Walks	9–24 months	3
g. Runs	13–36 months	3

**SP10. SKILL IN EATING

Observation	Age Range	Score
a. Oral-motor response/appropriate gag reflex	1–6 months	
b. Takes food appropriately into mouth	5–18 months	3
c. Lateralizes tongue with food	5–18 months	3
d. Swallows food	5–18 months	3
e. Chews	7–18 months	1

**SP11. SKILL IN DRINKING

Observation	Age Range	Score
a. Uses continuous, organized sucking pattern with bottle/breast	1–6 months	
b. Shows jaw, tongue, and lip control and stability with cup/glass drinking	9–36 months	1
c. Drinks with little liquid lost	11–36 months	1

**NM12. PICKING UP FINGER FOOD/SELF-FEEDING

Observation	Age Range	Score
a. Brings finger food to mouth by self	9–18 months	1
b. Rakes to pick up food	9–18 months	2
c. Uses 3-jaw chuck grasp	9–18 months	2
d. Uses index finger and thumb grasp	11–24 months	2

**NM13. SELF-FEEDING WITH EATING UTENSILS

Observation	Age Range	Score
a. Brings spoon to mouth	11–36 months	1
b. Puts spoonful of food in mouth independently	13–36 months	1
c. Uses pronated hand to hold spoon	13–36 months	1
d. Uses supinated hand to hold spoon	15–36 months	1

Unstructured Examiner-Child Play

SE14. QUALITY OF INTERACTION WITH UNFAMILIAR PEOPLE

Observation	Age Range	Score
a. Responds to smiling/soft talking	1–36 months	2
b. Initiates interaction	7–36 months	1
c. Maintains interaction	9–36 months	2
d. Relates to two or more unfamiliar people	9–36 months	2

SE15. ATTENTIVENESS TO PLAY ACTIVITIES

Observation	Age Range	Score
a. Attends to age-appropriate range of play events	1–36 months	2
b. Attends to play activities for age-appropriate periods of time	1–36 months	1

L16. RESPONSE TO COMMON ENVIRONMENTAL SOUNDS

Observation	Age Range	Score
a. Responds to voices in same or different room	1–36 months	3
b. Responds to common sounds in same or different room	1–36 months	3

NM17. QUALITY OF MOVEMENT

Observation	Age Range	Score
a. Moves into and out of developmental positions	3–36 months	3
b. Uses graded, smooth movement	3–36 months	3

NM18. LARGE MOTOR MILESTONES

Observation	Age Range	Score
a. Sits	5–36 months	3
b. Uses 4-point positions	7–36 months	3

NM19. HAND SKILLS

Observation	Age Range	Score
a. Brings hands to midline	3–12 months	
b. Reaches with right and left hands	3–12 months	
c. Grasps with right and left hands	3–12 months	
d. Transfers from hand to hand	5–12 months	
e. Releases objects with right and left hands	5–12 months	
f. Crosses midline with right and left hands	13–36 months	3

NM20. BODY SYMMETRY

Observation	Age Range	Score
a. On back	1–6 months	
b. On stomach	1–6 months	
c. In sitting	5–18 months	3
d. In 4-point creeping	7–18 months	3
e. In standing/upright/walking	11–36 months	3

NM21. TRANSITIONS INTO AND OUT OF VARIOUS POSITIONS

Observation	Age Range	Score
a. Moves out of sitting	9–24 months	3
b. Moves into sitting	9–24 months	3
c. Moves out of standing	13–36 months	3
d. Moves into standing	13–36 months	3

SP22. RESPONSE TO TOUCH

Observation	Age Range	Score
a. Responds to personal physical touch	1–36 months	2
b. Enjoys different textures	13–18 months	3
c. Walks on different surfaces	13–24 months	3

SE23. ATTENTION-GAINING BEHAVIORS

Observation	Age Range	Score
a. Uses positive nonverbal strategies to gain attention	5–36 months	2
b. Uses positive verbal strategies to gain attention	7–36 months	2

NM24. PROTECTIVE RESPONSES

Observation	Age Range	Score
a. Uses forward propping	5–12 months	
b. Uses lateral propping	5–12 months	
c. Uses backward equilibrium/balance reaction	9–12 months	

C25. PURPOSEFUL BEHAVIOR IN PLAY

Observation	Age Range	Score
a. Uses play to practice familiar/known skills and routines	7–36 months	2
b. Uses play to acquire/try new skills/tasks	9–36 months	2

L26. INTELLIGIBILITY OF SPEECH AND LANGUAGE

Observation	Age Range	Score
a. Single prompted/imitated expressions are understandable	11–36 months	1
b. Single-word spontaneous expressions are understandable	11–36 months	1
c. Multiword expressions are understandable	11–36 months	1

C27. PROBLEM-SOLVING SKILLS

Observation	Age Range	Score
a. Solves problems without assistance	11–36 months	1
b. Solves age-appropriate problems	11–36 months	1

L28. IMITATION SKILLS

Observation	Age Range	Score
a. Gestures	5–36 months	1
b. Vowels	5–36 months	2
c. Reduplicated babbling	9–18 months	2
d. Variegated babbling	9–18 months	2
e. Blends	9–36 months	2
f. Single words	11–36 months	1
g. Two-word combinations	17–36 months	1
h. Three-word combinations	23–36 months	

Structured Examiner-Child Interaction

L29. RESPONSE TO BELL

Observation	Age Range	Score
a. Alerts/locates bell on right side	1–36 months	4
b. Alerts/locates bell on left side	1–36 months	4

C30. ATTENTION TO FACES AND DESIGNS

Observation	Age Range	Score
a. Attends to human face	1–6 months	
b. Attends to checkerboard	1–6 months	
c. Attends to schematic face	1–6 months	
d. Responds to real image in mirror	3–18 months	3
e. Shows early responses to baby doll	5–18 months	2

SP31. TRACKING

Observation	Age Range	Score
a. Tracks horizontally	1–36 months	3
b. Tracks in circle	1–36 months	3
c. Shows smooth eye movement	1–36 months	3
d. Shows coordinated eye movement	1–36 months	3

L32. EARLY SOCIAL GAMES

Observation	Age Range	Score
a. Engages in vocal play with puppet	3–8 months	
b. Plays peek-a-boo	3–12 months	
c. Plays pat-a-cake	7–18 months	1

NM33. PLAY WITH RATTLES

Observation	Age Range	Score
a. Reaches for rattle	3–12 months	
b. Grasps rattle	3–12 months	
c. Transfers rattle hand to hand	5–12 months	
d. Releases rattle	5–12 months	

C34. RESPONSE TO HIDDEN OBJECTS

Observation	Age Range	Score
a. Finds partially covered rattle	5–12 months	
b. Finds completely covered rattle	7–12 months	

C35. EARLY UNDERSTANDING OF CAUSE AND EFFECT

Observation	Age Range	Score
a. Plays with pull toy	5–12 months	
b. Plays with pop-up pets box	9–24 months	1

C36. PLAY WITH BLOCKS AND SHAPE SORTER

Observation	Age Range	Score
a. Plays with blocks and shape sorter	9–18 months	3
b. Visual discrimination skills	11–36 months	

NM37. PLAY WITH BALLS

Observation	Age Range	Score
a. Rolls ball with intent	7–12 months	1
b. Throws ball with intent	13–36 months	1
c. Catches ball with intent	15–36 months	1

C38. PLAY WITH PICTURES AND PRINT

Observation	Age Range	Score
a. Responds to books	5–36 months	3
b. Responds to crayon and paper	9–36 months	1

SP39. PLAY WITH BUBBLE TUMBLER

Observation	Age Range	Score
a. Uses wand	13–36 months	
b. Blows bubbles	13–36 months	

C40. ADVANCED DOLL PLAY

Observation	Age Range	Score
a. Single play scenarios	13–36 months	2
b. Related play scenarios	13–36 months	1

C41. PROBLEM SOLVING

Observation	Age Range	Score
a. Seeks food behind one screen	13–36 months	2
b. Seeks food behind one of two screens	13–36 months	1
c. Seeks food inside clear container	13–36 months	1

**SP42. UNDRESSING AND DRESSING

Observation	Age Range	Score
a. Takes off socks	9–36 months	1
b. Puts on socks	13–36 months	1
c. Takes off shoes	13–36 months	1
d. Puts on toy hard hat	13–36 months	1
e. Puts on vest	13–36 months	1
f. Opens and closes vest fasteners	15–36 months	1

SE43. ADAPTABILITY

Observation	Age Range	Score
a. Makes transitions with interest	11–36 months	3
b. Attends during structured play	11–36 months	3

Partners in Play Scoring Worksheet 2

Child's name: ___Kyle Jones___   Evaluation date: ___6-1-05___   Chronological/adjusted age: ___20 mth. 18 mth.___ months

For each item administered, indicate + if the child attained a score of 3 or above and – for scores of 2 or less. Note that items are listed by developmental domain, which differs from the order on the record forms. Add up the number of +'s in each domain and enter that total.

Caregiver Report of Child Development

SOCIAL-EMOTIONAL (SE) ITEMS

Item	+/–
1. Attention to people	⊕
2. Attention to toys	–
3. Becoming fussy	⊕
4. Ability to calm	⊕
5. Sensitivity to sound/light/textures	⊕
6. Communication of needs	–
7. Adaptability	–
8. Showing emotions	–
9. Response to emotions	–
Subtotal	④

NEUROMOTOR (NM) ITEMS

Item	+/–
18. Early positions	+
19. Hand skills	–
20. Weight bearing	⊕
21. Transitions out of positions	⊕
22. Transitions into positions	⊕
23. Assistance needed with eating	–
24. Eating habits	–
25. Means of feeding	–
26. Mobility	⊕
27. Gross motor games	–
Subtotal	④

COMMUNICATION AND LANGUAGE (L) ITEMS

Item	+/–
35. Response to sounds	⊕
36. Phonemes produced	–
37. Communication strategies	⊕
38. Comprehension of names	⊕
39. Comprehension of other words	–
40. Verbal/nonverbal imitation	–
41. Babbling	⊕
42. Response to books	–
43. Comprehension of directions	–
44. Response to communication breakdown	–
45. Number of words produced	–
46. Expressive vocabulary	–
47. Word combinations	–
Subtotal	④

COGNITIVE (C) ITEMS

Item	+/–
10. Toys enjoyed	⊕
11. Quality of play	⊕
12. Playmates	–
13. Play initiation	–
14. Problem solving in play	–
15. Cause and effect in play	–
16. Exploring environment	–
17. Pretend play	–
Subtotal	②

SENSORY-PERCEPTUAL (SP) ITEMS

Item	+/–
28. Response to cuddling	⊕
29. Sensory input	⊕
30. Visual tracking	–
31. Manipulative toys	–
32. Assists with dressing	–
33. Proprioception	–
34. Pencil/crayon and paper activities	–
Subtotal	②

Unstructured Caregiver-Child Play

SOCIAL-EMOTIONAL (SE) ITEMS

Item	+/−
6a. Responds to smiling/soft talking	(+)
6b. Seeks comfort	(+)
7a. Periods of contentment	(+)
7b. Self-calming	−
7c. Initiates interaction	−
7d. Maintains interaction	−
Subtotal	(3)

COGNITIVE (C) ITEMS

Item	+/−
8a. Smiles at routines	(+)
8b. Engages in games	−
8c. Functional play	−
8d. Representational play	−
8e. Symbolic play	−
Subtotal	(1)

NEUROMOTOR (NM) ITEMS

Item	+/−
**12a. Bringing food to mouth	−
**12b. Raking food	−
**12c. 3-jaw chuck grasp	−
**12d. Pincer grasp	−
Subtotal	(0)

SENSORY-PERCEPTUAL (SP) ITEMS

Item	+/−
9a. Rolls to back	−
9b. Rolls to stomach	−
9c. Creeps	−
9d. Pulls up to stand	−
9e. Cruises	(+)
9f. Walks	(+)
9g. Runs	(+)
**10a. Gag reflex	−
**10b. Takes food into mouth	(+)
**10c. Lateralizes tongue in chewing	(+)
**10d. Swallows	(+)
**10e. Chews	−
**11a. Sucking pattern	−
**11b. Jaw stability in drinking	−
**11c. No liquid loss in drinking	−
**13a. Brings spoon to mouth	−
**13b. Inserts spoon in mouth	−
**13c. Pronated hand	−
**13d. Supinated hand	−
Subtotal	(6)

COMMUNICATION AND LANGUAGE (L) ITEMS

Item	+/−
1a. Differential vocalization	−
1b. Vocal play	(+)
1c. Reduplicated babbling	−
1d. Variegated babbling	−
1e. Gestures	−
1f. Jargon	−
1g. Uses requests	−
1h. Uses single words	−
1i. Uses 2-word phrases	−
1j. Uses 3-word phrases	−
1k. Dialogue	−
2a. Basic needs	(+)
2b. Social needs	−
3a. Responds to vocal play	−
3b. Responds to gestures	−
3c. Responds to 1-word directions	−
3d. Responds to 1-step directions	−
3e. Responds to 2-step directions	−
4a. Increase/decrease in vocalization	−
4b. Vocalizes one turn	−
4c. Vocalizes two turns	−
5a. Attends to caregiver	(+)
5b. Directs caregiver's attention	−
5c. Continues routine	−
5d. Shows humor	−
Subtotal	(3)

Unstructured Examiner-Child Play

SOCIAL-EMOTIONAL (SE) ITEMS

Item	+/−
14a. Responds to smiling/talking	−
14b. Initiates interaction	−
14c. Maintains interaction	−
14d. Relates to unfamiliar adults	−
15a. Attends to play	−
15b. Attention span	−
23a. Gains attention nonverbally	−
23b. Gains attention verbally	−
Subtotal	⓪

COGNITIVE (C) ITEMS

Item	+/−
25a. Uses routines in play	−
25b. Uses skills in play	−
27a. Solving problems independently	−
27b. Age-appropriate problem solving	−
Subtotal	⓪

NEUROMOTOR (NM) ITEMS

Item	+/−
17a. Transitions	⊕
17b. Smooth, graded movement	⊕
18a. Sitting	⊕
18b. 4-point positions	⊕
19a. Hands to midline	−
19b. Reaching	−
19c. Grasping	−
19d. Hand-to-hand transfers	−
19e. Releasing	−
19f. Crossing midline with hands	⊕
20a. Symmetry on back	−
20b. Symmetry on stomach	−
20c. Symmetry in sitting	⊕
20d. Symmetry in creeping	⊕
20e. Symmetry in standing/walking	⊕
21a. Transition out of sitting	⊕
21b. Transition into sitting	⊕
21c. Transition out of standing	⊕
21d. Transition into standing	⊕
24a. Forward propping	−
24b. Lateral propping	−
24c. Balance reaction	−
Subtotal	⑫

SENSORY-PERCEPTUAL (SP) ITEMS

Item	+/−
22a. Responds to touch	−
22b. Responds to textures	⊕
22c. Walks on different surfaces	⊕
Subtotal	②

COMMUNICATION AND LANGUAGE (L) ITEMS

Item	+/−
16a. Response to voices	⊕
16b. Response to sounds	⊕
26a. Intelligibility of imitated words	−
26b. Intelligibility of spontaneous words	−
26c. Intelligibility of multiword phrases	−
28a. Imitation of gestures	−
28b. Imitation of vowels	−
28c. Imitation of reduplicated babbling	−
28d. Imitation of variegated babbling	−
28e. Imitation of blends	−
28f. Imitation of single words	−
28g. Imitation of 2-word phrases	−
28h. Imitation of 3-word phrases	−
Subtotal	②

Structured Examiner-Child Interaction

SOCIAL-EMOTIONAL (SE) ITEMS

Item	+/−
43a. Activity transitions	(+)
43b. Attention to structured task	(+)
Subtotal	(2)

COGNITIVE (C) ITEMS

Item	+/−
30a. Attends to human face	−
30b. Attends to checkerboard	−
30c. Attends to schematic face	−
30d. Responds to image in mirror	(+)
30e. Responds to doll	−
34a. Finds partly covered rattle	−
34b. Finds fully covered rattle	−
35a. Pull toy	−
35b. Pop-up box	−
36a. Shape sorter/blocks	(+)
36b. Visual discrimination	−
38a. Responds to book	(+)
38b. Responds to crayon/paper	−
40a. Single scenarios with doll	−
40b. Related scenarios with doll	−
41a. Seeks food/one screen	−
41b. Seeks food/two screens	−
41c. Seeks food/clear container	−
41d. Garage play	−
Subtotal	(3)

NEUROMOTOR (NM) ITEMS

Item	+/−
33a. Reaches for rattle	−
33b. Grasps rattle	−
33c. Transfers rattle hand to hand	−
33d. Releases rattle	−
37a. Rolls ball	−
37b. Throws ball	−
37c. Catches ball	−
Subtotal	(0)

SENSORY-PERCEPTUAL (SP) ITEMS

Item	+/−
31a. Horizontal tracking	(+)
31b. Circular tracking	(+)
31c. Smooth eye movement	(+)
31d. Coordinated eye movement	(+)
39a. Uses wand	−
39b. Blows bubbles	−
**42a Takes off socks	−
**42b. Puts on socks	−
**42c. Takes off shoes	−
**42d. Puts on hat	−
**42e. Puts on vest	−
**42f. Vest fasteners	−
Subtotal	(4)

COMMUNICATION AND LANGUAGE (L) ITEMS

Item	+/−
29a. Locates bell/right	(+)
29b. Locates bell/left	(+)
32a. Vocal play w/puppet	−
32b. Peek-a-boo	−
32c. Pat-a-cake	−
Subtotal	(2)

Partners in Play Summary Worksheet

Child's name: ___Kyle Jones___   Evaluation date: ___6–1–05___

Chronological age: __20__ months   Adjusted age: __18__ months

Transfer the subtotals from Scoring Worksheet 2 to the appropriate cells in the top table and total each row to determine the number of items passed in each domain. Enter these totals in the bottom table, then consult the Index of Item Totals on the next page to locate the expected number of items passed. Divide the actual number passed by the expected number to determine the percentage of age-appropriate items passed.

Developmental Domain	Number of Items Passed in Caregiver Report	Number of Items Passed in Caregiver-Child Play	Number of Items Passed in Examiner-Child Play	Number of Items Passed in Examiner-Child Interaction	Total Items Passed
Social-Emotional	4	3	0	2	9
Cognitive	2	1	0	3	6
Neuromotor	4	0	12	0	16
Sensory-Perceptual	2	6	2	4	14
Language	4	3	2	2	11

SUBTOTALS AND TOTALS OF ITEMS PASSED

Developmental Domain	Number of Items Passed	Percent of Age-Appropriate Items Passed	Percent of Delay
Social-Emotional	⑨/ 25	36%	64%
Cognitive	⑥/ 29	21%	79%
Neuromotor	⑯/ 26	62%	38%
Sensory-Perceptual	⑭/ 36	39%	61%
Language	⑪/ 45	20%	76%

Index of Item Totals by Month

Determine the child's chronological age (or adjusted age, if appropriate) to the nearest month. For each domain, divide the number of items the child passed by the number given for the child's age in the following table to determine the percentage of delay.

Month	Primary Developmental Area Totals				
	NM	SP	C	L	SE
1	3	9	3	12	14
2	3	9	3	12	14
3	10	12	7	19	15
4	10	12	7	19	15
5	25	16	13	24	17
6	25	16	13	24	17
7	26	18	16	28	20
8	26	18	16	28	20
9	34	22	20	33	23
10	34	22	20	33	23
11	36	26	23	42	25
12	36	26	23	42	25
13	25	34	25	43	25
14	25	34	25	43	25
15	26	33	25	43	25
16	26	33	25	43	25
17	26	36	29	45	25
18**	26	36	29	45	25
19	20	29	26	38	25
20	20	29	26	38	25
21	20	29	27	38	25
22	20	29	27	38	25
23	22	29	27	40	25
24	22	29	27	40	25
25	16	27	26	39	25
26	16	27	26	39	25
27	16	27	26	39	25
28	16	27	26	39	25
29	16	27	26	39	25
30	16	27	26	39	25
31	16	27	26	39	25
32	16	27	26	39	25
33	16	27	26	39	25
34	16	27	26	39	25
35	16	27	26	39	25
36	16	27	26	39	25

In Brief Review

This chapter provided detailed instructions and guidelines for scoring and interpreting the *PIP* assessment. In brief review, the reader should remember that:

❖ The initial assessment of an infant or toddler is merely the first step in the overall evaluation process. If the child qualities for early intervention services, ongoing assessment will be an important guidepost for determining future goals, objectives, and strategies. In this regard, the *PIP* can be a helpful tool to track child progress and development.

❖ Flexibility is a key element of effective assessment of young children. This dimension will be vital to both families and their children. Teams should think about this aspect broadly in terms of adapting to the needs and challenges of individual children, the ethnic backgrounds and cultures of families, the settings for assessment, the time of day, and the numerous other considerations involved in planning and carrying out a child's evaluation.

❖ Families need to be involved actively in every phase of the evaluation and recommendation process of their children. This concept has been emphasized throughout each of the foregoing chapters. However, this consideration deserves repetition because the full benefit of early intervention for young children will ultimately depend on the actualization of this process for families. Ultimately, parents need to understand the goals and strategies of their child's programming so that these objectives can be carried out within the natural environment of the home.

❖ *Partners in Play* is an assessment that has been developed to address the need in early childhood special education for an instrument that recognizes and validates *informed clinical judgment*. However, it will be most effective when used in combination with multiple sources of information, gathered over time in the diverse natural settings of community and home, in partnership with those who are most familiar with the child.

References

Bagnato, S. J., Neisworth, J. T., & Munson, S. M. (1997). *LINKing assessment and early intervention: An authentic curriculum-based approach.* Baltimore, MD: Paul H. Brookes.

Bayley, N. (1993). *Bayley Scales of Infant Development* (2nd ed.). New York, NY: Psychological Corporation.

Ensher, G. L., & Clark, D. A. (1994). *Newborns at risk: Medical care and psychoeducational intervention* (2nd ed.). Gaithersburg, MD: Aspen.

Ensher, G. L., Bobish, T. P., Gardner, E. F., Michaels, C. A., Butler, K. G., Foertsch, D. J., & Cooper, C. (1998). *SDA: Syracuse dynamic assessment for birth to three.* Chicago, IL: Applied Symbolix.

Haarstad, C., & Thomas, W. (2003). *New American and refugee families when children have special needs.* Minot, ND: North Dakota Center for Persons with Disabilities, A University Center for Excellence for Persons with Developmental Disabilities at Minot State University, 1–18.

Hanson, M. J., & Lynch, E. W. (2004a). Family diversity, assessment, and cultural competence. In M. McLean, M. Wolery, & D. B. Bailey, Jr., (Eds.), *Assessing Infants and Preschoolers with Special Needs* (3rd ed.) (71–99). Upper Saddle River, NJ: Pearson/Merrill Prentice Hall.

Hanson, M. J., & Lynch, E. W. (2004b). *Understanding families: Approaches to diversity, disability, and risk.* Baltimore, MD: Paul H. Brookes.

Lynch, E. W., & Hanson, M. J. (2004). *Developing cross-cultural competence: A guide for working with children and their families* (3rd ed.). Baltimore, MD: Paul H. Brookes.

McLean, M., Wolery, M., & Bailey, D. B., Jr. (2004). *Assessing infants and preschoolers with special needs* (3rd ed.). Upper Saddle River, NJ: Pearson/Merrill Prentice Hall.

Meisels, S. J., & Fenichel, E. (Eds.). (1997). *New visions for the developmental assessment of infants and young children.* Washington, DC: National Center for Infants, Toddlers, and Families.

Reinson, C. L. T. (2002). *Parent perceptions and the assessment of developmental vulnerability.* Unpublished doctoral dissertation, Syracuse University, Syracuse, New York.

Shackelford, J. (2005). State and jurisdictional eligibility definitions for infants and toddlers with disabilities under IDEA. *NECTAC Notes, 18,* 1–15.

Slentz, K., Lewis, G., Fromme, C., Williams-Appleton, D., Milatchkov, L., & Shureen, A. (1997). Evaluation and assessment in early childhood special education: Children who are culturally and linguistically diverse. In T. Bergeson, B. J. Wise, D. H. Gill, & A. Shureen (Eds.). *Special education. . .a service, not a place.* Olympia, WA: Washington Office of State Superintendent of Public Instruction, 1–69.

Record Forms

Caregiver 1 Record Form: Parent Interview

Caregiver 2 Record Form: Child Development

Developmental Assessment Record Form

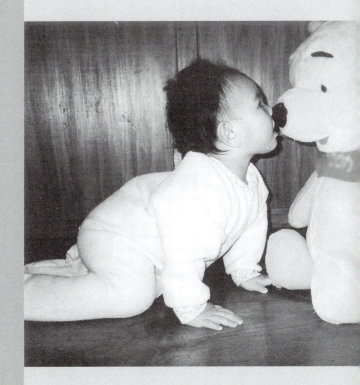

Caregiver 1 Record Form: Parent Interview

Evaluation date: ___ / ___ / ____   Interviewer's name: _____

Child's name: _____ Sex: _____
              First   Middle   Last   M/F

DOB: ____ / ____ / _____   Chronological age: _____months _____days   Adjusted age: _____months _____days

Race: _____   Ethnicity: _____

What language(s) are commonly spoken in the child's home? _____

PRIMARY CAREGIVERS

Full name: _____   Relationship to child: _____   DOB: ___ / ___ / ___

Full name: _____   Relationship to child: _____   DOB: ___ / ___ / ___

Home phone: _____   Work phone: _____   Other: _____

Home address: _____   City: _____   State: ___   Zip code: _____

Work address: _____   City: _____   State: ___   Zip code: _____

Education: _____

Child lives with caregiver(s): _____Full time _____Part time _____No

SIBLINGS

1. First Name _____ MI ___ Last _____ M/F ___ Age ___ Race _____ At Home? Y N

2. First Name _____ MI ___ Last _____ M/F ___ Age ___ Race _____ At Home? Y N

3. First Name _____ MI ___ Last _____ M/F ___ Age ___ Race _____ At Home? Y N

4. First Name _____ MI ___ Last _____ M/F ___ Age ___ Race _____ At Home? Y N

5. First Name _____ MI ___ Last _____ M/F ___ Age ___ Race _____ At Home? Y N

HEALTH SERVICE PROVIDERS

Primary Care Physician:_____   Phone: (   ) _____-_____   Fax: _____-_____

Other Physicians Currently Providing Medical Care

Name: _____ Phone: (   ) _____ - _____ Fax: _____ - _____ Specialty: _____

Name: _____ Phone: (   ) _____ - _____ Fax: _____ - _____ Specialty: _____

Name: _____ Phone: (   ) _____ - _____ Fax: _____ - _____ Specialty: _____

Public Health Nurse (if assigned):

Name: _____ Phone: (   ) _____ - _____ Fax: _____ - _____

AGENCIES PRESENTLY SERVING THE CHILD AND FAMILY

Name of Agency	Contact Person	Phone Number

PREVIOUS HEALTH-RELATED AND INTERVENTION SERVICES

Date	Services Received	Service Provider

FAMILY HISTORY OF PREMATURITY OR DEVELOPMENT PROBLEMS

Please describe below: _____

_____

_____

_____

_____

_____

Medical History of Child and Mother

PERINATAL HISTORY

1. Describe the frequency and nature of your visits to health care professionals during pregnancy with your child.

_____
_____
_____
_____

1st trimester:

_____
_____
_____
_____
_____

2nd trimester:

_____
_____
_____
_____
_____

3rd trimester:

_____
_____
_____
_____
_____

2. Describe any significant medical problems during pregnancy with your child.

Date	Problem	Outcome

3. Describe any significant medical problems during any other pregnancy.

_____
_____
_____
_____

4. Describe any family problems that occurred during pregnancy with your child.

_____
_____
_____
_____

5. Describe any use of drugs, tobacco, other toxins, or medications (prescription and nonprescription) during pregnancy with your child.

_____
_____
_____
_____

6. Describe any maternal hospitalizations during pregnancy with your child.

Dates　　　　　　　**Description of Problem**

_____
_____
_____
_____
_____
_____

DELIVERY AND BIRTH

7. Describe your child's birth: _____

_____

8. Setting of birth (e.g., hospital, home): _____

_____

9. Type of delivery (e.g., vaginal, cesarean): _____

_____

10. Term at birth: _____ Pre-term   _____ Full-term   _____ Post-term

    Gestational age: _____ weeks   Birth weight: _____ grams

11. Apgar score(s): 1 minute: _____   5 minutes: _____

12. Describe any medical problems you or your baby had at birth. _____

_____

13. If your baby was placed in a special nursery, give length of stay after birth.

       Level I: Neonatal newborn nursery   Dates _____

       Level II: Neonatal intensive care nursery   Dates _____

       Level III: Neonatal intensive care/regional nursery   Dates _____

       _____

14. Length of your hospitalization after delivery: _____

_____

INFANT CARE IMMEDIATELY AFTER DELIVERY

15. Describe the ease of visiting/caring for your baby during the hospital stay. _____

_____

_____

16. Describe your level of satisfaction with healthcare professionals during the hospital stay.   _____

_____

_____

Additional Comments:_____

_____

_____

_____

_____

_____

HOSPITAL DISCHARGE

17. Describe any special arrangements healthcare providers made on discharge from the hospital.

_____

_____

18. Describe the adequacy of information you received about how to care for your baby at home.

_____

_____

19. List any special services/programming arranged at the time of discharge.

_____

_____

20. Describe any problems experienced in caring for the baby immediately following discharge.

_____

_____

21. List any services not offered/received at the time of discharge that might have been helpful.

_____

_____

CHILD'S HEALTH HISTORY

22. Describe any problems you experienced in caring for your baby/child or any major illnesses your baby/child had.

Type of Problem	Frequency

23. List dates of hospitalization(s) and reason(s) (including emergency room visits).

Date	Reason for Hospitalization	Outcome
___ / ___ / ___	_____	_____
___ / ___ / ___	_____	_____
___ / ___ / ___	_____	_____
___ / ___ / ___	_____	_____

24. List any specialists seen.

Name	Specialty	Reason Seen	Dates
_____	_____	_____	_____
_____	_____	_____	_____
_____	_____	_____	_____
_____	_____	_____	_____
_____	_____	_____	_____
_____	_____	_____	_____

25. List all medications taken in the past.

Medication	Reason Prescribed	Date
_____	_____	___ / ___ / ___
_____	_____	___ / ___ / ___
_____	_____	___ / ___ / ___
_____	_____	___ / ___ / ___
_____	_____	___ / ___ / ___

CHILD'S CURRENT HEALTH

Weight: _____ pounds _____ ounces   Length/height: _____ feet _____ inches

Head circumference, if known _____

26. Describe your child's present general health.

_____
_____
_____
_____

27. List all known allergies.

_____
_____
_____
_____

28. List all current medications.

Medication	Reason Prescribed	Date
_____	_____	___ / ___ / ___
_____	_____	___ / ___ / ___
_____	_____	___ / ___ / ___
_____	_____	___ / ___ / ___
_____	_____	___ / ___ / ___

CHILD/FAMILY DEVELOPMENT AND ENVIRONMENT

29. List any medical/developmental problems family members experienced and any services they received.

Family Member	Problem	Services	Dates
_____	_____	_____	_____
_____	_____	_____	_____
_____	_____	_____	_____
_____	_____	_____	_____
_____	_____	_____	_____
_____	_____	_____	_____

30. List any circumstances in the family or environment that may have affected your baby or child.

_____

_____

_____

_____

_____

_____

31. Describe any childcare you have received and your level of satisfaction with the provider.

Child Provider/Setting	Frequency/Occasion (days per week)	Duration Per Day	History/Length of Care	Satisfaction with Care

32. List any present child/family service or support needs that are not being met.

_____

_____

_____

_____

_____

_____

_____

Caregiver 2 Record Form: Child Development

Evaluation date: _____

Child's name: _____

DOB: ____ / ____ / ____   Chronological age: ____months ____days   Adjusted age: ____months ____days

Address: _____

_____

Caregiver interviewed: _____   Relationship to child: _____

Caregiver's phone: Home: _____   Work: _____   Other: _____

Team member conducting interview: _____

Date of report: _____

Social-Emotional Development

SE1. How frequently does _____ attend to people?
(1–36 months)

Circle One	
Rarely/never	1
Sometimes	2
Usually	3
Most of the time/always	4

SE2. How frequently does _____ attend to toys or activities?
(1–36 months)

Circle One	
Rarely/never	1
Sometimes	2
Usually	3
Most of the time/always	4

SE3. How often does _____ become distressed or fussy during the day?
(1–36 months)

Circle One	
Most of the time/always	1
Usually	2
Sometimes	3
Rarely/never	4

SE4. Can you calm _____ when he/she becomes distressed?
(1–36 months)

Circle One	
Rarely/never	1
Sometimes	2
Usually	3
Most of the time/always	4

SE5. Is _____ unusually sensitive to specific situations or things in your home, such as sound, light, or different textures?
(1–36 months)

Circle One	
Most of the time/always	1
Usually	2
Sometimes	3
Rarely/never	4

SE6. How well does _____ communicate his/her needs and emotions?
(1–36 months)

Circle One	
Communicates little	1
Communication varies with need or situation/sometimes	2
Usually communicates well	3
Most of the time/always communicates well	4

SE7. How well is _____ able to adapt to new situations?
(1–36 months)

Circle One	
Always requires assistance from another	1
Usually/often requires assistance from another	2
Sometimes/varies with situation	3
Rarely/never requires assistance	4

SE8. How well does _____ show or express emotions with people?
(3–36 months)

Circle One	
Rarely/never	1
Sometimes	2
Usually	3
Most of the time/always	4

SE9. Does _____ respond to the emotions or feelings of other people?
(5–36 months)

Circle One	
Rarely/never	1
Sometimes	2
Usually	3
Most of the time/always	4

Notes:

_____

_____

_____

Cognitive Development

C10. What types of toys does _____ particularly enjoy?
(3–36 months)

Circle Any/All and Sum	
Large motor (e.g., balls)	1
Small motor (e.g., rattles, blocks, puzzles, beads)	1
Sensory (e.g., Koosh balls, light- or sound-producing toys)	1
Problem solving/cause-effect (e.g., busy boxes, pop-up boxes)	1
Pretend play (e.g., stuffed animals, dolls, dishes)	1
Total	3

C11. What qualities does _____ demonstrate in playing games with your family?
(3–36 months)

Circle Any/All and Sum	
Social/interactive (e.g., peek-a-boo, pat-a-cake, this little piggy)	1
Language (e.g., gestural, vocal play, turn taking)	1
Problem solving (e.g., hide and seek, hiding games)	1
Large motor (e.g., chase)	1
Games with simple routines (e.g., bedtime or bath-time routines)	1
Total	3

C12. Who does _____ like to play with?
(3–36 months)

Circle Any/All and Sum	
Primary caregivers	1
Siblings	1
Extended family	1
Adults/children outside the home	1
Pets	1
Total	1

C13. How well does _____ initiate play with others?
(5–36 months)

Circle One	
Always requires assistance from another	1
Usually/often requires assistance from another	2
Sometimes/varies with situation	3
Rarely/never requires assistance	4

C14. What examples of problem solving have you seen when _____ is playing?
(7–36 months)

Circle Any/All and Sum	
Looks for objects dropped out of sight	1
Plays with pull toys	1
Finds items moved from one place to another	1
Turns keys/tools to open doors/opens jars or drawers	1
Total	1

C15. What examples of cause-and-effect understanding have you seen in _____'s play?
(7–36 months)

Circle Any/All and Sum	
Turns on TV/VCR/radio/stereo with/without remote	1
Uses one object to reach another	1
Turns on light switch	1
Turns on mechanical toy (e.g., tape recorder)	1
Uses pull toys	1
Total	

C16. How does _____ explore his/her environment?
(7–36 months)

Circle Any/All and Sum	
Creeps to investigate	1
Looks inside or under covers/zippered bags	1
Plays with feely boxes	1
Visually searches/scans immediate surroundings	1
Total	2

C17. What examples of pretend play have you seen?
(13–36 months)

Circle Any/All and Sum	
Pretends that one object is another (e.g., pretending a box is an oven)	1
Pretends to be another person (e.g., mommy)	1
Acts out a familiar routine	1
Acts out a sequence of routines with dolls/stuffed animals	1
Total	

Notes:

_____

_____

_____

_____

Neuromotor Development

NM18. What early positions does _____ use?
(1–12 months)

Circle Any/All and Sum	
Back	1
Stomach	1
Sitting	1
Standing	1
Total	

NM19. What hand skills does _____ have?
(5–12 months)

Circle Any/All and Sum	
Brings hands to midline/ does finger plays	1
Grasps objects	1
Transfers objects from hand to hand	1
Releases/lets go of objects	1
Total	2

NM20. In what positions do you see _____ bearing weight?
(5–18 months)

Circle Any/All and Sum	
On stomach	1
In sitting (e.g., supporting weight with hands in front or to the side)	1
In independent sitting	1
In 4-point position	1
In independent sitting	1
Total	3

NM21. What positions does _____ move out of?
(5–36 months)

Circle Any/All and Sum	
Lying on back	1
Lying on stomach	1
Sitting	1
Creeping	1
Squatting	1
Standing	1
Total	5

NM22. What positions does _____ move into?
(5–36 months)

Circle Any/All and Sum	
To back	1
To stomach	1
Sitting	1
Creeping	1
Squatting	1
Standing	1
Total	3

NM23. How often does _____ need help eating?
(5–36 months)

Circle One	
Always requires assistance from another	1
Usually/often requires assistance from another	2
Sometimes/varies with situation	3
Rarely/never requires assistance	4

NM24. What are _____'s eating habits like (e.g., eating a variety of foods)?
(5–36 months)

Circle One	
Rarely/never eats well	1
Sometimes eats well	2
Usually/often eats well	3
Most of the time/always eats well	4

NM25. How do you feed _____?
(5–36 months)

Circle Any/All and Sum	
Bottle/breast feeds	1
Takes food from spoon	1
Uses fingers	1
Uses trainer or regular cup/glass	1
Total	2

NM26. How does _____ move from place to place?
(9–36 months)

Circle Any/All and Sum	
Rolls	1
Belly creeps	1
4-point creeps	1
Cruises along furniture/ people	1
Steps/walks	1
Total	3

NM27. What large movement games does _____ enjoy?
(9–36 months)

Circle Any/All and Sum	
Playing ball (e.g., rolls, throws, catches, kicks)	1
Tumbling	1
Rough-and-tumble (e.g., being tossed in the air and caught)	1
Jumping	1
Total	

Notes:

_____

_____

_____

_____

_____

Sensory-Perceptual Development

SP28. How does _____ react to being held and cuddled?
(1–36 months)

Circle One	
Rarely/never enjoys	1
Sometimes enjoys	2
Usually/often enjoys	3
Most of the time/always enjoys	4

SP29. What sensory experiences does _____ enjoy?
(1–36 months)

Circle Any/All and Sum	
Taking a bath	1
Cuddling/being covered with a blanket	1
Being held closely by a person	1
Touching a person	1
Being rocked/patted	1
Having hair combed/brushed	1
Total	3

SP30. How well is _____ able to follow your face and objects visually?
(1–36 months)

Circle Any/All and Sum	
Tracks left to right	1
Tracks right to left	1
Tracks up and down	1
Tracks in a circle	1
Has smooth and coordinated eye movements	1
Total	

SP31. What manipulative toys/materials does _____ enjoy playing with?
(5–36 months)

Circle Any/All and Sum	
Rattles	1
Blocks	1
Shape sorters	1
Fit-together toys (e.g., puzzles)	1
Modeling clay/paints/food	1
Total	2

SP32. How does _____ help with dressing and undressing?
(11–36 months)

Circle Any/All and Sum	
Takes off shoes/socks	1
Takes off 1 or 2 pieces of clothing	1
Puts on 1 or 2 pieces of clothing	1
Puts on socks/shoes	1
Does/undoes simple fasteners	1
Total	

SP33. Can you give examples of how _____ knows where his/her body is in space?
(7–36 months)

Circle Any/All and Sum	
Goes under tables	1
Climbs on chairs/furniture	1
Goes up and down stairs/turns self around	1
Creeps around furniture and people	1
Changes direction in movement	1
Total	

SP34. What does _____ do with pencil (or crayon) and paper activities?
(11–36 months)

Circle Any/All and Sum	
Holds pencil/crayon	1
Bangs pencil/crayon on paper	1
Scribbles	1
Imitates simple lines/figures	1
Draws simple pictures	1
Total	

Notes:

_____

_____

_____

_____

_____

_____

_____

_____

_____

Communication and Language Development

L35. What range of sounds does _____ respond to at home? (1–36 months)

Circle Any/All and Sum	
Voices in same or different room	1
Telephone ringing	1
Doorbell	1
TV/stereo/radio	1
Vacuum cleaner	1
Objects dropping/startles/locates	1
Total	3

L36. What single sounds have you heard _____ say? (1–8 months)

Circle Any/All and Sum (1 or more per set = 1 point)	
a, e, i	1
o, u, y	1
b, c, d	1
m, g, h	1
r, s, t	1
j, l, f	1
Total	

L37. How does _____ communicate with you and other people? (3–36 months)

Circle Any/All and Sum	
Cries/whines	1
Points/gestures	1
Looks/scans	1
Vocalizes	1
Verbalizes	1
Total	3

L38. What names of people does _____ recognize? (5–36 months)

Circle Any/All and Sum	
Own name	1
Mommy	1
Daddy	1
Names of siblings (List):	1
Others:	1
Total	5

L39. What words (other than names) does _____ understand? (List) (5–36 months)

Circle Any/All and Sum (1 or more per set = 1 point)	
People:	1
Action words:	1
Body parts:	1
Animals:	1
Foods/food related:	1
Total	

L40. What nonverbal or verbal expressions does _____ imitate? (5–36 months)

Circle Any/All and Sum	
Gestures (e.g., hi, bye, throwing kisses)	1
Single sounds (e.g., a, e, i, o, u, d, m)	1
Sound combinations (e.g., oh, ba, da)	1
Sound sequences (e.g., oh-oh, mama, dada, mada)	1
Total	

Notes:

_____

_____

_____

_____

_____

_____

_____

L41. What sound combinations does _____ say?
(7–36 months)

Circle Any/All and Sum (1 or more per set = 1 point)	
ba, ma, da	1
mama, dada (reduplicated babbling)	1
baga, tada, magada (variegated babbling)	1
Please note others:	1
Total	3

L42. What does _____ do with books?
(7–36 months)

Circle Any/All and Sum	
Turns pages	1
Scans/looks at pictures	1
Points/pats	1
Vocalizes randomly	1
Imitates pictured sounds/objects/living things	1
Verbalizes	1
Total	2

L43. What requests or directions does _____ understand?
(9–36 months)

Circle Any/All and Sum	
No-no	1
Come	1
Look/see	1
1-step (give examples):	1
2-step (give examples):	1
Total	1

L44. What does _____ do if you or someone else does not understand him/her?
(11–36 months)

Circle One	
Becomes frustrated	1
Cries/whines	2
Leads you to desired object/place/person	3
Gestures	4
Increases vocalizations	5
Repeats requests	6
Total	

L45. About how many words does _____ say?
(13–36 months)

Circle One	
1–5 words	1
6–10 words	2
11–25 words	3
26–50 words	4
Up to 100 words	5
Up to 200 words	6
300 words or more	7

L46. What words does _____ say? (List)
(13–36 months)

Circle Any/All and Sum (1 or more per set = 1 point)	
People:	1
Action words:	1
Body parts:	1
Animals:	1
Foods/eating:	1
Modifiers (e.g., all gone, big, mine):	1
Total	2

L47. How many words does _____ put together?
(17–36 months)

Circle One	
2 words	1
3 words	2
4 words	3
5 words	4
More than 5 words	5

Notes:

_____

_____

_____

_____

_____

_____

Partners in Play Developmental Assessment Record Form

Evaluation date: _____

Name of child: _____

Chronological age: _____months _____weeks   Adjusted age: _____months _____weeks

Address: _____

_____

Telephone # of Caregiver(s): (Home): _____

(Work): _____

Alternate Telephone #: _____

Name and Relationship to Child: _____

Date(s) of Evaluation: _____

Team Members Working with Child: _____

_____

Team Members Observing Child: _____

_____

Team Members Recording Information: _____

_____

Date of Report: _____

_____

Unstructured Caregiver-Child Play

L1. Strategies for Communication

a. Differential vocalization
(1 month – 6 months)

Circle One	
Not evident	1
Emerging	2
Developing	3
Well developed	4

b. Vocal play
(3 months – 18 months)

Circle One	
Not evident	1
Emerging	2
Developing	3
Well developed	4

c. Reduplicated babbling
(9 months – 18 months)

Circle One	
Not evident	1
Emerging	2
Developing	3
Well developed	4

d. Variegated babbling
(9 months – 18 months)

Circle One	
Not evident	1
Emerging	2
Developing	3
Well developed	4

e. Using gestures
(9 months – 36 months)

Circle One	
Not evident	1
Emerging	2
Developing	3
Well developed	4

f. Jargon-like vocalizations
(9 months – 36 months)

Circle One	
Not evident	1
Emerging	2
Developing	3
Well developed	4

g. Making requests
(11 months – 36 months)

Circle One	
Not evident	1
Emerging	2
Developing	3
Well developed	4

h. Using single words
(11 months – 36 months)

Circle One	
Not evident	1
Emerging	2
Developing	3
Well developed	4

i. Putting 2 words together
(11 months – 36 months)

Circle One	
Not evident	1
Emerging	2
Developing	3
Well developed	4

j. Putting 3 or more words together
(11 months – 36 months)

Circle One	
Not evident	1
Emerging	2
Developing	3
Well developed	4

k. Initiating/engaging in dialogue/discourse
(17 months – 36 months)

Circle One	
Not evident	1
Emerging	2
Developing	3
Well developed	4

L2. Communication of Needs/Intent

a. Making basic needs known (e.g., fatigue, hunger, change of position)
(1 month – 36 months)

Circle One	
Never/rarely	1
Sometimes	2
Usually/frequently	3
Most of the time/always	4

b. Making social needs known (e.g., desire to be picked up, to engage in play)
(1 month – 36 months)

Circle One	
Never/rarely	1
Sometimes	2
Usually/frequently	3
Most of the time/always	4

Notes:

_____

_____

_____

_____

_____

_____

_____

L3. Child's Understanding of Language or Communication
a. Responds to caregiver's vocal play
(3 months – 12 months)

Circle One	
Not evident	1
Emerging	2
Developing	3
Well developed	4

b. Responds to gestures (e.g., being beckoned to come)
(7 months – 36 months)

Circle One	
Not evident	1
Emerging	2
Developing	3
Well developed	4

c. Responds to single-word requests/ directions
(9 months – 36 months)

Circle One	
Not evident	1
Emerging	2
Developing	3
Well developed	4

d. Responds to 1-step directions
(13 months – 36 months)

Circle One	
Not evident	1
Emerging	2
Developing	3
Well developed	4

e. Responds to 2-step directions
(23 months – 36 months)

Circle One	
Not evident	1
Emerging	2
Developing	3
Well developed	4

L4. Vocalized Turn-Taking
a. Decreases/increases vocalizations in response to caregiver
(1 month – 6 months)

Circle One	
Not evident	1
Emerging	2
Developing	3
Well developed	4

b. Vocalizes across 1 turn
(1 month – 8 months)

Circle One	
Not evident	1
Emerging	2
Developing	3
Well developed	4

c. Vocalizes across 2 turns
(3 months – 18 months)

Circle One	
Not evident	1
Emerging	2
Developing	3
Well developed	4

L5. Joint Referencing with Caregiver
a. Attends to caregiver
(1 month – 18 months)

Circle One	
Not evident	1
Emerging	2
Developing	3
Well developed	4

b. Gains/directs attention of caregiver
(3 months – 18 months)

Circle One	
Not evident	1
Emerging	2
Developing	3
Well developed	4

c. Continues familiar routine with caregiver
(5 months – 24 months)

Circle One	
Not evident	1
Emerging	2
Developing	3
Well developed	4

d. Shows humor with caregiver
(7 months – 36 months)

Circle One	
Not evident	1
Emerging	2
Developing	3
Well developed	4

Notes:
_____
_____
_____
_____
_____
_____
_____

SE6. Quality of Social Interaction with Caregiver
a. Responds to smiling/soft talking (1 month – 36 months)

Circle One	
Never/rarely	1
Sometimes	2
Usually/frequently	3
Most of the time/always	4

b. Goes to caregiver for comfort (1 month – 36 months)

Circle One	
Never/rarely	1
Sometimes	2
Usually/frequently	3
Most of the time/always	4

SE7. Emotional Stability
a. Has periods of contentment during interaction with caregiver (1 month – 36 months)

Circle One	
Not evident	1
Emerging	2
Developing	3
Well developed	4

b. Able to self-calm (1 month – 36 months)

Circle One	
Not evident	1
Emerging	2
Developing	3
Well developed	4

c. Initiates interaction (7 months – 36 months)

Circle One	
Not evident	1
Emerging	2
Developing	3
Well developed	4

d. Maintains interaction (9 months – 36 months)

Circle One	
Not evident	1
Emerging	2
Developing	3
Well developed	4

C8. Play Strategies Observed
a. Smiles/laughs at engaging routines (5 months – 36 months)

Circle One	
Not evident	1
Emerging	2
Developing	3
Well developed	4

b. Engages in games/game-like play (5 months – 36 months)

Circle One	
Not evident	1
Emerging	2
Developing	3
Well developed	4

c. Shows appropriate functional play with toys/objects (17 months – 36 months)

Circle One	
Not evident	1
Emerging	2
Developing	3
Well developed	4

d. Represents 2 or more related events in play (17 months – 36 months)

Circle One	
Not evident	1
Emerging	2
Developing	3
Well developed	4

e. Engages in symbolic play with toys/caregiver (23 months – 36 months)

Circle One	
Not evident	1
Emerging	2
Developing	3
Well developed	4

Notes:

_____

_____

_____

_____

_____

_____

_____

SP9. Moving and Maneuvering in the Environment

a. Rolls from stomach to back
   (3 months – 12 months)

Circle One	
Not evident	1
Emerging	2
Developing	3
Well developed	4

b. Rolls from back to stomach
   (3 months – 12 months)

Circle One	
Not evident	1
Emerging	2
Developing	3
Well developed	4

c. Creeps
   (5 months – 12 months)

Circle One	
Not evident	1
Emerging	2
Developing	3
Well developed	4

d. Pulls up on people and furniture
   (7 months – 16 months)

Circle One	
Not evident	1
Emerging	2
Developing	3
Well developed	4

e. Cruises around people and furniture
   (9 months – 18 months)

Circle One	
Not evident	1
Emerging	2
Developing	3
Well developed	4

f. Walks
   (9 months – 24 months)

Circle One	
Not evident	1
Emerging	2
Developing	3
Well developed	4

g. Runs
   (13 months – 36 months)

Circle One	
Not evident	1
Emerging	2
Developing	3
Well developed	4

Notes:

_____

_____

_____

_____

SP10. **Skill in Eating

a. Oral-motor response/appropriate
   gag reflex
   (1 month – 6 months)

Circle One	
Never/rarely	1
Sometimes	2
Usually/frequently	3
Most of the time/always	4

b. Takes food appropriately into mouth
   (5 months – 18 months)

Circle One	
Not evident	1
Emerging	2
Developing	3
Well developed	4

c. Lateralizes tongue with food
   (5 months – 18 months)

Circle One	
Not evident	1
Emerging	2
Developing	3
Well developed	4

d. Swallows food
   (5 months – 18 months)

Circle One	
Not evident	1
Emerging	2
Developing	3
Well developed	4

e. Chews
   (7 months – 18 months)

Circle One	
Not evident	1
Emerging	2
Developing	3
Well developed	4

Notes:

_____

_____

_____

_____

_____

_____

SP11. **Drinking

a. Uses continuous, organized sucking
pattern with bottle/breast
(1 month – 6 months)

Circle One	
Not evident	1
Emerging	2
Developing	3
Well developed	4

b. Shows jaw, tongue, and lip control stable
with cup/glass drinking
(9 months – 36 months)

Circle One	
Never/rarely	1
Sometimes	2
Usually/frequently	3
Most of the time/always	4

c. Drinks with little liquid lost
(11 months – 36 months)

Circle One	
Never/rarely	1
Sometimes	2
Usually/frequently	3
Most of the time/always	4

NM 12. **Picking Up Finger Food/
Self-Feeding

a. Brings finger food to mouth
independently
(9 months – 18 months)

Circle One	
Not evident	1
Emerging	2
Developing	3
Well developed	4

b. Rakes to pick up food
(9 months – 18 months)

Circle One	
Not evident	1
Emerging	2
Developing	3
Well developed	4

c. Uses three-jaw chuck grasp
(9 months – 18 months)

Circle One	
Not evident	1
Emerging	2
Developing	3
Well developed	4

d. Uses index finger and thumb grasp
(11 months – 24 months)

Circle One	
Not evident	1
Emerging	2
Developing	3
Well developed	4

SP13. **Self-Feeding with Eating
Utensils

a. Brings spoon to mouth
(11 months – 36 months)

Circle One	
Not evident	1
Emerging	2
Developing	3
Well developed	4

b. Puts spoonful of food in mouth
independently
(13 months – 36 months)

Circle One	
Not evident	1
Emerging	2
Developing	3
Well developed	4

c. Uses pronated hand to hold spoon
(13 months – 36 months)

Circle One	
Not evident	1
Emerging	2
Developing	3
Well developed	4

d. Uses supinated hand to hold spoon
(15 months – 36 months)

Circle One	
Not evident	1
Emerging	2
Developing	3
Well developed	4

Notes:

_____

_____

_____

_____

_____

_____

Unstructured Examiner-Child Play

SE14. Quality of Interaction with Unfamiliar Person/s
a. Responds to smiling/soft talking
(1 month – 36 months)

Circle One	
Never/rarely	1
Sometimes	2
Usually/frequently	3
Most of the time/always	4

b. Initiates interaction
(7 months – 36 months)

Circle One	
Never/rarely	1
Sometimes	2
Usually/frequently	3
Most of the time/always	4

c. Maintains interaction
(9 months – 36 months)

Circle One	
Never/rarely	1
Sometimes	2
Usually/frequently	3
Most of the time/always	4

d. Relates to 2 or more unfamiliar persons
(9 months – 36 months)

Circle One	
Never/rarely	1
Sometimes	2
Usually/frequently	3
Most of the time/always	4

SE15. Attentiveness to Play Activities
a. Attends to age-appropriate range of play events
(1 month – 36 months)

Circle One	
Never/rarely	1
Sometimes	2
Usually/frequently	3
Most of the time/always	4

b. Attends to play activities for age-appropriate periods of time
(1 month – 36 months)

Circle One	
Most of the time/always requires assistance from another	1
Usually/often requires assistance from another	2
Varies with situation	3
Rarely/never requires assistance	4

L16. Response to Common Sounds in the Environment
a. Responds to voices in same or different room
(1 month – 36 months)

Circle One	
Never/rarely	1
Sometimes	2
Usually/frequently	3
Most of the time/always	4

b. Responds to common sounds in same or different rooms (e.g., telephone, television)
(1 month – 36 months)

Circle One	
Never/rarely	1
Sometimes	2
Usually/frequently	3
Most of the time/always	4

NM17. Quality of Movement
a. Moves in and out of developmental positions
(3 months – 36 months)

Circle One	
Never/rarely	1
Sometimes	2
Usually/frequently	3
Most of the time/always	4

b. Uses graded, smooth movement
(3 months – 36 months)

Circle One	
Not evident	1
Emerging	2
Developing	3
Well developed	4

Notes:

_____

_____

_____

_____

_____

NM18. Large Motor Milestones (without movement or maneuvering)

a. Sits
(5 months – 36 months)

Circle One	
Not evident	1
Emerging	2
Developing	3
Well developed	4

b. Uses 4-point positions
(7 months – 36 months)

Circle One	
Not evident	1
Emerging	2
Developing	3
Well developed	4

NM19. Hand Skills Observed

a. Brings hands to midline
(3 months – 12 months)

Circle One	
Not evident	1
Emerging	2
Developing	3
Well developed	4

b. Reaches with right and left hands
(3 months – 12 months)

Circle One	
Not evident	1
Emerging	2
Developing	3
Well developed	4

c. Grasps with right and left hands (Hand preference noted)
(3 months – 12 months)

Circle One	
Not evident	1
Emerging	2
Developing	3
Well developed	4

d. Transfers from hand to hand
(5 months – 12 months)

Circle One	
Not evident	1
Emerging	2
Developing	3
Well developed	4

e. Releases objects with right and left hands
(5 months – 12 months)

Circle One	
Not evident	1
Emerging	2
Developing	3
Well developed	4

f. Crosses midline with right and left hands
(13 months – 36 months)

Circle One	
Not evident	1
Emerging	2
Developing	3
Well developed	4

Notes:

_____
_____
_____
_____
_____
_____
_____
_____

NM20. Body Symmetry

a. On back
(1 month – 6 months)

Circle One	
Not evident	1
Emerging	2
Developing	3
Well developed	4

b. On stomach
(1 month – 6 months)

Circle One	
Not evident	1
Emerging	2
Developing	3
Well developed	4

c. In sitting
(5 months – 18 months)

Circle One	
Not evident	1
Emerging	2
Developing	3
Well developed	4

d. In 4-point creeping
(7 months – 18 months)

Circle One	
Not evident	1
Emerging	2
Developing	3
Well developed	4

e. In standing/upright/walking
(11 months – 36 months)

Circle One	
Not evident	1
Emerging	2
Developing	3
Well developed	4

NM21. Transitions into and out of Various Positions

a. Moves out of sitting
(9 months – 24 months)

Circle One	
Not evident	1
Emerging	2
Developing	3
Well developed	4

b. Moves into sitting
(9 months – 24 months)

Circle One	
Not evident	1
Emerging	2
Developing	3
Well developed	4

c. Moves out of standing
(13 months – 36 months)

Circle One	
Not evident	1
Emerging	2
Developing	3
Well developed	4

d. Moves into standing
(13 months – 36 months)

Circle One	
Not evident	1
Emerging	2
Developing	3
Well developed	4

SP22. Response to Touch

a. Responds to personal, physical touch (e.g., hugging)
(1 month – 36 months)

Circle One	
Never/rarely	1
Sometimes	2
Usually	3
Most of the time/always	4

b. Enjoys different textures
(13 months – 18 months)

Circle One	
Never/rarely	1
Sometimes	2
Usually	3
Most of the time/always	4

c. Walks on different surfaces
(13 months – 24 months)

Circle One	
Never/rarely	1
Sometimes	2
Usually	3
Most of the time/always	4

SE23. Attention-Gaining Behaviors Observed

a. Uses positive, nonverbal strategies to gain attention (e.g., eye gaze, reaching for, tugging)
(5 months – 36 months)

Circle One	
Not evident	1
Emerging	2
Developing	3
Well developed	4

b. Uses positive verbal strategies to gain attention
(7 months – 36 months)

Circle One	
Not evident	1
Emerging	2
Developing	3
Well developed	4

NM24. Protective Responses Observed

a. Uses forward propping
(5 months – 12 months)

Circle One	
Never/rarely	1
Sometimes	2
Usually/frequently	3
Most of the time/always	4

b. Uses lateral propping
(5 months – 12 months)

Circle One	
Not evident	1
Emerging	2
Developing	3
Well developed	4

c. Uses backward equilibrium/balance reaction
(9 months – 12 months)

Circle One	
Not evident	1
Emerging	2
Developing	3
Well developed	4

Notes:

_____

_____

_____

_____

_____

_____

_____

C25. Purposeful Behavior in Play
a. Uses play to practice familiar/known skills and routines
(7 months – 36 months)

Circle One	
Not evident	1
Emerging	2
Developing	3
Well developed	4

b. Uses play to acquire/try new skills/tasks
(9 months – 36 months)

Circle One	
Not evident	1
Emerging	2
Developing	3
Well developed	4

L26. Intelligibility of Speech and Language
a. Uses single prompted/imitated expressions that are understandable (e.g., bye-bye)
(11 months – 36 months)

Circle One	
About 10% or less of the time	1
About 25% of the time	2
About 50% of the time	3
About 75% or more of the time	4

b. Uses single spontaneous expressions (i.e., 1 word) that are understandable
(11 months – 36 months)

Circle One	
About 10% or less of the time	1
About 25% of the time	2
About 50% of the time	3
About 75% or more of the time	4

c. Uses understandable multiword expressions (spontaneous or prompted)
(11 months – 36 months)

Circle One	
About 10% or less of the time	1
About 25% of the time	2
About 50% of the time	3
About 75% or more of the time	4

C27. Problem-Solving Skills Observed
a. Solves problems without assistance (e.g., prompting, demonstration, hand-over-hand)
(11 months – 36 months)

Circle One	
Never/rarely	1
Sometimes	2
Usually/frequently	3
Most of the time/always	4

b. Solves age-appropriate problems
(11 months – 36 months)

Circle One	
Never/rarely	1
Sometimes	2
Usually/frequently	3
Most of the time/always	4

L28. Imitation Skills Observed
a. Uses gestures
(5 months – 36 months)

Circle One	
Not evident	1
Emerging	2
Developing	3
Well developed	4

b. Vowels
(5 months – 36 months)

Circle One	
Not evident	1
Emerging	2
Developing	3
Well developed	4

c. Reduplicated babbling
(9 months – 18 months)

Circle One	
Not evident	1
Emerging	2
Usually	3
Well developed	4

d. Variegated babbling
(9 months – 18 months)

Circle One	
Not evident	1
Emerging	2
Developing	3
Well developed	4

e. Blends
(9 months – 36 months)

Circle One	
Not evident	1
Emerging	2
Developing	3
Well developed	4

f. Single words
(11 months – 36 months)

Circle One	
Not evident	1
Emerging	2
Developing	3
Well developed	4

g. Two-word combinations
(17 months – 36 months)

Circle One	
Not evident	1
Emerging	2
Developing	3
Well developed	4

h. Three-word combinations
(23 months – 36 months)

Circle One	
Not evident	1
Emerging	2
Developing	3
Well developed	4

Structured Examiner-Child Play

L29. Response to Bell
a. Alerts/locates bell on right side
(1 month – 36 months)

Circle One	
Not evident	1
Responds 1 time	2
Responds inconsistently	3
Responds consistently	4

b. Alerts/locates bell on left side
(1 month – 36 months)

Circle One	
Not evident	1
Responds 1 time	2
Responds inconsistently	3
Responds consistently	4

C30. Attention to Faces and Designs
a. Attends to human face
(1 month – 6 months)

Circle One	
Not evident	1
Emerging	2
Developing	3
Well developed	4

b. Attends to checkerboard
(1 month – 6 months)

Circle One	
Not evident	1
Emerging	2
Developing	3
Well developed	4

c. Attends to schematic face (e.g., includes social/communicative response)
(1 month – 6 months)

Circle One	
Never/rarely	1
Emerging	2
Developing	3
Well developed	4

d. Responds to real image in mirror (e.g., includes social/communicative response)
(3 months – 18 months)

Circle One	
Not evident	1
Emerging	2
Developing	3
Well developed	4

e. Shows early responses to baby doll (e.g., holding, poking, touching, kissing)
(5 months – 18 months)

Circle One	
Not evident	1
Emerging	2
Developing	3
Well developed	4

SP31. Tracking
a. Tracks horizontally
(1 month – 36 months)

Circle One	
Not evident	1
Emerging	2
Developing	3
Well developed	4

b. Tracks in circle
(1 month – 36 months)

Circle One	
Not evident	1
Emerging	2
Developing	3
Well developed	4

c. Shows smooth eye movement
(1 month – 36 months)

Circle One	
Not evident	1
Emerging	2
Developing	3
Well developed	4

d. Shows coordinated eye movement
(1 month – 36 months)

Circle One	
Not evident	1
Emerging	2
Developing	3
Well developed	4

L32. Early Social Games
a. Engages in vocal play with toy puppet
(3 months – 8 months)

Circle One	
Not evident	1
Emerging	2
Developing	3
Well developed	4

b. Plays Peek-a-Boo
(3 months – 12 months)

Circle One	
Not evident	1
Emerging	2
Developing	3
Well developed	4

c. Plays Pat-a-Cake
(7 months – 18 months)

Circle One	
Not evident	1
Emerging	2
Developing	3
Well developed	4

Notes:
_____
_____
_____
_____
_____

NM33. Play with Rattles
a. Reaches for rattles
(3 months – 12 months)

Circle One	
Not evident	1
Emerging	2
Developing	3
Well developed	4

b. Grasps rattles
(3 months – 12 months)

Circle One	
Not evident	1
Emerging	2
Developing	3
Well developed	4

c. Transfers rattles
(5 months – 12 months)

Circle One	
Not evident	1
Emerging	2
Developing	3
Well developed	4

d. Releases rattles
(5 months – 12 months)

Circle One	
Not evident	1
Emerging	2
Developing	3
Well developed	4

C34. Response to Hidden Objects
a. Finds partially covered rattle
(5 months – 12 months)

Circle One	
Not evident	1
Emerging	2
Developing	3
Well developed	4

b. Finds completely covered rattle
(7 months – 12 months)

Circle One	
Not evident	1
Emerging	2
Developing	3
Well developed	4

C35. Early Understanding of Cause and Effect
a. Plays with pull toy
(5 months – 12 months)

Circle One	
No awareness evident	1
Holds string/ball only	2
Pulls without awareness	3
Pulls with awareness	4

b. Plays with pop-up pets box
(9 months – 24 months)

Circle One	
No awareness evident	1
Opens 1 lever	2
Opens 2 levers	3
Opens 3 levers	4
Opens 4 levers	5

C36. Play with Blocks and Shape Sorter
a. Plays with blocks and shape sorter
(9 months – 18 months)

Circle Any/All and Sum	
Holds	1
Bangs	1
Takes out of container	1
Puts into container	1
Stacks	1
Total	

Notes:

_____

_____

_____

_____

b. Displays visual discrimination with shape sorter
(11 months – 36 months)

Circle One	
Places 1 block near hole	1
Inserts 1 block through hole	2
Inserts 2 or 3 blocks near holes	3
Inserts 2 or 3 blocks through holes	4

NM37. Play with Balls
a. Rolls with intent
(7 months – 12 months)

Circle One	
Not evident	1
Emerging	2
Developing	3
Well developed	4

b. Throws ball with intent
(13 months – 36 months)

Circle One	
Not evident	1
Emerging	2
Usually	3
Well developed	4

c. Catches ball with intent
(15 months – 36 months)

Circle One	
Not evident	1
Emerging	2
Usually	3
Well developed	4

C38. Play with Pictures and Print
a. Responds to books
(7 months – 36 months)

Circle Any/All and Sum	
Shifts eye gaze/scans/studies	1
Turns pages	1
Points to pictures	1
Vocalizes/verbalizes in response to pictures	1
Total	

b. Responds to crayon and paper
(9 months – 36 months)

Circle Any/All and Sum	
Reaches for/holds crayon	1
Marks paper by banging	1
Makes strokes/circular lines	1
Imitates design/designs	1
Total	

SP39. Play with Bubble Tumbler
a. Uses wand
(13 months – 36 months)

Circle Any/All and Sum	
Reaches for/holds wand	1
Puts wand into container	1
Takes wand out of container	1
Brings wand near mouth	1
Total	

b. Blows bubbles
(13 months – 36 months)

Circle Any/All and Sum	
Puckers mouth	1
Imitates blowing with or without wand	1
Brings wand near mouth, then blows	1
Blows through wand/produces bubbles	1
Total	

C40. Advanced Doll Play
a. Displays single play scenarios (e.g., covering baby, feeding, rocking, dressing, undressing)
(13 months – 36 months)

Circle One	
Not evident	1
Emerging	2
Developing	3
Well developed	4

b. Displays related play scenarios (e.g., feeds/rocks, feeds/changes diaper, sings to baby/puts to bed)
(17 months – 36 months)

Circle One	
Not evident	1
Emerging	2
Developing	3
Well developed	4

C41. Problem-Solving
a. Seeks food/object behind one screen
(13 months – 36 months)

Circle One	
Not evident	1
Emerging	2
Developing	3
Well developed	4

b. Seeks food/object behind two screens
(13 months – 36 months)

Circle One	
Not evident	1
Emerging	2
Developing	3
Well developed	4

c. Seeks food inside clear container
(13 months – 36 months)

Circle One	
Not evident	1
Emerging	2
Developing	3
Well developed	4

d. Plays with toy garage
(17 months – 36 months)

Circle Any/All and Sum	
Attempts key	1
Inserts key	1
Turns key	1
Opens door	1
Exits car	1
Total	

Notes:

_____
_____
_____
_____
_____

SP42. Undressing and Dressing
a. Takes off socks
   (9 months – 36 months)

Circle One	
Not evident	1
Emerging	2
Developing	3
Well developed	4

b. Puts on socks
   (13 months – 36 months)

Circle One	
Not evident	1
Emerging	2
Developing	3
Well developed	4

c. Takes off shoes
   (13 months – 36 months)

Circle One	
Not evident	1
Emerging	2
Developing	3
Well developed	4

d. Puts on toy hard hat
   (13 months – 36 months)

Circle One	
Not evident	1
Emerging	2
Developing	3
Well developed	4

e. Puts on vest
   (13 months – 36 months)

Circle One	
Not evident	1
Emerging	2
Developing	3
Well developed	4

f. Opens and closes vest fasteners
   (15 months – 36 months)

Circle One	
Not evident	1
Emerging	2
Developing	3
Well developed	4

SE43. Adaptability
a. Makes transitions with interest
   (11 months – 36 months)

Circle One	
Never/rarely	1
Sometimes	2
Usually/frequently	3
Most of the time/always	4

b. Attends during structured play
   (11 months – 36 months)

Circle One	
Never/rarely	1
Sometimes	2
Usually/frequently	3
Most of the time/always	4

Notes:

_____

_____

_____

_____

_____

APPENDIX B
Scoring Worksheets

Partners in Play Scoring Worksheet 1

Child's name: _____   Evaluation date: _____

Chronological/adjusted age: _____ months

Photocopy and complete this worksheet to provide a permanent record of the child's performance.

Caregiver Report of Child Development

SOCIAL-EMOTIONAL SKILLS

Interview Question	Age Range	Score
1. How frequently does _____ attend to people?	1–36 months	
2. How frequently does _____ attend to toys or activities?	1–36 months	
3. How often does _____ become distressed or fussy during the day?	1–36 months	
4. Can you calm _____ when he/she becomes distressed?	1–36 months	
5. Is _____ unusually sensitive to specific situations or things in your home, such as sound, light, or different textures?	1–36 months	
6. How well does _____ communicate his/her needs and emotions?	1–36 months	
7. How well is _____ able to adapt to new situations?	1–36 months	
8. How well does _____ show or express emotions with people?	3–36 months	
9. Does _____ respond to the emotions or feelings of other people?	5–36 months	

COGNITIVE SKILLS

Interview Question	Age Range	Score
10. What types of toys does _____ particularly enjoy?	3–36 months	
11. What qualities does _____ demonstrate in playing games with your family?	3–36 months	
12. Who does _____ like to play with?	3–36 months	
13. How well does _____ initiate play with others?	5–36 months	
14. What examples of problem solving have you seen when _____ is playing?	7–36 months	
15. What examples of cause-and-effect understanding have you seen in _____'s play?	7–36 months	
16. How does _____ explore his/her environment?	7–36 months	
17. What examples of pretend play have you seen?	13–36 months	

NEUROMOTOR SKILLS

Interview Question	Age Range	Score
18. What early positions does _____ use?	1–12 months	
19. What hand skills does _____ have?	5–12 months	
20. In what positions do you see _____ bearing weight?	5–18 months	
21. What positions does _____ move out of?	5–36 months	
22. What positions does _____ move into?	5–36 months	
23. How often does _____ need help eating?	5–36 months	
24. What are _____'s eating habits like?	5–36 months	
25. How do you feed _____?	5–36 months	
26. How does _____ move from place to place?	9–36 months	
27. What large movement games does _____ enjoy?	9–36 months	

SENSORY-PERCEPTUAL SKILLS

Interview Question	Age Range	Score
28. How does _____ react to being held and cuddled?	1–36 months	
29. What sensory experiences does _____ enjoy?	1–36 months	
30. How well is _____ able to follow your face and objects visually?	1–36 months	
31. What manipulative toys/materials does _____ enjoy playing with?	5–36 months	
32. How does _____ help with dressing and undressing?	11–36 months	
33. Can you give examples of how _____ knows where his/her body is in space?	7–36 months	
34. What does _____ do with pencil/crayon and paper activities?	11–36 months	

LANGUAGE SKILLS

Interview Question	Age Range	Score
35. What range of sounds does _____ respond to at home?	1–36 months	
36. What single sounds have you heard _____ say?	1–8 months	
37. How does _____ communicate with you and other people?	3–36 months	
38. What names of people does _____ recognize?	5–36 months	
39. What words (other than names) does _____ understand?	5–36 months	
40. What nonverbal or verbal expressions does _____ imitate?	5–36 months	
41. What sound combinations does _____ say?	7–36 months	
42. What does _____ do with books?	7–36 months	
43. What requests or directions does _____ understand?	9–36 months	
44. What does _____ do if you or someone else does not understand him/her?	11–36 months	
45. About how many words does _____ say?	13–36 months	
46. What words does _____ say?	13–36 months	
47. How many words does _____ put together?	17–36 months	

Unstructured Caregiver-Child Play

L1. STRATEGIES FOR COMMUNICATION

Observation	Age Range	Score
a. Differential vocalization	1–6 months	
b. Vocal play	3–18 months	
c. Reduplicated babbling	9–18 months	
d. Variegated babbling	9–18 months	
e. Gestures	9–36 months	
f. Jargon-like vocalizations	9–36 months	
g. Makes requests	11–36 months	
h. Uses single words	11–36 months	
i. Puts two words together	11–36 months	
j. Puts three or more words together	17–36 months	
k. Initiates/engages in dialogue/discourse	17–36 months	

L2. COMMUNICATION OF NEEDS/INTENT

Observation	Age Range	Score
a. Makes basic needs known	1–36 months	
b. Makes social needs known	1–36 months	

L3. UNDERSTANDING OF LANGUAGE OR COMMUNICATION

Observation	Age Range	Score
a. Responds to caregiver's vocal play	3–12 months	
b. Responds to gestures	7–36 months	
c. Responds to single-word requests/directions	9–36 months	
d. Responds to 1-step directions	13–36 months	
e. Responds to 2-step directions	23–36 months	

L4. VOCALIZED TURN-TAKING

Observation	Age Range	Score
a. Decreases/increases vocalizations in response to caregiver	1–6 months	
b. Vocalizes across one turn	1–8 months	
c. Vocalizes across two turns	3–18 months	

L5. JOINT REFERENCING WITH CAREGIVER

Observation	Age Range	Score
a. Attends to caregiver	1–18 months	
b. Gains/directs attention of caregiver	3–18 months	
c. Continues familiar routine with caregiver	5–24 months	
d. Shows humor with caregiver	7–36 months	

SE6. QUALITY OF SOCIAL INTERACTION WITH CAREGIVER

Observation	Age Range	Score
a. Responds to smiling/soft talking	1–36 months	
b. Goes to caregiver for comfort	1–36 months	

SE7. EMOTIONAL STABILITY

Observation	Age Range	Score
a. Has periods of contentment during interaction with caregiver	1–36 months	
b. Able to self-calm	1–36 months	
c. Initiates interaction	7–36 months	
d. Maintains interaction	9–36 months	

C8. PLAY STRATEGIES OBSERVED

Observation	Age Range	Score
a. Smiles/laughs at engaging routines	5–36 months	
b. Engages in games/gamelike play	5–36 months	
c. Shows appropriate functional play with toys/objects	17–36 months	
d. Represents two or more related events in play	17–36 months	
e. Engages in symbolic play with toys/caregiver	23–36 months	

SP9. MOVING AND MANEUVERING IN THE ENVIRONMENT

Observation	Age Range	Score
a. Rolls from stomach to back	3–12 months	
b. Rolls from back to stomach	3–12 months	
c. Creeps	5–12 months	
d. Pulls up on people and furniture	7–16 months	
e. Cruises around people and furniture	9–18 months	
f. Walks	9–24 months	
g. Runs	13–36 months	

**SP10. SKILL IN EATING

Observation	Age Range	Score
a. Oral-motor response/appropriate gag reflex	1–6 months	
b. Takes food appropriately into mouth	5–18 months	
c. Lateralizes tongue with food	5–18 months	
d. Swallows food	5–18 months	
e. Chews	7–18 months	

**SP11. SKILL IN DRINKING

Observation	Age Range	Score
a. Uses continuous, organized sucking pattern with bottle/breast	1–6 months	
b. Shows jaw, tongue, and lip control and stability with cup/glass drinking	9–36 months	
c. Drinks with little liquid lost	11–36 months	

**NM12. PICKING UP FINGER FOOD/SELF-FEEDING

Observation	Age Range	Score
a. Brings finger food to mouth by self	9–18 months	
b. Rakes to pick up food	9–18 months	
c. Uses 3-jaw chuck grasp	9–18 months	
d. Uses index finger and thumb grasp	11–24 months	

**NM13. SELF-FEEDING WITH EATING UTENSILS

Observation	Age Range	Score
a. Brings spoon to mouth	11–36 months	
b. Puts spoonful of food in mouth independently	13–36 months	
c. Uses pronated hand to hold spoon	13–36 months	
d. Uses supinated hand to hold spoon	15–36 months	

Unstructured Examiner-Child Play

SE14. QUALITY OF INTERACTION WITH UNFAMILIAR PEOPLE

Observation	Age Range	Score
a. Responds to smiling/soft talking	1–36 months	
b. Initiates interaction	7–36 months	
c. Maintains interaction	9–36 months	
d. Relates to two or more unfamiliar people	9–36 months	

SE15. ATTENTIVENESS TO PLAY ACTIVITIES

Observation	Age Range	Score
a. Attends to age-appropriate range of play events	1–36 months	
b. Attends to play activities for age-appropriate periods of time	1–36 months	

L16. RESPONSE TO COMMON ENVIRONMENTAL SOUNDS

Observation	Age Range	Score
a. Responds to voices in same or different room	1–36 months	
b. Responds to common sounds in same or different room	1–36 months	

NM17. QUALITY OF MOVEMENT

Observation	Age Range	Score
a. Moves into and out of developmental positions	3–36 months	
b. Uses graded, smooth movement	3–36 months	

NM18. LARGE MOTOR MILESTONES

Observation	Age Range	Score
a. Sits	5–36 months	
b. Uses 4-point positions	7–36 months	

NM19. HAND SKILLS

Observation	Age Range	Score
a. Brings hands to midline	3–12 months	
b. Reaches with right and left hands	3–12 months	
c. Grasps with right and left hands	3–12 months	
d. Transfers from hand to hand	5–12 months	
e. Releases objects with right and left hands	5–12 months	
f. Crosses midline with right and left hands	13–36 months	

NM20. BODY SYMMETRY

Observation	Age Range	Score
a. On back	1–6 months	
b. On stomach	1–6 months	
c. In sitting	5–18 months	
d. In 4-point creeping	7–18 months	
e. In standing/upright/walking	11–36 months	

NM21. TRANSITIONS INTO AND OUT OF VARIOUS POSITIONS

Observation	Age Range	Score
a. Moves out of sitting	9–24 months	
b. Moves into sitting	9–24 months	
c. Moves out of standing	13–36 months	
d. Moves into standing	13–36 months	

SP22. RESPONSE TO TOUCH

Observation	Age Range	Score
a. Responds to personal physical touch	1–36 months	
b. Enjoys different textures	13–18 months	
c. Walks on different surfaces	13–24 months	

SE23. ATTENTION-GAINING BEHAVIORS

Observation	Age Range	Score
a. Uses positive nonverbal strategies to gain attention	5–36 months	
b. Uses positive verbal strategies to gain attention	7–36 months	

NM24. PROTECTIVE RESPONSES

Observation	Age Range	Score
a. Uses forward propping	5–12 months	
b. Uses lateral propping	5–12 months	
c. Uses backward equilibrium/balance reaction	9–12 months	

C25. PURPOSEFUL BEHAVIOR IN PLAY

Observation	Age Range	Score
a. Uses play to practice familiar/known skills and routines	7–36 months	
b. Uses play to acquire/try new skills/tasks	9–36 months	

L26. INTELLIGIBILITY OF SPEECH AND LANGUAGE

Observation	Age Range	Score
a. Single prompted/imitated expressions are understandable	11–36 months	
b. Single-word spontaneous expressions are understandable	11–36 months	
c. Multiword expressions are understandable	11–36 months	

C27. PROBLEM-SOLVING SKILLS

Observation	Age Range	Score
a. Solves problems without assistance	11–36 months	
b. Solves age-appropriate problems	11–36 months	

L28. IMITATION SKILLS

Observation	Age Range	Score
a. Gestures	5–36 months	
b. Vowels	5–36 months	
c. Reduplicated babbling	9–18 months	
d. Variegated babbling	9–18 months	
e. Blends	9–36 months	
f. Single words	11–36 months	
g. Two-word combinations	17–36 months	
h. Three-word combinations	23–36 months	

Structured Examiner-Child Interaction

L29. RESPONSE TO BELL

Observation	Age Range	Score
a. Alerts/locates bell on right side	1–36 months	
b. Alerts/locates bell on left side	1–36 months	

C30. ATTENTION TO FACES AND DESIGNS

Observation	Age Range	Score
a. Attends to human face	1–6 months	
b. Attends to checkerboard	1–6 months	
c. Attends to schematic face	1–6 months	
d. Responds to real image in mirror	3–18 months	
e. Shows early responses to baby doll	5–18 months	

SP31. TRACKING

Observation	Age Range	Score
a. Tracks horizontally	1–36 months	
b. Tracks in circle	1–36 months	
c. Shows smooth eye movement	1–36 months	
d. Shows coordinated eye movement	1–36 months	

L32. EARLY SOCIAL GAMES

Observation	Age Range	Score
a. Engages in vocal play with puppet	3–8 months	
b. Plays peek-a-boo	3–12 months	
c. Plays pat-a-cake	7–18 months	

NM33. PLAY WITH RATTLES

Observation	Age Range	Score
a. Reaches for rattle	3–12 months	
b. Grasps rattle	3–12 months	
c. Transfers rattle hand to hand	5–12 months	
d. Releases rattle	5–12 months	

C34. RESPONSE TO HIDDEN OBJECTS

Observation	Age Range	Score
a. Finds partially covered rattle	5–12 months	
b. Finds completely covered rattle	7–12 months	

C35. EARLY UNDERSTANDING OF CAUSE AND EFFECT

Observation	Age Range	Score
a. Plays with pull toy	5–12 months	
b. Plays with pop-up pets box	9–24 months	

C36. PLAY WITH BLOCKS AND SHAPE SORTER

Observation	Age Range	Score
a. Plays with blocks and shape sorter	9–18 months	
b. Visual discrimination skills	11–36 months	

NM37. PLAY WITH BALLS

Observation	Age Range	Score
a. Rolls ball with intent	7–12 months	
b. Throws ball with intent	13–36 months	
c. Catches ball with intent	15–36 months	

C38. PLAY WITH PICTURES AND PRINT

Observation	Age Range	Score
a. Responds to books	5–36 months	
b. Responds to crayon and paper	9–36 months	

SP39. PLAY WITH BUBBLE TUMBLER

Observation	Age Range	Score
a. Uses wand	13–36 months	
b. Blows bubbles	13–36 months	

C40. ADVANCED DOLL PLAY

Observation	Age Range	Score
a. Single play scenarios	13–36 months	
b. Related play scenarios	13–36 months	

C41. PROBLEM SOLVING

Observation	Age Range	Score
a. Seeks food behind one screen	13–36 months	
b. Seeks food behind one of two screens	13–36 months	
c. Seeks food inside clear container	13–36 months	

**SP42. UNDRESSING AND DRESSING

Observation	Age Range	Score
a. Takes off socks	9–36 months	
b. Puts on socks	13–36 months	
c. Takes off shoes	13–36 months	
d. Puts on toy hard hat	13–36 months	
e. Puts on vest	13–36 months	
f. Opens and closes vest fasteners	15–36 months	

SE43. ADAPTABILITY

Observation	Age Range	Score
a. Makes transitions with interest	11–36 months	
b. Attends during structured play	11–36 months	

Partners in Play Scoring Worksheet 2

Child's name: _____   Evaluation date: _____   Chronological/adjusted age: _____ months

For each item administered, indicate + if the child attained a score of 3 or above and − for scores of 2 or less. Note that items are listed by developmental domain, which differs from the order on the record forms. Add up the number of +'s in each domain and enter that total.

Caregiver Report of Child Development

SOCIAL-EMOTIONAL (SE) ITEMS

Item	+/−
1. Attention to people	
2. Attention to toys	
3. Becoming fussy	
4. Ability to calm	
5. Sensitivity to sound/light/textures	
6. Communication of needs	
7. Adaptability	
8. Showing emotions	
9. Response to emotions	
Subtotal	

NEUROMOTOR (NM) ITEMS

Item	+/−
18. Early positions	
19. Hand skills	
20. Weight bearing	
21. Transitions out of positions	
22. Transitions into positions	
23. Assistance needed with eating	
24. Eating habits	
25. Means of feeding	
26. Mobility	
27. Gross motor games	
Subtotal	

COMMUNICATION AND LANGUAGE (L) ITEMS

Item	+/−
35. Response to sounds	
36. Phonemes produced	
37. Communication strategies	
38. Comprehension of names	
39. Comprehension of other words	
40. Verbal/nonverbal imitation	
41. Babbling	
42. Response to books	
43. Comprehension of directions	
44. Response to communication breakdown	
45. Number of words produced	
46. Expressive vocabulary	
47. Word combinations	
Subtotal	

COGNITIVE (C) ITEMS

Item	+/−
10. Toys enjoyed	
11. Quality of play	
12. Playmates	
13. Play initiation	
14. Problem solving in play	
15. Cause and effect in play	
16. Exploring environment	
17. Pretend play	
Subtotal	

SENSORY-PERCEPTUAL (SP) ITEMS

Item	+/−
28. Response to cuddling	
29. Sensory input	
30. Visual tracking	
31. Manipulative toys	
32. Assists with dressing	
33. Proprioception	
34. Pencil/crayon and paper activities	
Subtotal	

Unstructured Caregiver-Child Play

SOCIAL-EMOTIONAL (SE) ITEMS

Item	+/–
6a. Responds to smiling/soft talking	
6b. Seeks comfort	
7a. Periods of contentment	
7b. Self-calming	
7c. Initiates interaction	
7d. Maintains interaction	
Subtotal	

COGNITIVE (C) ITEMS

Item	+/–
8a. Smiles at routines	
8b. Engages in games	
8c. Functional play	
8d. Representational play	
8e. Symbolic play	
Subtotal	

NEUROMOTOR (NM) ITEMS

Item	+/–
**12a. Bringing food to mouth	
**12b. Raking food	
**12c. 3-jaw chuck grasp	
**12d. Pincer grasp	
Subtotal	

SENSORY-PERCEPTUAL (SP) ITEMS

Item	+/–
9a. Rolls to back	
9b. Rolls to stomach	
9c. Creeps	
9d. Pulls up to stand	
9e. Cruises	
9f. Walks	
9g. Runs	
**10a. Gag reflex	
**10b. Takes food into mouth	
**10c. Lateralizes tongue in chewing	
**10d. Swallows	
**10e. Chews	
**11a. Sucking pattern	
**11b. Jaw stability in drinking	
**11c. No liquid loss in drinking	
**13a. Brings spoon to mouth	
**13b. Inserts spoon in mouth	
**13c. Pronated hand	
**13d. Supinated hand	
Subtotal	

COMMUNICATION AND LANGUAGE (L) ITEMS

Item	+/–
1a. Differential vocalization	
1b. Vocal play	
1c. Reduplicated babbling	
1d. Variegated babbling	
1e. Gestures	
1f. Jargon	
1g. Uses requests	
1h. Uses single words	
1i. Uses 2-word phrases	
1j. Uses 3-word phrases	
1k. Dialogue	
2a. Basic needs	
2b. Social needs	
3a. Responds to vocal play	
3b. Responds to gestures	
3c. Responds to 1-word directions	
3d. Responds to 1-step directions	
3e. Responds to 2-step directions	
4a. Increase/decrease in vocalization	
4b. Vocalizes one turn	
4c. Vocalizes two turns	
5a. Attends to caregiver	
5b. Directs caregiver's attention	
5c. Continues routine	
5d. Shows humor	
Subtotal	

Unstructured Examiner-Child Play

SOCIAL-EMOTIONAL (SE) ITEMS

Item	+/−
14a. Responds to smiling/talking	
14b. Initiates interaction	
14c. Maintains interaction	
14d. Relates to unfamiliar adults	
15a. Attends to play	
15b. Attention span	
23a. Gains attention nonverbally	
23b. Gains attention verbally	
Subtotal	

COGNITIVE (C) ITEMS

Item	+/−
25a. Uses routines in play	
25b. Uses skills in play	
27a. Solving problems independently	
27b. Age-appropriate problem solving	
Subtotal	

NEUROMOTOR (NM) ITEMS

Item	+/−
17a. Transitions	
17b. Smooth, graded movement	
18a. Sitting	
18b. 4-point positions	
19a. Hands to midline	
19b. Reaching	
19c. Grasping	
19d. Hand-to-hand transfers	
19e. Releasing	
19f. Crossing midline with hands	
20a. Symmetry on back	
20b. Symmetry on stomach	
20c. Symmetry in sitting	
20d. Symmetry in creeping	
20e. Symmetry in standing/walking	
21a. Transition out of sitting	
21b. Transition into sitting	
21c. Transition out of standing	
21d. Transition into standing	
24a. Forward propping	
24b. Lateral propping	
24c. Balance reaction	
Subtotal	

SENSORY-PERCEPTUAL (SP) ITEMS

Item	+/−
22a. Responds to touch	
22b. Responds to textures	
22c. Walks on different surfaces	
Subtotal	

COMMUNICATION AND LANGUAGE (L) ITEMS

Item	+/−
16a. Response to voices	
16b. Response to sounds	
26a. Intelligibility of imitated words	
26b. Intelligibility of spontaneous words	
26c. Intelligibility of multiword phrases	
28a. Imitation of gestures	
28b. Imitation of vowels	
28c. Imitation of reduplicated babbling	
28d. Imitation of variegated babbling	
28e. Imitation of blends	
28f. Imitation of single words	
28g. Imitation of 2-word phrases	
28h. Imitation of 3-word phrases	
Subtotal	

Structured Examiner-Child Interaction

SOCIAL-EMOTIONAL (SE) ITEMS

Item	+/−
43a. Activity transitions	
43b. Attention to structured task	
Subtotal	

COGNITIVE (C) ITEMS

Item	+/−
30a. Attends to human face	
30b. Attends to checkerboard	
30c. Attends to schematic face	
30d. Responds to image in mirror	
30e. Responds to doll	
34a. Finds partly covered rattle	
34b. Finds fully covered rattle	
35a. Pull toy	
35b. Pop-up box	
36a. Shape sorter/blocks	
36b. Visual discrimination	
38a. Responds to book	
38b. Responds to crayon/paper	
40a. Single scenarios with doll	
40b. Related scenarios with doll	
41a. Seeks food/one screen	
41b. Seeks food/two screens	
41c. Seeks food/clear container	
41d. Garage play	
Subtotal	

NEUROMOTOR (NM) ITEMS

Item	+/−
33a. Reaches for rattle	
33b. Grasps rattle	
33c. Transfers rattle hand to hand	
33d. Releases rattle	
37a. Rolls ball	
37b. Throws ball	
37c. Catches ball	
Subtotal	

SENSORY-PERCEPTUAL (SP) ITEMS

Item	+/−
31a. Horizontal tracking	
31b. Circular tracking	
31c. Smooth eye movement	
31d. Coordinated eye movement	
39a. Uses wand	
39b. Blows bubbles	
**42a Takes off socks	
**42b. Puts on socks	
**42c. Takes off shoes	
**42d. Puts on hat	
**42e. Puts on vest	
**42f. Vest fasteners	
Subtotal	

COMMUNICATION AND LANGUAGE (L) ITEMS

Item	+/−
29a. Locates bell/right	
29b. Locates bell/left	
32a. Vocal play w/puppet	
32b. Peek-a-boo	
32c. Pat-a-cake	
Subtotal	

Partners in Play Summary Worksheet

Child's name: _____   Evaluation date: _____

Chronological age: _____months   Adjusted age: _____months

Transfer the subtotals from Scoring Worksheet 2 to the appropriate cells in the top table and total each row to determine the number of items passed in each domain. Enter these totals in the bottom table, then consult the Index of Item Totals on the next page to locate the expected number of items passed. Divide the actual number passed by the expected number to determine the percentage of age-appropriate items passed.

Developmental Domain	Number of Items Passed in Caregiver Report	Number of Items Passed in Caregiver-Child Play	Number of Items Passed in Examiner-Child Play	Number of Items Passed in Examiner-Child Interaction	Total Items Passed
Social-Emotional					
Cognitive					
Neuromotor					
Sensory-Perceptual					
Language					

SUBTOTALS AND TOTALS OF ITEMS PASSED

Developmental Domain	Number of Items Passed	Percent of Age-Appropriate Items Passed	Percent of Delay
Social-Emotional			
Cognitive			
Neuromotor			
Sensory-Perceptual			
Language			

Index of Item Totals by Month

Determine the child's chronological age (or adjusted age, if appropriate) to the nearest month. For each domain, divide the number of items the child passed by the number given for the child's age in the following table to determine the percentage of delay.

Month	Primary Developmental Area Totals				
	NM	SP	C	L	SE
1	3	9	3	12	14
2	3	9	3	12	14
3	10	12	7	19	15
4	10	12	7	19	15
5	25	16	13	24	17
6	25	16	13	24	17
7	26	18	16	28	20
8	26	18	16	28	20
9	34	22	20	33	23
10	34	22	20	33	23
11	36	26	23	42	25
12	36	26	23	42	25
13	25	34	25	43	25
14	25	34	25	43	25
15	26	33	25	43	25
16	26	33	25	43	25
17	26	36	29	45	25
18**	26	36	29	45	25
19	20	29	26	38	25
20	20	29	26	38	25
21	20	29	27	38	25
22	20	29	27	38	25
23	22	29	27	40	25
24	22	29	27	40	25
25	16	27	26	39	25
26	16	27	26	39	25
27	16	27	26	39	25
28	16	27	26	39	25
29	16	27	26	39	25
30	16	27	26	39	25
31	16	27	26	39	25
32	16	27	26	39	25
33	16	27	26	39	25
34	16	27	26	39	25
35	16	27	26	39	25
36	16	27	26	39	25

Appendix C

Glossary of Terms and Blackline Drawings for the *PIP* Assessment

183

Unstructured Caregiver-Child Play

1. *Differential vocalization:* Any infant vocalizations other than crying, including grunts, squeals, sighs, changes in pitch, single vowel sounds, and early consonant-vowel (CV) combinations.

2. *Vocal play:* Vocalizations such as raspberries, early- or later-developing CV combinations, or reduplicated syllables.

3. *Reduplicated babbling:* Repetition of the same CV syllable in a single vocalization; e.g., "dadada," "bababa."

4. *Variegated babbling:* Production of a combination of different CV syllable combinations in a vocalization; e.g., "babadaga."

5. *Jargon-like vocalizations:* A stream of vocalizations that greatly resembles speech in intonation and inflection but contains few or no real words.

6. *Joint referencing with caregiver:* A shared focus of attention between the child and caregiver. The child or caregiver may comment on an object or point of reference; e.g., the child may reach toward a ball, look at the caregiver, and then look back at the ball. The caregiver then may say "ball" and roll the ball toward the child.

7. *Symbolic play:* The ability to represent an object/event with something else in play through speech, language, cognitive problem solving, and action.

8. *Creeps:* Moves on hands and knees, with stomach lifted off the floor or ground.

9. *Cruises:* Steps sideways, while standing and holding onto a supporting surface such as a piece of furniture.

10. *Lateralizes tongue with food:* Moves the tongue from side to side while masticating to propel food between the biting surfaces of the teeth.

11. *Chews:* Shows a mature pattern of mastication, characterized by circular and diagonal jaw movement.

12. *Continuous, organized sucking pattern:* A mature pattern of taking liquids from a bottle or breast, characterized by up and down movements of the tongue and smaller up and down movements of the jaw.

13. *Jaw, tongue, lip control and stability:* In drinking from a cup, the ability to stabilize the lip of the cup in the mouth without biting it or spilling liquid; internal control of the jaw is present in drinking, with minimal up and down movement of the tongue and jaw. Loss of liquid is rare and may occur only when the cup or glass is taken from the mouth.

14. *Rakes to pick up food:* Drags a prone hand across the surface to pick up finger food, rather than grasping it (see Figure 1).

Figure 1
Rakes with fingers.

15. *Uses three-jaw chuck grasp:*   Picks up finger food with thumb, index, and middle fingers (see Figure 2).

Figure 2
Uses three-jaw chuck grasp.

16. *Uses index finger and thumb grasp:*   Picks up food with a mature two-finger pincer grasp (see Figure 3).

Figure 3
Tip

17. *Pronated hand:*   Hand is in front of trunk with the palm side of hand facing down. Grasps the spoon in a whole-hand grip with the palm facing down.

18. *Supinated hand:*   Hand is in front of trunk with palm side of hand facing up. Grasps the spoon in a mature grasp with the palm turned in.

Unstructured Examiner/Play Facilitator-Child Activities

19. *Graded, smooth movement:*   Regular, fluid movements without signs of loose, weak movements, tightness (stiff, tense movements); jerkiness (disjointed movements); or tremulousness (shaky, quivering movements).

20. *4-Point positions:*   Positions involving weightbearing on hands and knees simultaneously.

21. *W-sits:*   Sits with legs at sides in the form of a "W" (see Figure 4).

Figure 4
W-sitting

22. *Sits on feet:* Sits with legs bent and under self; sits on feet (see Figure 5).

Figure 5
Sitting on feet

23. *Ring-sits:* Sits with legs bent and feet meeting; legs form a circle or ring (see Figure 6).

Figure 6
Ring-sitting

24. *Sits cross-legged:* Sits with legs folded and crossed in front. This position also is called tailor-sitting (see Figure 7).

Figure 7
Cross-legged

25. *Side-sits:* Sits with legs bent and to one side (see Figure 8).

Figure 8
Side-sitting

26. *Long-sits:*   Sits with both legs straight and in front (see Figure 9).

Figure 9
Long-sitting

27. *Midline:*   An imaginary line down the center of the body from head to foot.

28. *Crosses midline:*   Shows eye or hand/arm movements across midline to the opposite side of the body.

29. *Body symmetry on back:*   Body is uniform on the right and left sides (see Figure 10).

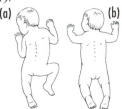

Figure 10
(a) Asymmetry (b) Symmetry

30. *Body symmetry on stomach:*   Body is uniform on the right and left sides (see Figure 11).

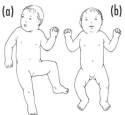

Figure 11
(a) Asymmetry (b) Symmetry

31. *Moves out of sitting:*   See Figure 12.

Figure 12
(a) Vaults forward into prone or 4-point.
(b) Rotates into prone or 4-point.

32. *Moves into sitting:*   See Figure 13.

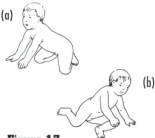

Figure 13
(a) Pushes back from prone or 4-point.
(b) Rotates from prone or 4-point.

33. *Forward propping:*   In sitting position, supports weight with both arms and hands in front of the body (see Figure 14).

Figure 14
Forward propping

34. *Lateral propping:*   In sitting position, supports weight on one arm and hand to the right or left side of the body (see Figure 15).

Figure 15
Lateral propping

35. *Backward equilibrium:*   With displacement of the child's center of gravity backward, the back curls forward or the arms extend behind the body (see Figure 16).

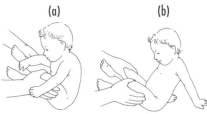

Figure 16
(a) Curls forward to save self.
(b) Extends arms backward.

Structured Examiner-Child Play

36. *Criteria for Imitation of Designs, Item C38b:* See Figure 17.

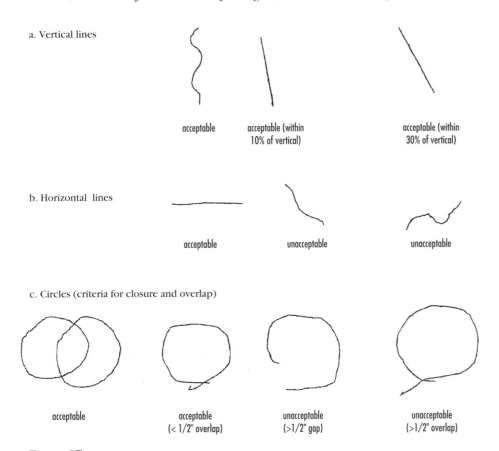

a. Vertical lines

        acceptable   acceptable (within 10% of vertical)   acceptable (within 30% of vertical)

b. Horizontal lines

        acceptable   unacceptable   unacceptable

c. Circles (criteria for closure and overlap)

    acceptable   acceptable (< 1/2" overlap)   unacceptable (>1/2" gap)   unacceptable (>1/2" overlap)

Figure 17

State and Jurisdictional Eligibility Definitions for Infants and Toddlers with Disabilities Under IDEA March 2005

National Early Childhood
TA Center
NECTAC Notes
Issue no. 20
February 2006

State and Jurisdictional Eligibility Definitions for Infants and Toddlers with Disabilities Under IDEA

by Jo Shackelford

A major challenge to state and jurisdictional policy makers in implementing the Early Intervention Program for Infants and Toddlers with Disabilities, Part C under the Individuals with Disabilities Education Improvement Act of 2004 (IDEA, 2004), continues to to be determining definitions of developmental delay and criteria of eligibility for services to young children, birth through 2 years of age, and their families. Under Part C, participating states and jurisdictions must provide services to two groups of children: those who are experiencing developmental delays, and those who have a diagnosed mental or physical condition that has a high probability of resulting in developmental delay. In addition, states may choose to serve children who are at risk of experiencing a substantial developmental delay if early intervention services are not provided. *(See Table 1 on page 2 for the statutory language relating to eligibility of infants and toddlers under Part C of the Individuals with Disabilities Education Improvement Act of 2004. Please note that as of November, 2005, federal regulations for this reauthorization have not been proposed. However, there were no substantive changes in the law in this area that would suggest regulatory changes. When the regulations are available this paper will be revised accordingly.)*

The task of defining eligible population has been a challenge for states. Eligibility criteria influence the numbers and types of children needing or receiving services, the types of services provided, and ultimately the cost of the early intervention system. Over the years, several states have revised their definitions: some have narrowed their eligibility criteria and others have expanded them. Soon after the creation of the Early Intervention Program under IDEA, many states were interested in serving children at risk, but fears of highly increased numbers of eligible children, and therefore, highly increased costs, reduced the number of states that included children at risk in their eligibility definition. Several states that are not serving children at risk under their definition indicate that they will monitor the development of these children and refer them for early intervention services as delays are manifested.

The National Early Childhood Technical Assistance Center

Issue No. 20 *NECTAC Notes* February 2006, page 2

This paper discusses how the 50 states and 6 jurisdictions that participate in the Part C program define developmental delay and, as applicable, at risk in their definition of eligibility for services. Table 2 displays a summary of states' and jurisdictions' definitions of developmental delay and, as applicable, their approaches to serving children who are at risk of having substantial developmental delay.

Criteria for Definitions of Developmental Delay

Although the IDEA statute for Part C specifies the developmental areas that are to be included in states' definitions of developmental delay *(see Table 1)*, states must identify appropriate diagnostic instruments, procedures (including the use of informed clinical opinion), and levels of functioning or other criteria that will be used to determine eligibility. A review of state eligibility definitions under Part C reveals that states are expressing criteria for delay quantitatively — such as (a) the difference between chronological age and actual performance level expressed as a percentage of chronological age, (b) delay expressed as performance at a certain number of months below chronological age, or (c) delay as indicated by standard deviation below the mean on a norm-referenced instrument — and qualitatively — such as delay indicated by atypical development or observed atypical behaviors. One state has developed a matrix of criteria for delay, differentiating the amount of delay according to the age of the child in months. The rationale for this is that a 25% delay in a 1-year-old's development, for example, is quite different from a 25% delay in a 3-year-old's development (Harbin, Gallagher, & Terry, 1991; Shonkoff & Meisels, 1991).

Table 1 Definitions Related to Eligibility Under Part C of the IDEA Amendments of 2004

Under Part C of IDEA, states *must provide* services to any child "under 3 years of age who needs early intervention services" (IDEA 2004, §632(5)(A)) because the child:

"(i) is experiencing developmental delays, as measured by appropriate diagnostic instruments and procedures in 1 or more of the areas of cognitive development, physical development, communication development, social or emotional development, and adaptive development; or

(ii) has a diagnosed physical or mental condition which has a high probability of resulting in developmental delay" (IDEA 2004, §632(5)(A)).

A state also *may provide* services, at its discretion, to at-risk infants and toddlers. An at-risk infant or toddler is defined under Part C as "an individual under 3 years of age who would be at risk of experiencing a substantial developmental delay if early intervention services were not pro-vided to the individual" (IDEA 2004, §632(1)).

There is wide variability in the type of quantitative criteria states use to describe developmental delay, and there also is a wide range in the level of delay states require for eligibility. Common measurements of level of delay are 25% delay or 2 standard deviations (SD) below the mean in one or more developmental areas, or 20% delay or 1.5 SD in two or more areas. Traditional assessment instruments, yielding scores in standard deviations or developmental age in months, may not adequately address some developmental domains, or may not be comparable across developmental domains or across age levels (Benn, 1994; Brown & Brown, 1993). For this reason, some states have included qualitative criteria for determining developmental delay. This type of criterion includes findings of atypical behavior.

Because there is an insufficient number of reliable and valid instruments for the birth-through-2 age group and questionable predictive validity for available instruments, determining delay by traditional assessment can be problematic (Benn, 1994; Shonkoff & Meisels, 1991). For that reason, the existing Part C regulations require that informed clinical opinion be included for eligibility determination (see 34 C.F.R. 303.322(c)(2)). Informed clinical opinion relies on qualitative and quantitative information to determine the need for early intervention services, and typically is derived from the consensus of a multidisciplinary team that includes parents and information from multiple sources (Benn, 1994; Harbin et al., 1991). Several states' policies specify only informed clinical opinion as the criterion for eligibility without providing quantitative criteria.

Inclusion of Risk Factors

Three categories of risk for adverse developmental outcomes that are frequently described by states are conditions of established risk, biological/medical risk, and environmental risk. Children with an established physical or mental condition with a high probability of resulting in developmental delay are, under IDEA, eligible for services. If a state decides to include in its eligibility definition children with other risk factors, it must delineate the criteria and procedures (including the use of informed clinical opinion) that will be used to identify those children. The statute encourages states "to expand opportunities for children under 3 years of age who would be at risk of having substantial developmental delay if they did not receive early intervention services" (IDEA 2004, §631(b)(4)). The statute also allows states that do not serve infants and toddlers who are at risk to use IDEA funds to identify, evaluate, refer, and conduct periodic follow-up on each referral to determine any changes in eligibility status (IDEA 2004, §638(5)).

Conditions of Established Risk. IDEA requires states to provide services to children who have conditions of established risk. A condition of established risk is defined as a "diagnosed physical or mental condition which has a high probability of resulting in developmental delay" (IDEA 2004, §632(5)(A)(ii)). These conditions include, but are not limited to, "chromosomal abnormalities; genetic or congenital disorders; severe sensory impairments, including hearing and vision; inborn errors of metabolism; disorders reflecting disturbance of the development of the nervous system; congenital infections; disorders secondary to exposure to toxic substances, including fetal alcohol syndrome; and severe attachment disorders" (see 34 C.F.R. §303.16, Note 1). Children in this category are eligible for services under Part C of IDEA by virtue of their diagnosis, regardless of whether a measurable delay is present.

Although many states have mirrored the Part C regulatory language in listing diagnosed conditions in their eligibility definitions, several states have included many other conditions in their eligibility definitions. This may be because there is less agreement among professionals about what other conditions might be included in this category versus the biological/medical risk category. Accompanying their list of diagnosed conditions, many states use the phrase "but is not limited to the following" to allow flexibility for other conditions to be accepted for eligibility.

Biological/medical risk. Because children with a history of significant biological or medical conditions or events have a greater chance of developing a delay or a disability than children in the general population, states may include them under the optional eligibility category of at risk. Examples of biological/medical risk conditions that states have listed include low birthweight, intraventricular hemorrhage at birth, chronic lung disease, and failure to thrive.

Biological/medical risk conditions do not invariably lead to developmental delay, and many children who have a history of biological events will do well developmentally with or without services (Shonkoff & Meisels, 1991). Therefore, a comprehensive child and family evaluation by a multidisciplinary team (MDT) is necessary to determine (a) eligibility and (b) the appropriate intervention services (Shonkoff & Meisels, 1991).

Environmental Risk. Children at environmental risk include those whose caregiving circumstances and current family situation place them at greater risk for delay than the general population. As with biological/ medical risk, states are not required, but may chose to include children at environmental risk under the optional eligibility category of at risk. Examples of environmental risk factors may include parental substance abuse, family social disorganization, poverty, homelessness, parental developmental disability, parental age, parental educational attainment, and child abuse or neglect.

The 2004 reauthorization of IDEA added a requirement that states have policies and procedures to refer children for early intervention services who are involved in substantiated child abuse or neglect, or affected by illegal substance abuse or withdrawal symptoms resulting from prenatal drug exposure (IDEA 2004, §637(a)(6)). Federal regulations addressing this new requirement will be forthcoming.

As with children at biological/medical risk, environmental risk factors do not invariably result in delay or disability. Therefore, an MDT's comprehensive evaluation is essential to determining eligibility and appropriate services.

Single vs. Multiple Risk Factors. No single event or risk factor reliably predicts developmental outcome. The greater the number of both biological/medical and/or environmental risk factors, the greater the developmental risk. Research shows, however, that there can be factors in a child's caregiving environment that may mediate the impact of risk factors. These may include temperament of the child, high self- esteem, good emotional relationship with at least one parent, and successful learning experiences (Brown & Brown, 1993; Knudtson et al., 1990). Assessments should address multiple and cumulative risk criteria, both biological and environmental, and consider the resilience or protective factors, within a context of change over time (Kochanek, Kabacoff & Lipsitt, 1990; Shonkoff & Meisels, 1991).

Some states that choose to serve children who are eligible under optional at risk categories use a multiple risk model with a range of three to five risk factors required for eligibility for services. A few states require less delay for eligibility when environmental and/or biological/medical risk factors also are present.

Table of States' Part C Definitions

Table 2, at the end of this paper, summarizes the policies of states and other governing jurisdictions regarding the definition of developmental delay for Part C eligibility and the provision of services for at risk children. The author gathered this information from the most recent copy of states' Part C applications or from personal communication with Part C coordinators. The Table is divided into three categories: Level of Developmental Delay Required for Eligibility, Serving At Risk, and Comments.

Level of Developmental Delay Required for Eligibility. State criteria for delay are indicated in different ways. Those measured by assessment instruments are expressed in standard deviation (SD), percent delay, delay in months, or percentile scores. Other determinants include informed clinical opinion or the judgment of an MDT. Areas refer to the five developmental areas cited in the law: "cognitive development, physical development, communication development, social or emotional development, and adaptive development" (IDEA 2004, §632(5)(A)(i)).

Serving At Risk. Whether or not a state has elected to serve at risk children under its Part C program is indicated. If a state is serving only particular categories of at risk (e.g., biological/medical risk and/or environmental risk), the eligible category as identified by the state is indicated. Please note that diagnosed physical or mental condition with high probability of resulting in developmental delay, commonly referred to as "established conditions," is an eligibility category required under Part C and, thus, is not included in this Table.

Comments. This column provides several kinds of information. For those states that have elected not to serve at risk under Part C, the intent to track, screen, or monitor this population is described if the state has so indicated. Other relevant observations about a state's eligibility criteria also are included, such as state-developed lists of risk factors or established conditions.

State definitions are current as of publication date, but may change as states redefine their eligible population. NECTAC maintains files on states' Part C eligibility criteria and can provide updated information on request.

References

Benn, R. (1994). Conceptualizing eligibility for early intervention services. In D. M. Bryant & M. A. Graham (Eds.), *Implementing early intervention* (pp. 18-45). New York: Guilford Press.

Brown, W., & Brown, C. (1993). Defining eligibility for early intervention. In W. Brown, S. K. Thurman, & F. Pearl (Eds.), *Family-centered early intervention with infants and toddlers: Innovative cross-disciplinary approaches* (pp. 21-42). Baltimore: Paul H. Brookes Publishing Co.

Early Intervention Program for Infants and Toddlers with Disabilities Rule, 34 C.F.R. §303 (2001).

Harbin, G. L., Gallagher, J. J., & Terry, D. V. (1991). Defining the eligible population: Policy issues and challenges. *Journal of Early Intervention, 15*(1), 13-20.

The Individuals with Disabilities Education Improvement Act of 2004, Pub. L. No. 108-446, §632, 118 Stat. 2744 (2004).

Kochanek, T., Kabacoff, R., & Lipsitt, L. (1990). Early identification of developmentally disabled and at risk preschool children. *Exceptional Children, 56*(6), 528-538.

Knudtson, F., Strong, M., Wiegardt, E., Grier, R., & Bennett, B. (1990, January 10). *Definition of developmental delay and high risk factors study, Task B Report: Literature review.* [Available from Mike Zito, Early Intervention Program, State Department of Developmental Services, P.O. Box 944202, Sacramento, CA 95814; or Patricia Spikes-Calvin, Berkeley Planning Associates, 440 Grand Avenue, Suite 500, Oakland, CA 94610.]

Shonkoff, J., & Meisels, S. (1991). Defining eligibility for services under Public Law 99-457. *Journal of Early Intervention, 15*(1), 21-25.

Citation

Please cite as:

Shackelford, J. (2006). *State and jurisdictional eligibility definitions for infants and toddlers with disabilities under IDEA* (NECTAC Notes No. 20). Chapel Hill: The University of North Carolina, FPG Child Development Institute, National Early Childhood Technical Assistance Center.

NECTAC Notes No. 20 is an update of NECTAC Notes No. 19 dated November 2005. The current edition includes changes to two states' eligibility criteria. We are aware of 3 states having proposed changes, or considering changes. As these are finalized, we will incorporate them into future editions of this paper.

About the Author

Jo Shackelford is a Technical Assistance Specialist at NECTAC. Her research interests include Part C eligibility, interagency coordination, and health issues.

NECTAC Notes is produced and distributed by the National Early Childhood Technical Assistance Center (NECTAC), pursuant to contract ED-01-CO-0112 with the Office of Special Education Programs, U.S. Department of Education (ED).

Contractors undertaking projects under government sponsorship are encouraged to express their judgment in professional and technical matters. Opinions expressed do not necessarily represent the Department of Education's position or policy.

This document appears at http://www.nectac.org/pubs/pdfs/nnotes20.pdf and updates to the data herein will be announced at http://www.nectac.org/pubs/.

Paper copies of this document are available from NECTAC at cost. A list of currently available NECTAC publications can be viewed at our site on the World Wide Web or requested from us. NECTAC is committed to making the information it disseminates fully accessible to all individuals. To acquire this publication in an alternate format, please contact the Publications Coordinator in Chapel Hill.

NECTAC is a program of the FPG Child Development Institute at The University of North Carolina at Chapel Hill. The address is:

Campus Box 8040, UNC-CH
Chapel Hill, NC 27599-8040
919-962-2001 * phone
919-843-3269 *TDD
919-966-7463 * fax
nectac@unc.edu
* www.nectac.org

Principal Investigator: Pascal Trohanis
Contracting Officer's Representative at OSEP: Peggy Cvach
Contract Specialist at U.S. ED: Stephan Lewis
Publications Coordinator: Caroline Armijo

Table 2 State and Jurisdictional Eligibility Definitions Under Part C of IDEA[1, 2]

State	Level of Developmental Delay Required for Eligibility[3]	Serving At-Risk	Comments
Alabama	25% delay in one or more areas	NO	
Alaska	50% delay or equivalent standard deviation (SD) below the norm in one area; multidisciplinary team (MDT) clinical opinion to document atypical development	NO	Provides services to at risk, based on available funding through the Infant Learning Program; collaborative efforts with Early Head Start, Healthy Families Alaska, and child care resource and referral agencies
American Samoa	25% delay or 1.5 SD in one or more developmental areas; or professional judgment	YES (biological and environmental)	Biological risk is defined as medical conditions that increase the risk of developmental delay. Environmental risks are physical, social or economic factors which may result in developmental delay. Some require only one risk factor; some require five or more risk factors
Arizona	50% delay in one or more areas	NO	
Arkansas	25% delay in one or more areas; informed clinical opinion	NO	
California	Significant difference between expected level of development and current level of functioning as determined by qualified MDT, including parents; atypical development determined by informed clinical opinion	YES (biological)	Serves high risk due to a combination of two or more biological factors determined by the multidisciplinary team
Colorado	Significant delay in one or more developmental domains; "Significant delay" shall mean development that qualified personnel determine to be outside the range of "normal" or "typical" as for a same age peer.	NO	
Connecticut	As measured on a standardized test, 2 SD in one area; or 1.5 SD in two areas; or informed clinical opinion of at least two qualified professionals to substantiate	NO	Enrollment in the Ages and Stages tracking program is offered to any family whose child is found not eligible,

(Continued)

Table 2 (*Continued*)

State	Level of Developmental Delay Required for Eligibility[3]	Serving At-Risk	Comments
Connecticut	the equivalent delay for children for whom use of standardized instruments is not applicable		and families can request another evaluation after three months. Children with birth weights 750–1000g, children with certain conditions and a mild delay, and children with a minus 2 SD in expressive language only with biological risk factors, are offered quarterly "follow-along" visits to monitor the child's development
Delaware	25% delay in one area; and/or MDT clinical judgment; and/or standardized test scores (when available) of 1.75 SD below the mean. Children with expressive language delays only are not eligible except based on clinical judgment	NO	Provides a list of established conditions. Provides eligibility guidelines for infants and toddlers with delays in expressive language, "Delaware Guidelines for Young Children with Communication Delays"
District of Columbia	50% delay in one or more areas; informed clinical opinion	NO	
Federated States of Micronesia — Currently not eligible for this federal program.			
Florida	1.5 SD in one area or 25% delay in months of age in one area; or informed clinical opinion	NO	
Georgia	2 SD in one area; 1.5 SD in two areas; or informed clinical opinion	NO	Provides an extensive annotated list of established physical/mental conditions
Guam	2 SD or 30% delay in one area; 1.5 SD or 22% delay in two areas; or informed clinical opinion by at least two qualified professionals	YES (biological and environmental)	Provides an extensive list of established physical, mental conditions as well as a list of biological risk factors. A list of environmental risk conditions is provided. Some require only one risk factor; others require five or more environmental risk factors.

Hawaii	MDT consensus; no level of SD or % delay specified	YES (biological and environmental)	Biological risk: means prenatal, perinatal, neonatal, or early developmental events suggestive of biological insults to the developing central nervous system; a diagnosed physical or mental condition that has a high probability of resulting in developmental delay including very low birth weight (1,500 grams or less). Environmental risk: means physical, social or economic factors which may limit development. One of the following conditions: parental age less than 16; any existing physical, developmental, emotional, or psychiatric disability in primary caregiver; substance abuse by primary caregiver; or risk for child abuse or neglect *Or* Two of the following conditions: Birth weight 1500–2500 grams; parental age16-18 and less than high school education; presence of physical, developmental, emotional, or psychiatric disability in a sibling or any family member in the home; economically disadvantaged family; single parent; or, incarceration of a primary caregiver
Idaho	30% below age norm or 6 months delay, whichever is less adjusted for prematurity, or 2 SD in one area; 1.5 SD in two areas; informed clinical opinion	NO	Screens and tracks at risk. These children may be eligible "based on informed clinical opinion for those infants and toddlers having a combination of risk factors that taken together make developmental delay highly possible." An extensive list of established conditions is provided
Illinois	30% delay in one or more areas; or informed clinical opinion by MDT	NO	A list of established medical conditions is provided

(Continued)

Table 2 (*Continued*)

State	Level of Developmental Delay Required for Eligibility[3]	Serving At-Risk	Comments
Indiana	1.5 SD in one area or 20% below chronological age; 1 SD in two areas or 15% below chronological age in two areas; informed clinical opinion	YES (biological)	Eight biological risk factors are defined. Only one risk factor is necessary for eligibility
Iowa	25% below age in one or more areas based on informed clinical opinion of an MDT or a known condition with a high probability of resulting in later delays in development based on informed clinical opinion	NO	
Kansas	25% delay or 1.5 SD in one or more areas; 20% delay or 1 SD in two areas; clinical judgment of MDT	NO	Tracking, monitoring, and serving at risk are based on local option and availability of local funding
Kentucky	2 SD in one area; 1.5 SD in two areas; informed clinical opinion; if formal testing does not meet eligibility criteria but concerns remain, a more intensive level of evaluation may be requested	NO	Provides a list of established conditions
Louisiana	2 SD below the mean or 33% below age in months in one area; or 1.5 SD below the mean or 25% below age in months in two or more areas; Informed clinical opinion may be used to establish eligibility when use of standardized instruments is not applicable and when child exhibits atypical behavior that cannot be measured by standardized test. Informed clinical opinion must be from at least two qualified professionals from different disciplines, other than Family Support Coordinator, to substantiate the equivalent delay of 2 SD in one area	NO	Children who are initially eligible by informed clinical opinion must be re-evaluated annually to document significant developmental delay, and if not eligible will exit the system Examples of atypical behavior provided; List of established conditions
Maine	A delay of approximately 2.0 or more SD's below the mean or delay of 25% below chronological age in at least one area; or a delay of approximately 1.5 SD's below the mean or 15% below chronological age in at least two areas	NO	

State	Criteria	At risk eligible for this federal program	At-risk description
Marshall Islands	—	—	Currently not eligible for this federal program
Maryland	25% delay in one or more areas; a typical development/behavior	NO	Tracks and refers at risk children
Massachusetts	25% delay as, measured by an approved instrument yielding age equivalent scores, in one or more areas of development; or 1 SD below the norm, as measured by an approved instrument yielding SD scores, in one or more areas of development; or if child has questionable quality of developmental skills and functioning based on clinical judgment of MDT	Yes (biological and environmental)	A child found to be eligible based on clinical judgment can receive services for up to 6 months. For services to continue after this period, eligibility must be determined based on, diagnosis developmental delay or risk factors. Eligibility based on risk requires the presence of four risk factors from lists of child characteristics and family characteristics
Michigan	Developmental delay will be determined by informed clinical judgment of a MDT which includes parent(s); multiple sources of information required which include at a minimum: (1) developmental history as currently reported by the parent(s) and/or primary caregiver; (2) observational assessment; (3) recent health status appraisal; (4) An appropriate formal assessment measure (standardized developmental test, inventory or behavioral checklist); This formal measure shall not be used as the sole criterion to determine the absence of delay	NO	At risk not entitled to services under Part C, but local service areas may choose to serve this population. Biological and environmental risk factors are described. Children are considered at risk for substantial developmental delay based on parental and/or professional judgment and presence of four or more risk factors
Minnesota	Children birth through 2 are eligible if they have a medically diagnosed syndrome or condition known to hinder normal development or if they have a delay in overall development demonstrated by a composite score of 1.5 SD or more below the mean on an evaluation **or** if less than 18 months and they have a delay in motor development that is demonstrated by a composite score of more than 2.0 SD below the mean. The child's needs must be supported by observation and corroboration of the evaluation or medical diagnosis must be made with a developmental history and at least one other evaluation procedure	NO	

(Continued)

Table 2 (*Continued*)

State	Level of Developmental Delay Required for Eligibility[3]	Serving At-Risk	Comments
Mississippi	1.5 SD or 25% delay in one or more areas; informed clinical opinion	NO	Tracks and refers at risk children
Missouri	50% delay in one area; for prematurity, the adjusted chronological age (which is calculated by deducting one-half of the prematurity from the child's chronological age) should be assigned for a period of up to 12 months or longer if recommended by the child's physician	NO	List of established conditions
Montana	50% delay in one area or 25% delay in two areas; informed clinical opinion	NO	
Nebraska	2.0 SD below the mean in one area; 1.3 SD below the mean in two areas or informed clinical opinion of qualified professionals in consultation with the family	NO	
Nevada	50% delay in one area or 25% delay in two areas, adjusted for gestational age less than 36 weeks	NO	
New Hampshire	Atypical behaviors documented by qualified personnel; or 33% delay in one or more areas	YES (biological and environmental)	At risk means child is experiencing five or more documented diagnoses, events, or circumstances affecting the child or parent. A list is included
New Jersey	33% delay in one area; 25% delay in two or more areas based on corrected age for infants born before 38 weeks gestation and applying until age 24 months	NO	Legal requirement to report children with birth defects to special child health registry and case management

State	Developmental Delay Criteria	At Risk	Description
New Mexico	25% delay in one area after correction for prematurity	YES (biological and environmental)	Biological Risk – early medical conditions as documented by a physician or other primary health care provider, which are known to produce developmental delays in some children; Environmental Risk – two or more physical, social and/or economic factors in the environment which pose a substantial threat to the child's development. The team which determines eligibility based on environmental risk must include representation from two or more agencies with relevant knowledge of the child, family and environmental risk factors.
New York	1) 12-month delay in one area, or 2) 33% delay in one area or 25% delay in two areas, or 3) 2 SD in one area or 1.5 SD in two areas, or 4) informed clinical opinion by MDT	NO	
North Carolina	1.5 SD in one area or 20% delay in months for birth to 36 months; atypical development	YES (biological and environmental)	Uses the term High Risk Potential and requires three risk indicators. Defines atypical development including "substantiated physical, sexual abuse, and other environmental situations that raise significant concern regarding a child's emotional well-being."
North Dakota	50% delay in one area; 25% delay in two or more areas; informed clinical opinion	NO	
Northern Mariana Islands	25% delay in one or more developmental domains; clinical opinion of qualified professionals may establish eligibility	NO	Defines qualified professionals. Assists with tracking and monitoring infants and toddlers at risk

(Continued)

Table 2 (*Continued*)

State	Level of Developmental Delay Required for Eligibility[3]	Serving At-Risk	Comments
Ohio	Experiencing a delay in one or more areas as measured by a developmental evaluation tool and informed clinical opinion	NO	Provides a list of established conditions
Oklahoma	50% delay in one area; 25% delay in two or more areas	NO	
Oregon	2 SD in one area; or 1.5 SD in two or more areas; or meets the minimum criteria for one of the following disability categories in Oregon Administrative Rule (OAR) 581-015-0051: autism spectrum disorder, deaf blindness, hearing impairment, orthopedic impairment or visual impairment	NO	
Palau — Currently not eligible for this federal program			
Pennsylvania	25% delay or 1.5 SD in one area; informed clinical opinion	NO	Children at risk are eligible for tracking and periodic screening. Defines at risk
Puerto Rico	Quantitative and qualitative criteria listed for each area. *Growth development deviations*: percentiles specified *Motor skills*: 2.0 SD or 33% delay; 1.5 SD or 25% delay with other delays *Visual and bearing impairment*: clinical judgment *Cognitive*: 2.0 SD or 33% delay; 1.5 SD or 25% delay with other delays; developmental index between 1-2.0 SD plus consistent delays in other areas; informed clinical opinion based on atypical development or observed behaviors *Communication*: 2.0 SD or 33% delay; 1.5 SD or 25% delay with other delays; informed clinical opinion *Social-Emotional*: informed clinical opinion *Adaptive*: informed clinical opinion	NO	Tracks children at risk and conducts periodic followup at risk clinics. Uses medical (biological) risk factors

State			
Rhode Island	2.0 SD or 33% delay in one or more areas; 1.5 SD or 25% delay in two areas; or clinical opinion	NO	Describes single and multiple established conditions. Single conditions involve diagnoses which are known to result in developmental delay. Multiple established conditions include all diagnoses, events, and circumstances which, in combination, are known to result in developmental delay. Definition does not include children who are at risk. List of child- and parent-centered conditions. Four or more positive findings are considered guidelines for eligibility
South Carolina	33% below chronological/adjusted age in at least one area; or 25% below chronological/adjusted age in two or more areas	NO	Provides a table of established conditions with diagnostic criteria for eligibility
South Dakota	25% below normal age range or 6-month delay, or demonstrating at least a 1.5 SD delay in one or more areas	NO	
Tennessee	25% below chronological age in two or more areas; or 40% below chronological age in one area; informed clinical opinion	NO	
Texas	Atypical development or delay in one or more areas (specific level of delay determined by test performance): documented atypical responses or behaviors; Ages 2 months or less — Ages 2–12 months — 2-month delay in one area; Ages 13–24 months — 3-month delay in one area; Ages 25–36 months — 4 month delay in one area	NO	Adjusts for prematurity up to 12 months. May not adjust for more than 2 months prematurity. Includes criteria for atypical development
Utah	1.5 SD at or below the mean, or at or below the 7th percentile in one or more areas; clinical opinion determined by at least two professionals representing different disciplines and at lease one must hold the EI Specialist II credential; must have expertise in areas of stated concern	NO	Tracks and monitors at risk. Provides a list of established conditions

(Continued)

Table 2 (*Continued*)

State	Level of Developmental Delay Required for Eligibility[3]	Serving At-Risk	Comments
Vermont	Clearly observable and measurable delay in one or more areas at the level that child's future success in home, school, or community cannot be assured without provision of early intervention services; clinical judgment including family input	NO	Provides a list of conditions at high probability for developmental delay. Lists exit criteria
Virgin Islands	25% delay in one or more areas, standardized test scores of 1.5 SD below norm, or documented informed clinical opinion or established condition	NO	Defines criteria for informed clinical opinion. Includes a list of established conditions
Virginia	25% below chronological or adjusted age in one or more areas; or show atypical development; informed clinical opinion	NO	
Washington	1.5 SD or 25% delay in one or more areas; criteria listed for hearing and vision impairment	NO	Provides family resources coordination (FRC) for all families referred from the time a concern is identified through completion of evaluation/ assessments. If the child is determined not to be eligible, FRC services are no longer continued. Includes a list of established conditions
West Virginia	A substantial developmental delay or atypical development in one or more areas, determined by a MDT including parents, and supported by observation, measurement, and/or clinical judgment.	YES (biological and environmental)	Provides a list of established conditions. At risk category requires at least four risk factors. Includes a list of risk factors
Wisconsin	25% delay or 1.3 SD in one area; or atypical development as determined by MDT with informed clinical opinion	NO	Defines atypical development. Multidisciplinary team determines established conditions with physician report. Provides examples of established conditions in state rule
Wyoming	1.5 SD or 25% delay in one or more areas; clinical opinion	NO	

1. *Source:* Survey of Part C Coordinators and/or definition from most recent OSEP-approved application; data current as of October 2005.
2. *Note:* Diagnosed physical or mental condition with high probability of resulting in developmental delay, commonly referred to as "established conditions," is an eligibility category required under Part C and, thus, is not included in this table.
3. "Areas" refer to the five developmental areas — physical, communication, cognitive, social or emotional, and adaptive — that are cited in the law.

Index